FOREWORD BY NEHAL BHUTA

International criminal law is a field of international law which has never been more institutionalized, and more established. Multiple international and hybrid tribunals have been created over the last 30 years, and the field now boasts its own journals, textbooks and digests of jurisprudence. It is a domain of international law which has well and truly stabilized as a recurrent field of activity, both scholarly and institutional – in a relatively short period of time. Yet it is a field which is also always somehow in crisis, in terms of its consistent application, its susceptibility to the changing winds of power politics, and continuous criticism of either its excessive or insufficient ambition. If international law is a "discipline of crisis",[1] as Judge Hilary Charlesworth observed more than 20 years ago, international criminal law is perhaps its most crisis-dependent subfield (although perhaps international humanitarian law should share pole position in such a race).

The tempo of a crisis-oriented field means that slower, deliberate scholarship is often a lower priority. But its importance is therefore even greater. A discipline constantly reacting and responding to some new atrocity or dynamic of political contestation, easily neglects reflection on its foundations, purpose and nature; as a result, it either simply repeats its founding myths and assumptions, which calcify and become brittle, or it becomes unable to articulate a foundational response to each new contingency. In either case, it does not bode well for the future of the field.

In this deeply researched and reflective book, Dr. Song revisits one of the fundamental assumptions of the field of international criminal law: that its philosophical foundations can be meaningfully rooted in a modern conception of cosmopolitan thought. She shows that such an assumption suffers from a range of difficulties. First, it rests on an overly simplified and unhistorical understanding of what cosmopolitanism was, and is. Dr. Song demonstrates that modern cosmopolitanism does not sit easily with a project of criminal law and criminal punishment, and also that, in any event, the positive law of war crimes cannot easily be tethered to cosmopolitan roots – either in terms of genealogy, or in terms of philosophical reconstruction.

---

1 Hilary Charlesworth, "International Law: A Discipline of Crisis", in *Modern Law Review*, 2002, vol. 65, no. 3, p. 377.

Second, and more profoundly, Dr. Song challenges the extent to which a cosmopolitan law of international crimes can truly grapple with the challenges of human agency during armed conflict. She draws on a social psychological and organizational sociology literature to consider how human agency is shaped by military institutions and the nature of war as an organized and bureaucratized exercise of violence. The kinds of human agency constructed by a weakly cosmopolitan international criminal law may well not be the ones that are created and maintained through the institutions of war-making.

The implication of this unflinching and unvarnished analysis is not that international criminal law is a hopeless endeavour. Rather, it is a call for a better understanding of the place of legal norms within the shaping of institutions and organizations devoted to war (such as ministries of defence). Law and social psychology cannot be ships passing in the night, but must meet in some institutional contexts and be able to shape one another. Easy claims about 'humanity law' or grand cosmopolitan visions of the moral agency of the human soldier, require tempering. This is not in the name of a cynical realism which repudiates the possibility of law, but, paradoxically, as a means of protecting the enterprise of international criminal law against such cynical reason.

Nehal Bhuta

Professor and Chair of Public International Law
University of Edinburgh

FOREWORD BY CLAUS KREß

"[I]f international law is, in some ways, at the vanishing point of law, the law of war is, perhaps even more conspicuously, at the vanishing point of international law."[1] In her impressive book, Dr. Song Tianying takes Hersch Lauterpacht's well-known statement one step further and asks: "Can cosmopolitan law exist and operate in war?". This is a highly pertinent and truly fascinating question. Highly pertinent because cosmopolitanism offers a most plausible way for giving full meaning to the morality of the law on war crimes, and truly fascinating because, as the author puts it succinctly, a "cosmopolitan war crimes law is inherently paradoxical". Dr. Song unfolds this paradox in a masterful sequence of enchantment and disenchantment.

In her enchanting picture of cosmopolitan war crimes law, the author, drawing on a deep familiarity with the relevant discourse in moral and political philosophy, skilfully displays a thin cosmopolitan moral community which transcends the State and instead places the individual human being at the centre. The confrontation of this normative construction with the reality of warfare, however, leads to disenchantment. For, as Dr. Song points out, "[w]ar begins where cosmopolitanism cracks: particular identity is prioritized over human identity, particular interests over universal interests, and exchange of brute force over rational communication". Relying now on rich insights gained by a meticulous study of the relevant literature of sociology and moral psychology, the author shows up to what point the social condition of war challenges the human agency of the individual soldier and puts him or her in a position of 'bad moral luck'. For, to cite Dr. Song, war "strengthens internal cohesion and weakens, if not eliminates, the already fragile cosmopolitan solidarity", and "[m]ilitary life diminishes individual capacity and will to think and act as an independent moral agent".

The author could have left her analysis at this point of artful deconstruction. But her scholarly ambition goes further than that. She believes in a space "between the arrogance of dogmatism, and the despair of skepticism",[2] and, in this spirit, she calls for a serious effort of 're-enchantment'. On the doctrinal level, the author pleads, to name just one important example, for duly considering the

---

1 Hersch Lauterpacht, "The Problem of the Revision of the Law of War", in *British Yearbook of International Law*, 1952–1953, vol. 29, p. 382.

2 Francis Bacon, "Novum Organum", in *The Works*, ed. and trans. by Basil Montague, Volume 3, Parry & MacMillan, Philadelphia, 1854, p. 343.

soldier's concrete 'cognitive environment' in the application of the legal standard of 'manifest illegality' of superior orders in the Statute of the International Criminal Court. As she demonstrates convincingly, such an approach would not contradict the existence of a cosmopolitan legal standard, but it would open the door for duly recognizing the possibility that the 'moral distance' between the abstract standard and the concrete position of a foot soldier might be too long. To nevertheless inflict punishment would not be just and it would risk instrumentalizing criminal law to 'scapegoat' individuals at the bottom of the hierarchical structure.

And, on the legal policy level, Dr. Song makes a powerful case for giving the (leadership) crime of aggression its right place within the overall architecture of international criminal law: "For war crimes prosecution not to distract the public from the true moral cost of war, it is crucial to prosecute the crime of aggression, where applicable". Not only at this juncture, the reader appreciates that the very considerable value of this coherently structured and eloquently written study extends beyond the realm of war crimes law *stricto sensu*. In fact, the study makes an important contribution to a better understanding of international criminal law in its entirety.

One more, and certainly not the least value of this splendid book lies in its humility: Dr. Song's style is free of even the slightest touch of intellectual triumphalism and she also approaches 'her' body of law with all due modesty: "Criminal law is necessary but certainly not enough in dealing with atrocities. It should not give us the illusion that it can alone align the motivation of actors to refrain from committing war crimes. To be fully informed in finding solutions to war crimes, we need to look beyond the regime of criminal law".

Claus Kreß

Professor of International Law and Criminal Law
Chair for German and International Criminal Law
Director, Institute of International Peace and Security Law
University of Cologne

TABLE OF CONTENTS

1

Introduction: Why a *Cosmopolitan* War Crimes Law?

Can cosmopolitan law exist and operate in war? This book asks a simple but counter-intuitive question. This question is addressed in two parts: first, how can a cosmopolitan law be conceived in relation to war? And second, what are the empirical challenges in its implementation?

1.1. Why Cosmopolitanism in War?

1.1.1. The Search for Law's Moral Meaning

The project of a cosmopolitan war crimes law seeks to make law "morally meaningful".[1] Subject to changing political and social conditions, legal rules and practices are inevitably complex, fragmentary and often inconsistent. In contrast to the "transient, unstructured, pragmatic"[2] legal reality is legal philosophy's never-ending effort to find "system and coherence in legal doctrine".[3] One of the important rationalization tasks for legal philosophers is to find moral meaning in rules. It would be "self-defeating" for law to claim only legality and not "moral correctness" or justice.[4] The claim to correctness is integral to any norm as "justificatory reasons".[5] For law not to be "mere abstraction" or an alien imposition, it must have moral content.[6] For this purpose, moral and political theories can offer a certain "valuational frame of reference" or "matrix of justice".[7] Internal moral meaning is central to *criminal law* which proclaims social solidarity in vital moral issues. For war crimes law, the quality of its moral message

---

1 Roger Cotterrell, *Law's Community: Legal Theory in Sociological Perspective*, Oxford University Press, 1997, pp. 2–22.

2 *Ibid.*, pp. 91–110.

3 *Ibid.*, pp. 274–295.

4 Joxerramon Bengoetxea, "Legal Theory and Sociology of Law", in Jiří Přibáň (ed.), *Research Handbook on the Sociology of Law*, Edward Elgar Publishing, Cheltenham, 2020, p. 16.

5 *Ibid.*

6 Émile Durkheim, *Textes. Tome 2: Religion, Morale, Anomie*, Les Éditions de Minuit, Paris, 1975, p. 277, cited in Cotterrell, 1997, pp. 296–314, see *supra* note 1.

7 Albena Azmanova, "The Costs of the Democratic Turn in Political Theory", in Benjamin Martill and Sebastian Schindler (eds.), *Theory as Ideology in International Relations: The Politics of Knowledge*, Routledge, Abingdon, 2020, pp. 99, 102.

is directly linked to its legitimacy and mobilizing force. The moral message can be varied depending on the perspective of the interpreter.

Different moral, political theories can capitalize the development of war crimes law. Despite its popularity among certain practitioners and scholars, a cosmopolitan approach is not necessary in understanding and developing international criminal law. It is just one of the descriptive and prescriptive approaches to the law. To better appreciate the cosmopolitan approach, we need not only ask where it comes from and what its main values are, but also have an idea about its competing approaches. This section offers a succinct comparative perspective to give context to the cosmopolitan approach. The next sections turn to its sources and substance.

I would like to draw on David Held's three conceptions of international law as a mere illustration of different understandings: the law of States, international law with liberal constraints, and an emerging cosmopolitan law. These theories are both explanatory and normative. The first approach, that of the law of States, sees the law of war crimes as purely State-made, the evolution of which is a direct result of and justified by State consent. This line of reasoning is based on the "Westphalian regime" consisting of free and equal States who enjoy "supreme authority" within their territories and "recognize no temporal authority superior to themselves".[8] International law feeds into and sips from the "political mythology"[9] of the sovereign State. The law of war crimes are measures of limited co-operation among States, with its content dictated by the will of States. Non-State actors and individuals have no legitimate role to play in this Westphalian world order.

The second approach, according to Held, is often referred to as liberal internationalism. It holds the State to liberal standards of "self-determination, democracy, and human rights".[10] In this understanding, international law regulates individuals, States and non-State actors across sovereign territories.[11] In the liberal international order, State sovereignty is circumscribed by international law formulated by States themselves. The function and role of the State are

[8] David Held, "Law of States, Law of Peoples: Three Models of Sovereignty", in Neil Walker (ed.), *Relocating Sovereignty*, Routledge, Abingdon, 2006, pp. 383–384. For more on the "Westphalia model of the international law", see Claus Kreß, "Major Post-Westphalian Shifts and Some Important Neo-Westphalian Hesitations in the State Practice on the International Law on the Use of Force", in *Journal on the Use of Force and International Law*, 2014, vol. 1, no. 1, pp. 11–54.

[9] Florian Edelmann, "'I See Something You Don't See': Niklas Luhmann's Social Theory Between Observation and Meta-Critique", in Martill and Schindler (eds.), 2020, p. 74, see *supra* note 7.

[10] Held, 2006, p. 5, see *supra* note 8.

[11] *Ibid.*, p. 11.

"reconstituted" or "reconfigured" with the extension of classic liberal concerns to the international realm.[12] War crimes law is part of the self-imposed standards and constraints on State sovereignty. The liberal internationalist framework does not envisage that a supranational authority could articulate or enforce international law.[13]

The third approach holds that war crimes law should be a part of a cosmopolitan global order. It is based on cosmopolitan moral and political outlooks which see the individual person as the ultimate unit of moral concern and as a member of humankind. All human beings are equal irrespective of their place of birth or residence.[14] Like liberal internationalism, the cosmopolitan approach is committed to universal standards, rights and dignity of persons, *et cetera*, but it reverses the primacy of State in global politics *vis-à-vis* individuals. War crimes law is thus seen as expression of cosmopolitan values which centre on the interests and responsibility of individuals.

David Held calls the first conception of international law, "law of states", and the third, "law of peoples" or cosmopolitan law; the second conception being somewhere in between. Held's broad-stroke characterization captures three streams of legal and political theories which have large following and generate many debates in the field of international law. They present a spectrum of war crimes law's moral message which ranges from the morality of the State to the morality of the human person. As Ulrich Beck puts it:

> The two images of world society – on the one hand, world society as a *patchwork quilt of nation-states* (that is, the sum of sovereign nation-states), and on the other, the one world society, at once individualized as well as globalized, conceived as *cosmopolitan order of human rights* – clash and spark a worldwide intellectual and political conflict.[15]

In these debates, cosmopolitanism is often seen as an antidote to the view that world politics is nothing but power, self-interest and contingency.[16] In many ways, a cosmopolitan legal order seems to better suit the "narrative of

[12] *Ibid.*, p. 14.

[13] *Ibid.*, p. 14.

[14] *Ibid.*, pp. 23–24. See, for example, Sergio Dellavalle, "In Defence of Cosmopolitan Law", Occasional Paper Series No. 16, Torkel Opsahl Academic EPublisher, Brussels, 2024 (http://www.toaep.org/ops-pdf/16-dellavalle/).

[15] Ulrich Beck, "The Cosmopolitan Perspective: Sociology of the Second Age of Modernity", in *British Journal of Sociology*, 2000, vol. 51, no. 1, p. 85.

[16] Robert Fine, *Cosmopolitanism*, Routledge, Abingdon, 2007, p. 21.

judicialization, legalization, and globalization"[17] which projects progressivism and optimism.

1.1.2. Cosmopolitanism and War: Two Extremes

At first glance, cosmopolitanism is the least likely moral message to be dispensed by laws of war. Although moral message for law needs to be appealing, cosmopolitanism seems extreme in the context of war. It is, however, quite understandable if one considers the circumstances of international crimes. Core international crimes include genocide, war crimes, crimes against humanity, and the crime of aggression. They typically take place in conflicts between groups, where national, ethnical, religious and tribal identities collide most violently. The humanity of members of the enemy group is cast in doubt and eventually denied. Cosmopolitanism tells participants in the conflict to extend respect for most fundamental human rights to the enemy group. It also reminds the whole world that certain intergroup violence concerns everyone because they touch the very core of our humanity. Cosmopolitanism provides the basis for a species-wide solidarity which supports the criminalization and punishment of grave inter-human violence in group conflicts.

Therefore, theoretically, cosmopolitanism can perform three functions in war crimes law interpretation. It first seeks to perform a *preventive* function by telling participants in group violence that there are certain limits to treating your enemy, who is as human as you are. It also performs a *justificatory* function by explaining why the world community should be concerned with grave local violence. It finally performs a *motivational* function by appealing to all of humanity to rally behind international criminal law which is the ultimate guarantee of basic human rights.

On the other hand, this paradoxical necessity of cosmopolitanism in war raises an obvious question: can the cosmopolitan approach *actually* perform these functions? Indeed, the normative ambition of cosmopolitanism may not be matched by its efficacy. Its presumed theoretical necessity cannot guarantee its realization. After all, if cosmopolitanism really works, war or intergroup conflicts would not occur. Out of many possible approaches to answering this question, the present book takes the perspective of moral psychology. I examine the feasibility of such a theory *vis-à-vis* individual moral agents, especially participants in war.

[17] Bryant G. Garth, "Issues of Empire, Contestation, and Hierarchy in the Globalization of Law", in Moshe Hirsch and Andrew Lang (eds.), *Research Handbook on the Sociology of International Law*, Edward Elgar Publishing, Cheltenham, 2018, p. 19.

1.2. Cosmopolitan Ethos in the Field of International Criminal Law

Cosmopolitan references are familiar to the field of international criminal law.[18] As is illustrated in Chapters 3 and 4 below, the stated purposes of many war-related international treaties demonstrate cosmopolitan spirit. The Statute of the International Criminal Court ('ICC'), a landmark institution for international criminal justice, affirms cosmopolitan solidarity among all peoples. Its Preamble recognizes that "all peoples are united by common bonds".[19] Many participants in this discourse – such as scholars, judges, lawyers and activists – embrace and promote international criminal justice as a cosmopolitan project. For example, ICC judges in the *Al Mahdi* case recognize a planet-wide interest in United Nations ('UN') Educational, Scientific and Cultural Organization ('UNESCO') heritage sites whose destruction concerns the international community as a whole.[20] Claus Kreß argues that international criminal courts exercise jurisdiction over core international crimes on behalf of the international community as a whole.[21] Kai Ambos suggests that international criminal law be based on a "valued-based world order" and a cosmopolitan society composed of world citizens.[22] Similarly, Ryan Long sees international criminal law as expressing public values of humanity.[23] Owiso Owiso proposes to use cosmopolitanism as a theoretical basis for collective action in ensuring accountability for international crimes.[24] Ryan Liss argues that international criminal law should

---

[18] Robinson offers an overview of cosmopolitan references in international criminal law literature. See Darryl Robinson, "A Cosmopolitan Liberal Account of International Criminal Law", in *Leiden Journal of International Law*, 2013, vol. 26, no. 1, pp. 138–139.

[19] See Rome Statute of the International Criminal Court, 17 July 1998, Preamble (https://www.legal-tools.org/doc/7b9af9/).

[20] International Criminal Court, *Prosecutor v. Ahmad Al Faqi Al Mahdi*, Trial Chamber, Judgment and Sentence, 27 September 2016, ICC-01/12-01/15-171, para. 80 (https://www.legal-tools.org/doc/042397/).

[21] Claus Kreß, "Preliminary Observations on the ICC Appeals Chamber's Judgment of 6 May 2019 in the Jordan Referral re Al-Bashir Appeal", Occasional Paper Series No. 8, Torkel Opsahl Academic EPublisher, Brussels, 2019, p. 19 (https://www.toaep.org/ops-pdf/8-kress/).

[22] Kai Ambos, "Punishment without a Sovereign? The *Ius Puniendi* Issue of International Criminal Law: A First Contribution towards a Consistent Theory of International Criminal Law", in *Oxford Journal of Legal Studies*, 2013, vol. 33, no. 2, p. 314.

[23] Ryan Long, "Responsibility, Authority, and the Community of Moral Agents in Domestic and International Criminal Law", in *International Criminal Law Review*, 2014, vol. 14, nos. 4–5, p. 854. Long takes candidate values to include reciprocity, respect, bodily integrity, freedom of conscience, and autonomy.

[24] Owiso Owiso, "Obligations to 'Strangers': Reconceptualizing Cosmopolitanism as a Basis for Collective (Regional-Level) Accountability for International Crimes", in *Journal of International Criminal Justice*, 2023, vol. 21, no. 1, pp. 1–28.

be seen as a Kantian cosmopolitan right in reverse.[25] Such examples of cosmopolitan references in the field of international criminal justice are closely examined in later chapters.

A number of scholars have described and reflected upon the cosmopolitan ethos in the field. Darryl Robinson sees common inspirations of cosmopolitanism and international criminal law: promotion of universal human values and relativization of State sovereignty.[26] Fréderic Mégret describes international criminal law as "a project of cosmopolitan individual responsibility".[27] Gerry Simpson discerns a tendency to cast international war crimes trials in a cosmopolitan light.[28] Payam Akhavan notices that 'progressive' development of the law, more than strict interpretation, is regarded as "heroic".[29] Through her extensive ethnographic work, Kjersti Lohne reveals a "cosmopolitan penal imaginary" which motivates and legitimizes many projects of non-governmental organizations on international criminal justice.[30] In their description of the cosmopolitan trend, these scholars tend to maintain a somewhat critical distance.

1.3. International Criminal Justice in the Eyes of Cosmopolitan Theorists

Not only do international lawyers seek cosmopolitan justifications, cosmopolitan theorists also see the value of international criminal justice as a potential cosmopolitan project. Daniele Archibugi, a prominent political theorist who advances cosmopolitan democracy, seeks to guide the development of international criminal justice in the cosmopolitan direction in his article "A Cosmopolitan Perspective on Global Criminal Justice".[31] Another advocate for cosmopolitan democracy, David Held, proposes a global legal system of criminal law and an international criminal court to realize his eight cosmopolitan democratic

25 Ryan Liss, "International Criminal Law as Cosmopolitan Right in Reverse", in *Jurisprudence*, 2024, vol. 15, no. 3, pp. 387–397.

26 See Robinson, 2013, pp. 138–139, *supra* note 18.

27 Frédéric Mégret, "The Subjects of International Criminal Law", in Philip Kastner (ed.), *International Criminal Law in Context*, Routledge, Abingdon, 2017, p. 37.

28 See Gerry Simpson, *Law, War and Crime*, Polity Press, Cambridge, 2007.

29 See Payam Akhavan, "The Perils of Progressive Jurisprudence: The *Nullum Crimen Sine Lege* Principle in International Criminal Law", in *Current Legal Problems*, 2022, vol. 20, no. 1, p. 24.

30 See Kjersti Lohne, *Advocates of Humanity: Human Rights NGOs in International Criminal Justice*, Oxford University Press, 2019.

31 See Daniele Archibugi, "A Cosmopolitan Perspective on Global Criminal Justice", in George Andreopoulos and Henry F. Carey (eds.), *Justice and World Order Reassessing Richard Falk's Scholarship and Advocacy*, Routledge, Abingdon, 2022, pp. 83 ff.

principles.[32] Jürgen Habermas argues for a thin cosmopolitan solidarity which is limited to maintaining peace and protecting human rights. Such a *negative* solidarity is supported by "moral outrage toward egregious human rights violations and manifest acts of aggression".[33] It can substantiate a cosmopolitan understanding of international criminal law as recognizing "negative duties of a universalistic morality of justice".[34] Pavlos Eleftheriadis links Kant's cosmopolitan law to the idea of international accountability and argues that there is an emerging Kantian cosmopolitan law in existing human rights law.[35] Chapter 3 discusses the link between such cosmopolitan theories and a cosmopolitan criminal law in detail.

1.4. Philosophical and Sociological Presuppositions in Cosmopolitan War Crimes Law

In this book, I would like to expand the discussion on the cosmopolitan approach to international criminal law, in particular, war crimes law, by elaborating cosmopolitan philosophical and sociological presuppositions and their application in the context of war. While "certain mantras"[36] – often inspired by a kind of cosmopolitan ethos – have been repeated to provide moral foundations for punishing international crimes, they remain formalistic and superficial. Despite frequent invocation of a cosmopolitan community – both in theory and in practice – to justify the punishment of war crimes, specific components and structure of such a community are unclear. Drawing on existing cosmopolitan theories, the book gives an in-depth account of possible moral and political models of a cosmopolitan community. It shows how cosmopolitan solidarity can support criminal law's right to punish and protection of intrinsic values of human beings in inter-group conflict.

After laying out some central tenets of cosmopolitan thinking in Chapter 2, I turn to interactions between cosmopolitanism and war crimes law in two

---

[32] David Held, *Democracy and the Global Order: From the Modern State to Cosmopolitan Governance*, Stanford University Press, 1995, pp. 267 ff. The eight cosmopolitan democratic principles are: (1) equal worth and dignity; (2) active agency; (3) personal responsibility and accountability; (4) consent; (5) reflexive deliberation and collective decision-making through voting procedures; (6) inclusiveness and subsidiarity; (7) avoidance of serious harm and the amelioration of urgent need; and (8) sustainability.

[33] Jürgen Habermas, *The Divided West*, ed. and trans. by Ciaran Cronin, Polity Press, Cambridge, 2006, p. 143; Jürgen Habermas, *The Postnational Constellation*, ed. and trans. by Evald Ojaveer, Polity Press, Cambridge, 2001, p. 143.

[34] *Ibid.*

[35] Pavlos Eleftheriadis, "Cosmopolitan Law", in *European Law Journal*, 2003, vol. 9, no. 2, pp. 255, 260–262.

[36] Frédéric Mégret, "What is the Specific Evil of Aggression?", in Claus Kreß and Stefan Barriga (eds.), *The Crime of Aggression: A Commentary*, Cambridge University Press, 2016, p. 1399.

aspects: social foundations of the law and values protected by the law. Chapter 3 investigates possible ways to conceive and organize a cosmopolitan community as a prerequisite for a cosmopolitan war crimes law. Chapter 4 explicates strategies of criminalization which seek compromise between cosmopolitan values and dictates of war.

It is important to clarify at the start that I do not present my description of the cosmopolitan approach as the only possible way to conceive a cosmopolitan war crimes law. Rather, this book presents one version of war crimes law which conforms to cosmopolitan ideology and is sufficiently informed by positive law and practice. It explores, for the purposes of war crimes law, normative possibilities presented by cosmopolitan theories and appendant challenges.

1.5. Moral Psychology of Human Agents in War

What empirical challenges does war impose on a cosmopolitan war crimes law? The normative strengths of cosmopolitan legal inspirations are contrasted with human agents' cognitive and motivational weaknesses in war. I proceed to show a possible *moral distance* between a cosmopolitan conception of the law and the specific normative environment of war. Through extensive psychological evidence, individual accounts of soldiers, and war studies, Chapters 5–7 show that war subverts the normative environment and exacerbates human vulnerabilities. The viability and ultimate legitimacy of the project of a cosmopolitan war crimes law are linked to the moral nature of human beings. Participants in war may not have the normative competence to consider the reason of cosmopolitan law.

Chapter 8 explains the consequences of the *moral distance* between cosmopolitan war crimes law and the embedded military personnel. It considers how criminal law can be practiced in a way that shows greater sensitivity to the unique social environment in war. Chapter 9 evaluates moral and legal authorities of a cosmopolitan war crimes law and compatibility between cosmopolitanism, criminal law and war. It concludes by reflecting on the intrinsic merits and defects in the cosmopolitan characterization of war crimes law.

2

The Universal, the Individual, the Rational: A Cosmopolitan Approach to War Crimes Law

This chapter describes the central tenets of cosmopolitanism for the purposes of the book. It then confronts cosmopolitan thinking with conceptual challenges posed by war.

Contemporary cosmopolitanism first of all assumes a common *moral* community consisted of all human beings. It means certain moral values are valid for all people no matter who they are and where they live. As a result, we have certain cosmopolitan obligations to distant strangers with whom we have no special relationship of any kind. Cosmopolitanism includes moral and political orientations. It is an interpretation of the world and at the same time a powerful normative force for change. It projects the idea of a universal human community as possible and good.

2.1. A Quest for Universality: Commonality over Differences

This section gives an overview of the intellectual heritage, problematization of the world, and search for moral authority of cosmopolitan thinking. It discerns two main strategies of cosmopolitan thinking: describing common human features as morally relevant and essential; and downplaying human differences, particularly those of cultural and social nature.

2.1.1. Western Heritage of Contemporary Cosmopolitanism

The quest for universality is a distinctly human struggle. People have different visions for universality in different times and spaces. The kind of cosmopolitanism that inspires international criminal law has largely Western heritage. Other cultures have their way of conceiving the universal which may be related to but nevertheless different from the one described here. The philosopher Zhao Tingyang, for example, describes Chinese historical notion of 'tianxia' (天下), or "all under heaven", as a borderless world.[1] The relevant Chinese tradition sees difference as enriching, and harmonious co-existence and interactions among all the particulars as cosmopolitan.[2] Cosmopolitan moral concerns may

[1] Zhao Tingyang, *All Under Heaven: The Tianxia System for a Possible World Order*, trans. by Joseph E. Harroff, University of California Press, Berkeley, 2021.

[2] Xiang Shuchen, *Chinese Cosmopolitanism: The History and Philosophy of an Idea*, Princeton University Press, 2023, pp. 24–25.

also be extended to animals, plants and even non-living things.[3] An important difference among cosmopolitan ideals is the morally relevant criteria to be included in the universal community: it can be cultural, biological, spiritual, *et cetera*. Another important difference is the content of universal moral concern. For example, is it harmonious and mutually enriching co-existence of groups, or survival and flourishing of individual persons, living things or non-living things?

Alternative conceptions of the universal can reveal the strengths and weaknesses of the current one; they help us realize that the cosmopolitanism which is familiar to international criminal law is neither necessary nor absolute. However, in this book, I will focus on the Western conception of cosmopolitanism as it is most akin to the theory and practice of international criminal law as we know it. It is therefore a particular kind of cosmopolitanism that is envisaged and studied here.

The kind of contemporary cosmopolitanism described here has a distinctly biological basis: it regards the naturally born human body, which generates common human features, as morally relevant. In other words, the primary unit for moral concern is the physical human being. The universal moral standards that follow are centred on the individual human being, in particular, the preservation of bodily and mental integrity.

Cosmopolitan ideas can be found in classical antiquity. The original Greek word *kosmopolites* means 'citizen of the world'. It is attributed to Diogenes the Cynic. When asked where he comes from, Diogenes replies, "I am a citizen of the world [*kosmopolites*]".[4] This statement reverberates throughout the history of Western cosmopolitanism.[5] It imagines a form of belonging which goes beyond the community to which one is born – a belonging that attaches to all of humanity. It relativizes one's own culture and identity and challenges the inside-outside distinction of a particular community.[6] A century later, the Stoics take up Diogenes' cosmopolitanism with "an enduring political orientation".[7] The

3 In some cultures, cosmopolitanism includes all living things or even things in the moral universe and see them not as distinct categories, but in a natural continuum. See, for example, Xiang, 2023, p. 110, *supra* note 2. Xiang summarizes an important stream of Chinese philosophy as seeing "a fundamental commensurability or oneness underlying all things, whether animals, demons, or non-Chinese". She describes "a pervasive view in the Chinese classics is that animals are in some ways sensitive to human virtue" (p. 170).

4 Cited in Noah Feldman, "Cosmopolitan Law?", in *The Yale Law Journal*, 2007, vol. 116, no. 1022, p. 1027.

5 Gerard Delanty, *The Cosmopolitan Imagination: The Renewal of Critical Social Theory*, Cambridge University Press, 2009, p. 20.

6 *Ibid*., p. 21.

7 *Ibid*.

Stoics believe that the social nature of human beings makes unity and solidarity of a cosmopolitan community possible.[8] According to Martha Nussbaum, the Stoics aspire to be citizens not of a particular polis, but to give "first allegiance to no mere form of government, no temporal power, but to the moral community made up by the humanity of all human beings".[9] The influence of the Stoic cosmopolitan ideal on the Graeco-Roman civilization is expressed in the notion *oikoumene*, which means "the whole world" or "the inhabited world" and envisions an extended community beyond the immediate one.[10]

While cosmopolitanism is a marginal stream of thought in antiquity, it becomes integrated into the movement of modernity.[11] Its political and cultural orientations develop further under the influence of secularism, geographical discoveries and scientific progress.[12] From the Renaissance to the Enlightenment, the cosmopolitan spirit spreads throughout Europe.[13] The humanists, such as Erasmus, revive the ancient cosmopolitan beliefs in human unity and the possibility of extended communal bonds based on common human nature.[14] New theories of political authority and social relations emerge in light of optimistic conceptions of human nature.[15] In particular, the writings of Grotius and Pufendorf on an emerging theory of international law display a kind of political and legal cosmopolitanism limited to avoiding war.[16] The Enlightenment spirit favours allegiance to a wider human community rather than a closed community. Diogenes' claim of 'a citizen of the world' is invoked by many eighteenth-century thinkers, such as Voltaire and Hume.[17] It is believed that the Enlightenment

---

8 *Ibid.*

9 Martha C. Nussbaum, "Patriotism and Cosmopolitanism", in Joshua Cohen (ed.), *For Love of Country: Debating the Limits of Patriotism*, Beacon Press, Boston, 1996, p. 7.

10 Cited in Delanty, 2009, p. 24, see *supra* note 5. More on Greek and Roman cosmopolitanism in relation to international criminal law, see Morten Bergsmo, Emiliano J. Buis and Song Tianying, "Protected Interests in International Criminal Law", in Morten Bergsmo, Emiliano J. Buis and Song Tianying (eds.), *Philosophical Foundations of International Criminal Law: Legally-Protected Interests*, Torkel Opsahl Academic EPublisher, Brussels, 2022, pp. 1 ff. (https://www.toaep.org/ps-pdf/36-bergsmo-buis-song).

11 Delanty, 2009, p. 29, see *supra* note 5. The distinction between civilization and barbarism was widely accepted throughout most of Western history. The "discourse of barbarism" creates "a complex system of signifiers denoting the ethnically, psychologically, and politically 'other'". See Edith Hall, *Inventing the Barbarian*, Oxford University Press, 1991, cited in Xiang, 2023, p. 75, *supra* note 2.

12 *Ibid.*

13 *Ibid.*

14 *Ibid.*, p. 30.

15 *Ibid.*

16 *Ibid.*

17 *Ibid.*, p. 36.

cultivated "an attitude of world openness" and "a transcendental sensibility around the centrality of the human person and rights".[18] Kant's cosmopolitanism, for example, posits that all human beings are united in their common moral nature and purpose.[19]

The term 'cosmopolitanism' is "rediscovered" and gradually taken up by recent political scientists in the critical discourse on globalization.[20] Cosmopolitanism is introduced to formulate strategies in dealing with globalization and its negative consequences.[21] Many contemporary cosmopolitan theories carry a distinct Kantian legacy. The last 30 years have witnessed the growing importance of Kantian cosmopolitanism in the global justice debate. Enlightenment cosmopolitan ideals are found to be pertinent to the contemporary world of globalization, legitimacy challenges of State sovereignty, and the emerging role of non-State actors.[22] This "new cosmopolitanism" draws on the Kantian cosmopolitan right and places on top of its agenda human rights, international law, global governance and inter-State peace.[23] It takes strength from the liberal multilateral order, but is more radical in its structural design and normative claims.[24]

Another source of contemporary cosmopolitan debate is John Rawls' 1971 book *A Theory of Justice*. It is an unexpected upshot of cosmopolitan thinking because Rawls' *A Theory of Justice* is about distributive justice within a State. Yet Rawls' idea of intra-State justice triggers discussions of global justice.[25] In Rawls' hypothesis of an "original position", when members of a society can choose – behind a veil of ignorance – a redistribution system, they would rationally choose a system where the worst-off person can be as comfortable as he would have been under equal redistribution of resources. Charles Beitz and

---

18 *Ibid.*

19 *Ibid.*

20 Edgar Grande, "Cosmopolitan Political Science", in *The British Journal of Sociology*, 2006, vol. 57, no. 1, pp. 87 ff. More on Anglo-American influence on the global justice discourse, see Samuel Moyn, "The Political Origins of Global Justice", in Joel Isaac *et al.* (eds.), *The Worlds of American Intellectual History*, Oxford University Press, 2016, pp. 133–153.

21 Grande, 2006, see *supra* note 20.

22 Robert Fine, *Cosmopolitanism*, Routledge, Abingdon, 2007, p. 4.

23 *Ibid.*, p. 1.

24 Grande, 2006, p. 88, see *supra* note 20.

25 Rawls himself later argues for State-centred principles of international justice in John Rawls, *The Law of Peoples: With "The Idea of Public Reason Revisited"*, Harvard University Press, Cambridge, 2001.

Thomas Pogge seek to extend Rawls's theory of distributive justice globally,[26] while Brian Barry claims that Rawls' theory is flawed because it cannot address issues of international justice.[27] These and other arguments against Rawls' thesis herald the "heroic" breach of "the frontiers of justice" in a distinctly cosmopolitan spirit.[28]

Various cosmopolitan agendas emerge in fields such as distributive justice, democracy, peace, humanitarian intervention, global criminal justice, and migration.[29] Most contemporary cosmopolitans share the view that all human beings have equal moral standing in the species-wide community. This "egalitarian individualism"[30] challenges the Westphalian State sovereignty and the "national presuppositions and prejudices"[31] that come with it in traditional legal and political theories. As mentioned in the beginning of this section, cosmopolitanism, of course, does not have to be solely or even mainly individual-oriented. Though, the individualistic vision of contemporary cosmopolitanism has, to a great extent, won the competition among rival cosmopolitanisms in many areas.[32] I now turn to the notion 'human identity' as the material basis for contemporary cosmopolitan theories.

2.1.2. Human Identity Consisting of Common Human Features

What does the human identity consist of? A simple answer is that humankind is an aggregate of members of a biological species. This answer is not satisfying for our moral philosophical inquiry because humankind as such is not different from 'animalkind'. Sharing a biological species is only the starting point. What

[26] See Charles R. Beitz, *Political Theory and International Relations*, Princeton University Press, 1979; Thomas W. Pogge, *Realizing Rawls*, Cornell University Press, Ithaca, 1989. Articles by these authors include Charles R. Beitz, "Bounded Morality: Justice and the State in World Politics", in *International Organization*, 1979, vol. 33, no. 3, pp. 405–424; Thomas Pogge, "Rawls and Global Justice", in *Canadian Journal of Philosophy*, 1988, vol. 18, no. 2, pp. 227–256.

[27] See Brian Barry, *Theories of Justice: A Treaties on Social Justice*, Volume 1, Harvester Wheatsheaf, Berkeley, 1989.

[28] Moyn, 2016, see *supra* note 20.

[29] See, for example, list made by Daniele Archibugi, "A Cosmopolitan Perspective on Global Criminal Justice", IRPPS Working Paper No. 75, 2015, p. 63. For more on cosmopolitan projects, see Ulrich Beck and Natan Sznaider, "A Literature on Cosmopolitanism: An Overview", in *The British Journal of Sociology*, 2006, vol. 57, no. 1, pp. 153–164.

[30] David Held, "Principles of Cosmopolitan Order", in Gillian Brock and Harry Brighouse (eds.), *Global Justice and Cosmopolitanism: An Introduction*, Cambridge University Press, 2005, p. 12.

[31] Fine, 2007, p. 2, see *supra* note 22.

[32] Samuel Moyn, "The Universal Declaration of Human Rights of 1948 in the History of Cosmopolitanism", in *Critical Inquiry*, 2014, vol. 40, no. 4, p. 377.

is distinctly 'human' has to be elaborated to warrant corresponding universal moral standards. Such uniquely *human* quality has been described in different ways: "the inalienable features of our common humanity",[33] "the fundamental 'human' element of our common humanity",[34] "the most stable components of atemporal human nature",[35] or in less essentialist terms such as "human universals or universal human constants".[36]

Throughout history, the quest of common features particular to humans, or what being 'human' entails, has never ceased. The social, moral and intellectual dimensions of being human are familiar candidates; compassion, creativity, spirituality, selfishness, and hedonism also make frequent appearance. Richard Norman uses "basic responses" such as anger and laughter as the starting point for his evaluation.[37]

The ways in which human identity is studied have also changed throughout time. The focus of human identity moves away from early metaphysical questions about the cosmos and closer to empirical studies such as anthropology, sociology and psychology. In his theory on crimes against humanity, David J. Luban explains his characterization of human beings as political animals is "wholly naturalist", anchored in empirical observations and "common sense".[38] Scientists and philosophers have been searching for "psychological universals", or the "psychic unity" of humanity.[39] Bhikhu Parekh interprets human identity as constituted by "human universals or universal human constants" such as human capacities, desires, needs, *et cetera*.[40] According to Parekh, human universals are presupposed and instantiated by all cultures and societies.[41] The idea of human universals integrates psychological, anthropological, sociological and philosophical perspectives. In the rest of this sub-section, I draw on Parekh's list of human universals consisting of *capacities*, *needs* and *desires*, as an

33 Daniel Chernilo, *The Natural Law Foundations of Modern Social Theory*, Cambridge University Press, 2013, p. 4.

34 *Ibid.*

35 *Ibid.*, p. 74.

36 Bhikhu Parekh, "Non-Ethnocentric Universalism", in Tim Dunne and Nicholas J. Wheeler (eds.), *Human Rights in Global Politics*, Cambridge University Press, 1999, p. 142.

37 Richard Norman, *Ethics, Killing and War*, Cambridge University Press, 1995, p. 20.

38 David J. Luban, "A Theory of Crimes Against Humanity", in *Yale Journal of International Law*, 2004, vol. 29, p. 111.

39 Daniel M.T. Fessler and Edouard Machery, "Culture and Cognition", in Eric Margolis (ed.), *The Oxford Handbook of Philosophy of Cognitive Science*, Oxford University Press, 2012, pp. 503–504.

40 Parekh, 1999, p. 142, see *supra* note 36.

41 *Ibid.*

illustration of the notion of human identity.[42] Notably, many of these human universals are pertinent to the interpretation and legitimation of a cosmopolitan war crimes law and have been repeatedly referenced in legal practice.

Conceptions of human agency proceed from conceptions of human capacities. Parekh illustrates the following human capacities: "the capacities to think, reason, use language, judge, dream dreams, form visions of the good life, acknowledge and discharge duties", and to enter into moral and emotional relations with each other.[43] These are intellectual, rational, imaginary, emotional, moral, and sensual capacities universally displayed by human beings. These capacities are developed in society and are exclusive to the human species.[44] They make humans "meaning-creating and culture-building beings".[45] There is a tendency to emphasize mental qualities, explicitly or implicitly, to reveal what is unique with being human.[46] While seeing mental capacities as distinctly human, we should not forget that the more primitive sentient capacities – capacities to feel pain and pleasure – can also have a social aspect. Pain and pleasure can be quite subjective. Human beings can attach meanings to pain and pleasure in ways that animals cannot.

The uniquely human capacities concern both oneself and one's relationship with other human beings. They have both inward and outward application. Or, as Catherine Lu puts it, "humans are part authors of themselves and their world".[47] Looking inward, human beings possess strong self-consciousness in that they are capable of forming overall conceptions of their lives. Every human being has a past and a future, thus a unique experience of life. Through their activities and experiences, human beings give meaning and character to the natural biological process from birth to death.[48] For example, humans are capable of self-development through spiritual, philosophical, scientific, artistic or literary explorations. Human beings create meaning not only for their inner selves, but also for their social and natural environment. They are capable of

42 For more on how human universals relate to human nature and human culture, see Donald E. Brown, "Human Universals, Human Nature & Human Culture", in *Daedalus*, 2004, vol. 133, no. 4, pp. 47–54.

43 Parekh, 1999, p. 143, see *supra* note 36.

44 *Ibid.*, p. 142.

45 *Ibid.*, p. 144.

46 This section does not examine the immensely controversial question of individuals who do not possess the required level of consciousness or rationality, which is a topic in its own right. As Parekh says, even people with mental problems are mad or sick in a uniquely human way. See also the detailed discussion in Norman, 1995, *supra* note 37.

47 Catherine Lu, "The One and Many Faces of Cosmopolitanism", in *The Journal of Political Philosophy*, 2000, vol. 8, no. 2, p. 254.

48 Norman, 1995, p. 59, see *supra* note 37.

understanding and changing the world. They interact with society and nature in profound and uniquely human ways.[49]

In addition to common capacities, human beings share certain desires and needs. The desires and needs can be natural or social, physical or mental. Humans as living beings desire survival, health, seek sexual satisfaction, need rest, physical activities, *et cetera.*[50] As social beings, they desire "self-respect, the good opinion of others, friendship, love and forming relations with those they like (and avoiding those they do not like)".[51] In light of the human universals described above, certain common conditions are essential for all human beings to survive and flourish.[52]

Although the concept of human identity is often intended to provide material grounds for determining moral principles, it is not devoid of normative input. These characterizations are inevitably teleological given how the question is posed. For example, despite that the concept of human universals is presented as a neutral description of human identity, disagreements over human universals can be as ideological as they are epistemological. Philosophers have cautioned against confounding norms and facts.[53] That is, values and moral principles cannot be derived from facts, or factual conceptions. The role of facts is said to inform normative exercises, to provide "the indispensable raw material and context" for human evaluation.[54] Facts are considered necessary, not determinative of normative decision. However, description is inevitably preceded by, and conflated with, norm. Normative presumptions can give rise to different descriptions of the same facts. The same facts can be the basis of different normative assessments and propositions. Norman warns against ascribing "a false universality to forms of behaviour which are in fact culturally specific". Such 'false universality' is in turn used to "legitimise particular social institutions by making them appear inevitable".[55] Luban reminds us of the dangers of overconfident assertions of "certain central aspects of human condition" as obvious and

[49] Parekh, 1999, p. 143, see *supra* note 36.

[50] *Ibid.*, p. 144.

[51] *Ibid.*

[52] *Ibid.*, p. 145.

[53] For example, Kant rejects the belief that moral commands can be deduced from human properties: "a metaphysics of morals cannot be based upon an anthropology but still can be applied to it" (cited in Chernilo, 2013, p. 122, see *supra* note 33). John Finnis firmly states that there can never be "'inference' from universality of human nature to values" (John Finnis, *Natural Law and Natural Rights*, Oxford University Press, 2011, p. 81).

[54] Parekh, 1999, p. 142, see *supra* note 36.

[55] Norman, 1995, p. 19, see *supra* note 37.

banal.[56] This is why empirical studies are not simply induction from facts – and philosophical reasoning not purely deduction from an idea.

Moral reasoning, in so far as it is a characterization of "actions and situations as being of a certain kind",[57] is a combination of moral principles and empirical facts. The description of human identity is therefore a cosmopolitan *insight*. It is called an 'insight' because it bears a normative predisposition. The investigation of common human features is guided by and lends substance to the idea of a universal human identity. Without universalism, the investigation of human features lacks direction; without demonstrable common features, universality is empty. The construction of human identity here prioritizes common human features over cultural and social differences. Commonality is given moral priority over differences to justify universal moral standards. How people perceive basic human condition directly affects their hypothesis for inter-human relations. For example, many cosmopolitans interpret differences among human groups as a driving force, rather than obstacle, for unity. They believe that commonality always triumphs over difference, and universality over particularity in inter-group encounters. Chernilo observes a "self-propelling capacity" of universalism: "the more it was able to recognise differences empirically, the more it sought to foster the belief in universal equality".[58] Gerard Delanty similarly argues: "The diversity of peoples and the pursuit of a civilizational unity was the central animus that inspired cosmopolitan thought in several civilizations".[59] As we will see in the last section of this chapter, this normative predisposition is somewhat out of place in war. Whether people see other human beings as fellow members of humanity or as enemies with irreconcilable differences, may be influenced by the normative environment.

2.2. A Cosmopolitanism of the Universal, the Individual, and the Rational

Bearing in mind the normative strategy to prioritize commonality over differences within the human species, I proceed to highlight three key features of cosmopolitanism studied here: that it is (1) universalistic in its reach, (2) individualistic in its standing, and (3) rationalistic in its conception of human agency. The normative triad is crucial to the conception of a cosmopolitan war crimes law in Chapters 3 and 4.

[56] Luban, 2004, p. 28, see *supra* note 38.

[57] Norman, 1995, p. 35, see *supra* note 37.

[58] Chernilo, 2013, p. 85, see *supra* note 33.

[59] Delanty, 2009, p. 20, see *supra* note 5.

2.2.1. Universal in Normative Reach

Cosmopolitans are persons "whose primary allegiance is to the worldwide community of human beings".[60] The idea of human identity is a universalistic way to understand the human species. It embodies the belief in "fundamental unity" of all human beings, a unity that is beyond the physiological constitution of human beings.[61] It provides a way of extending our sense of belonging beyond the immediate environment. Eric Voegelin says: "Without universality, there would be no mankind other than the aggregate of members of a biological species; there would be no more a history of mankind than there is a history of catkind or horsekind".[62] And Daniel Chernilo adds: "it is only through an idea of universality that we transcend our biological likeness and become able to recognise each other as human beings".[63] Unity of humankind is enabled by human capacity for fellowship.[64] Cosmopolitans believe that human imagination is never satisfied with limited communities – it seeks to transcend boundaries and reach the widest range possible, that is, a cosmopolis encompassing all human beings.

Parekh gives reason for unity of humankind as a preferred normative choice. According to Parekh, moral or social exclusion builds artificial barriers among human groups which are impossible to sustain. The exclusivist view is vulnerable because it has to maintain that some human groups are so different from others that they cannot inhabit the same moral universe. Such claim is false and can only be justified by further falsehoods. And falsehoods are "sustained by suppressing inner doubts, moral feelings and critical reflection, by encouraging morbid fears and irrational obsessions, etc., all of which take a heavy psychological and moral toll on those involved".[65] Social exclusion is not only untenable but also undesirable. The exclusivist mindset has grave consequences for human beings: it "breeds aggressiveness, hatred, intolerance and desire for domination, and leads to violence and bloodshed".[66] Indeed, moral exclusion is a familiar logic of genocidal ideology or armed conflict between groups. Human unity should be promoted if we do not want genocide, ethnic cleansing or war.

Universality of human features also means certain norms should apply to all human beings without distinction. Kant, for example, relies on the idea of human identity to support his argument that all human beings should always

[60] Nussbaum, 1996, p. 4, see *supra* note 9.

[61] Chernilo, 2013, p. 4, see *supra* note 33.

[62] Cited in *ibid.*

[63] Chernilo, 2013, p. 224, see *supra* note 33.

[64] Parekh, 1999, p. 149, see *supra* note 36.

[65] *Ibid.*, p. 146.

[66] *Ibid.*

treat each other as ends and never as means.[67] Claus Nielsen characterizes this kind of cosmopolitanism as "non-relational", that is, an inter-personal relationship that is not relative to social circumstances.[68] Non-relational cosmopolitanism seeks to apply principles of (liberal) domestic justice globally. It is argued that since all human beings have common "morally relevant properties", moral values should attach equally and universally to all.[69] Similarly, principles derived from Rawls' original position should apply globally because the original position uses a universalistic conception of human beings – it presupposes "a capacity for a sense of justice" and "a capacity to form, to revise and rationally to pursue a conception of the good" in human beings generally.[70]

The universalist dimension of cosmopolitanism can serve to relativize political and territorial boundaries. Boaventura de Sousa Santos proclaims that "[w]e have the right to be equal whenever difference diminishes us".[71] The concept of 'State' has dominated political theory for a long time.[72] As the universal form of political organization, the State exercises "political and ethical monopoly over a territory and population".[73] The principle of sovereignty promotes "rigid, hierarchical and closed forms of political practice, subjectivity, identity and community".[74] The three "epochal" inter-State wars of the twentieth century have entrenched the Westphalian State-system.[75] Cosmopolitan thinking challenges conventional moral boundaries presumed in political theories. The ethics of sovereignty is said to be one of "absolute exclusion", which is built on "a spatial metaphysics of same and other, citizen and enemy, identity and difference".[76] The exclusivist logic of State sovereignty results in an unjustifiable gap between intra-State and inter-State norms and reality: "Inside the state is community, morality, politics, freedom etc., and outside is anarchy, power, war,

[67] Chernilo, 2013, p. 129, see *supra* note 33.

[68] Claus Nielsen, "Justifying Cosmopolitanism: A Methodological Critique", in Laura Valentini (ed.), *Justice in a Globalized World: A Normative Framework*, Oxford University Press, 2011, p. 46.

[69] Cited in *ibid.*

[70] Cited in *ibid.*, p. 48.

[71] Boaventura de Sousa Santos, "Nuestra America", in *Theory, Culture & Society*, 2001, vol. 18, nos. 2–3, p. 193.

[72] Feldman, 2007, p. 1027, see *supra* note 4.

[73] Richard Shapcott, *Justice, Community and Dialogue in International Relations*, Cambridge University Press, 2001, p. 65.

[74] *Ibid.*

[75] Feldman, 2007, p. 1027, see *supra* note 4.

[76] Cited in Shapcott, 2001, p. 65, see *supra* note 73.

danger, difference and insecurity".[77] It is argued that moral and political discourses need not be constrained by the dichotomies and exclusions dictated by the principle of sovereignty. Many cosmopolitans have come to see nationality as "a 'morally arbitrary' feature of persons in the same way as their hair colour or the social class of their parents".[78] It is morally arbitrary because a person is not morally responsible for his or her nationality.[79] Simon Caney says that "people should not be penalized because of the vagaries of happenstance, and their fortunes should not be set by factors like nationality and citizenship".[80] Unequal treatment on the basis of morally arbitrary features such as the nationality is considered unjustified.[81]

2.2.2. The Individual as the Source of Norms and Behaviours

The individual person is at the centre of cosmopolitan thought. Universality and rationality are embodied in the human person. Every human being has intrinsic moral worth and should be treated with equal consideration. Human beings are capable of creating meaning through intellectual, moral, artistic, spiritual and social activities. To confer worth on human beings is to value the capacity to create worthy things and lead worthy lives.[82] Universalism is achieved through 'normative individualism'. 'Normative individualism', as Roland Pierik and Wouter Werner explain, means exactly that "persons are taken to be 'self-originating sources of valid claims' and, as such, as the ultimate units of concern".[83] It is argued that every human being should have "a global stature" independent of social and cultural contingencies.[84] As such normative individualism distinguishes the kind of cosmopolitanism described here from theories which ascribe intrinsic moral values to "ethnic or religious communities, the family, the state, traditions, etc.".[85]

---

77 *Ibid.*

78 David Miller, *National Responsibility and Global Justice*, Oxford University Press, 2007, p. 31.

79 *Ibid.*

80 Cited in *ibid.*, p. 32.

81 *Ibid.*

82 Parekh, 1999, p. 147, see *supra* note 36.

83 Roland Pierik and Wouter Werner, "Cosmopolitanism in Context: An Introduction", in Roland Pierik and Wouter Werner (eds.), *Cosmopolitanism in Context: Perspectives from International Law and Political Theory*, Cambridge University Press, 2010, p. 2. Pierik and Werner point out that the phrase "self-originating sources of valid claims" is coined by John Rawls in "Kantian Constructivism in Moral Theory", in *Journal of Philosophy*, 1980, vol. 77, no. 9, p. 543.

84 See Pierik and Werner, 2010, p. 1, *supra* note 83.

85 *Ibid.*, p. 2.

The human person is the ultimate scale for the normative assessment of institutions, values and practices. Reliance on human identity – not social, cultural contexts – to determine moral rules assumes the primacy of human persons over social institutions and circumstances. Parekh explains that the reason why we value human creations such as cultural, historical objects, or cultural and spiritual communities is because we value the human capacity to create worth, not the objects or institutions themselves.[86] Parekh argues that no cultural community can deny human worth altogether because it would deny the worth of the community.[87] Being a human creation, the cultural community cannot claim worth of "its beliefs, practices and achievements without valuing both the capacities that made these possible and their human bearers".[88] Charles Beitz similarly argues that the interests of persons are fundamental and those of the State are derived from individual interests.[89] From this basis, he keeps questioning the empirical and normative significance of State boundaries in politics and morality.[90]

Every human being has dignity and worth, needs certain conditions to lead a meaningful life, and deserves equal moral consideration.[91] One should not pursue one's goals in violation of others' dignity, worth or well-being. The cosmopolitan position requires formal equality among all persons – every individual is a holder of the same rights and duties.[92] Invoking certain notions of human nature presupposes that human nature is stable and personal passions, motives, interests and capacities are primary in understanding human action and forming normative guidance.

The cosmopolitan individual is inevitably abstract. Cosmopolitan thinking privileges the "generalised" other over the "concrete other" – general in terms of common capacities, desires and needs; "concrete" in terms of social and cultural embeddedness.[93] Universal individualism carries heritage of Western philosophy from Hobbes to Rawls.[94] It is an individualism that does not recognise distinct individuals.

[86] Parekh, 1999, p. 147, see *supra* note 36.

[87] *Ibid.*, p. 148.

[88] *Ibid.*

[89] Beitz, 1979, p. 64, see *supra* note 26.

[90] See Catherine Lu's analysis of Beitz's work in "Cosmopolitan Liberalism and the Faces of Injustice in International Relations", in *Review of International Studies*, 2005, vol. 31, no. 2, p. 402.

[91] Parekh, 1999, p. 149, see *supra* note 36.

[92] Shapcott, 2001, p. 35, see *supra* note 73.

[93] *Ibid.*

[94] *Ibid.*

The individual is the ultimate source not only of cosmopolitan values, but also of normative judgment and behaviour. As we will see in the following chapters, the centrality of the individual coincides with proliferation of criminal law at international level.

2.2.3. Rationality as a Force for Normative Unity

Contemporary cosmopolitanism can be seen as "the prolongation of rationalist thought" which is characteristic of the Western way of thinking.[95] Rational capacity is a generic category. It can refer to a cluster of closely related mental capacities which enable abstract thinking, belief-formation, decision-making, normative reasoning, planning, self-control, *et cetera*. Human reason figures prominently in the source and content of moral principles. A lasting heritage of the Enlightenment is that moral values are grounded in human rationality more than religious or naturalistic origins. Every human being with rational capacity has access to the most fundamental norms of right and wrong – fundamental as touching the core of our human identity. The content and validity of these underived moral values are considered as recognizable by our innate moral capacity. We need not look outside ourselves to find answers to the most basic questions of right and wrong. These fundamentals cannot be proven, nor are they demonstrable or falsifiable; they are immanent to the human experience. They come close to moral intuition but are not characterized as such. As Norwegian philosopher Arne Johan Vetlesen puts it: "we, simply as human beings with some experience with others (and with ourselves), know what evil is; we know, that is, what it means to intentionally inflict pain and suffering on someone else".[96] Similarly, Norman emphasizes the inherent wrongfulness of killing: it cannot be proven, nor can there be an argument offered to someone who doubts it; the only thing that can be pointed to is "the fact that most people just *do* regard it in that way".[97] Jürgen Habermas confirms this capacity for moral experience:

> what moral and, especially, immoral action means is something we experience and learn prior to all philosophy; it confronts us no less compellingly in compassion for the hurt integrity of others than in suffering over one's own afflicted identity or in anxiety at its being endangered.[98]

---

95 See, for example, Tariq Ramadan's argument in *Islam, the West, and the Challenges of Modernity*, trans. by Saïd Amghar, The Islamic Foundation, Markfield, 2009, p. 130, fn. 36.

96 Arne Johan Vetlesen, *Evil and Human Agency*, Cambridge University Press, 2009, p. 3.

97 Norman, 1995, p. 70, see *supra* note 37.

98 Cited in Vetlesen, 2009, p. 3, see *supra* note 96.

In addition to the innate capacity to access core values, moral reasoning is said to also follow certain prior principles of logic. All human studies, be it natural or social, rely on some sort of underived principles from which all the other inferences within the discipline can be made. The first principles of human reason come from "an imaginary moral universe whose status is quite mysterious" and form "an external demand which we have to obey, a self-sufficient moral requirement which imposes itself on us".[99] These prior principles are not falsifiable, and can only be presumed to be valid. Principles of elementary formal logic, for example, are relied upon by natural sciences and other disciplines.[100] John Finnis illustrates seven principles of rational thinking:

> One such principle is that the principles of logic, for example the forms of deductive inference, are to be used and adhered to in all one's thinking, even though no non-circular proof of their validity is possible (since any proof would employ them). Another is that an adequate reason why anything is so rather than otherwise is to be expected, unless one has a reason not to expect such a reason [...]. A third is that self-defeating theses are to be abandoned [...]. A fourth is that phenomena are to be regarded as real unless there is some reason to distinguish between appearance and reality. A fifth is that a full description of data is to be preferred to partial descriptions, and that an account or explanation of phenomena is not to be accepted if it requires or postulates something inconsistent with the data for which it is supposed to account. A sixth is that a method of interpretation which is successful is to be relied upon in further similar cases until contrary reason appears. A seventh is that theoretical accounts which are simple, predictively successful, and explanatorily powerful are to be accepted in preference to other accounts.[101]

These elementary principles of theoretical rationality means that moral reasoning is intuitive but not necessarily *arbitrary*. Parekh points out that the reasoning exercise "is guided by methodically collected and carefully scrutinised facts, demands of consistency, rules of valid inference, and a balanced assessment of the arguments for and against different views".[102] According to Parekh, "[e]very step it takes in its journey to its conclusions is guided by and justified

[99] Norman, 1995, p. 26, see *supra* note 37.

[100] Finnis, 2011, p. 68, see *supra* note 53. See also, David Estlund, "Methodological Moralism in Political Philosophy", in *Critical Review of International Social and Political Philosophy*, 2017, vol. 20, no. 3, pp. 365–379.

[101] Finnis, 2011, p. 68, see *supra* note 53.

[102] Bhikhu Parekh, *Ethnocentric Political Theory: The Pursuit of Flawed Universals*, Springer, Cham, 2019, p. 59.

in terms of reasons based on these".[103] This means that "all moral reasoning is comparative in nature and involves showing why we should live by some values rather than others".[104] In debates about moral values, being reasonable is to give good reasons for defending or rejecting a moral value; being unreasonable is to reject certain values without giving good reasons, or refuse to accept others' good reasons because it does not warrant one's own preferred conclusions.[105] For example, reasons may include "assessment of our moral capacities, the likely consequences of pursuing different values, their compatibility, the ease with which they can be combined into a coherent way of life, past and present experiences of societies who live by them".[106] It is "clearly unreasonable" to give reasons which are "flimsy, self-serving, based on crude prejudices or ignorance of relevant facts".[107]

Moral reasoning is therefore impartial in its nature and immanent in its origin. It is impartial as it operates according to objective principles of logic, independent of "the agent's feelings, emotions, local situations and circumstances".[108] It is immanent because it originates from natural human capacities. Human beings are endowed with the ability to distinguish between the moral and immoral in the most fundamental matters. The impartial and immanent reason gives force to species-wide *unity* in moral reasoning. That is, fundamental moral values can be discerned by all human beings and be implemented according to the same logical principles. For many cosmopolitan thinkers, the invincible human reason makes unity of humankind possible or even inevitable. Kant, for example, claims that the moral nature of human beings can guarantee the creation of republican governments on the basis of which a wider republican world order can be established.[109] The method of moral reasoning, according to some cosmopolitans, applies to "all thinking subjects, all nations, all epochs, and all cultures".[110] Self-interest, cultural influences, emotional attachments, *et cetera*, are all regarded as contingencies to be transcended.[111] The normative capacity conceived as such is detached from particular circumstances, from social environment, and even from human agents themselves insofar as their preferences and emotions are concerned. Such rational capacity enables the agent to

[103] *Ibid.*
[104] Parekh, 1999, p. 142, see *supra* note 36.
[105] *Ibid.*, p. 143.
[106] *Ibid.*, p. 142.
[107] *Ibid.*, p. 143.
[108] Parekh, 2019, p. 59, see *supra* note 102.
[109] Delanty, 2009, p. 32, see *supra* note 5.
[110] Cited in Lu, 2000, p. 249, see *supra* note 47.
[111] Parekh, 2019, p. 11, see *supra* note 102.

assess cultural and social influences objectively and critically. Ideally, rational capacity facilitates understanding, positive recognition and objective evaluation of the Other, especially those from different cultural and normative backgrounds.[112]

Determination of human agency must proceed from a certain conception of rational capacity. If moral truth is universal and accessible to ordinary human beings, it should create universal standards for human judgment and agency. Human agency grounded in rationality is universal, invariable and not restricted to or impacted by specific circumstances. However, if the stability and impartiality of moral reasoning are inflated, so is the uniting force of moral reasoning. Questions arise as to whether moral reason is a uniting or a dividing force. As we will see in later chapters, the abstract, *a priori* understanding of the moral nature of the human species underlies a cosmopolitan war crimes law's conception of human agency.

2.3. Challenges to Universalism, Individualism and Rationalism: War as Antithesis to Cosmopolitanism

> The cosmopolitan condition is just the condition of peace made permanent. The idea of the cosmopolitan constitution which guarantees 'a union of all peoples under public laws' has the meaning of a 'genuine,' definitive, and not merely provisional condition of peace.[113]

Inter-group encounter can produce cosmopolitanism or war. Human beings can be seen to have a common identity or incompatible identities. While cosmopolitanism highlights commonality, war maximizes difference. While cosmopolitanism is a quest for universality, war is one for hostility. While cosmopolitanism can inspire common goods, war means everyone for himself. As such, cosmopolitanism and war are mutually exclusive. They are at the opposing ends of the range of possible human relationships. Existence and justification of war present both empirical and philosophical challenges to cosmopolitan principles. War demonstrates absolute and insurmountable barriers among human groups. As Habermas's quote at the beginning of this section suggests, peace is an essential component of the cosmopolitan condition.

In a world with numerous human communities, conflict is a permanent theme. War, a particularly severe kind of conflict, carries inter-group animosity to the extreme. The rational, physical and social capacities of human beings can be readily channelled into inter-group war. If, according to the cosmopolitans,

---

[112] Delanty, 2009, p. 86, see *supra* note 5.

[113] Jürgen Habermas, *The Divided West*, ed. and trans. by Ciaran Cronin, Polity Press, Cambridge, 2006, p. 121.

human unity is constitutive of the human conditions, the same can be said about war. War is nothing but human. Political scientist Jean-Pierre Derriennic writes:

> War is a typically human activity. It is specific to a rational, physical and social being: rational, thus capable of formulating aims for his acts and of entering into conflict with his fellows for a wide variety of stakes; physical, thus capable of inflicting and being subjected to violence; social, thus capable of organization and co-operation, without which violence would remain individual and fragmented.[114]

War challenges the idea of unity of humankind. It is a zero-sum game where one's victory is another's defeat. War can be fought for just causes. It means unity of humankind can be breached in the most violent, and possibly irreparable way, for an even 'greater good'. Such greater goods can be human life and dignity, or survival of certain communities, as in the case of humanitarian intervention. War thus brings out potential rivalries within the conceptual trinity of universalism, individualism and rationalism of cosmopolitan morality.

War strengthens moral bonds within the group and alienates the enemy. It typically requires its participants to banish members of the enemy group from their moral universe. The agent recognizes no other relationship than the one with his fellow group members as placing normative demands upon him.[115] The relationship with members of enemy groups is seen as "devoid of moral import".[116] Morality becomes "an exclusively intra-group"[117] matter.

War challenges the worth of the individual. War, regardless of its ultimate goal, is prosecuted on the assumption of the supremacy of the collective good over the individual good. The protagonists of war are (typically) States – the public entity, not individuals. Organized violence is carried out for the sake of the political community and at the expense of individual lives. Individuals – especially soldiers – are mere instruments of war. The worth and dignity of the individual become secondary. There are collective identities and common goals, not individual human identity and personal ends. The individual's moral standing depends on the moral standing of his or her group. Human life and dignity are dispensable in the violent struggle between groups. Killing and humiliating the enemy become "supremely meaningful" forms of violence for participants

---

[114] Jean-Pierre Derriennic, *Les Guerres Civiles*, Presses de Sciences Po, Paris, 2001, cited in Jean-Jacques Frésard, *The Roots of Behaviour in War: A Survey of the Literature*, International Committee of the Red Cross, Geneva, 2004, p. 38.

[115] Vetlesen, 2009, p. 173, see *supra* note 96.

[116] *Ibid.*

[117] *Ibid.*, p. 174.

in war.[118] Human agency is collectivized by and disappears into the collective struggle.

War challenges the universality of objective reason. There are differences which cannot be resolved by rational dialogue in search of the objective truth. Cosmopolitan reason may seem remote and even aloof in front of historical, cultural, emotional or psychological forces. War affirms the strength of physical violence, not the Habermasian "unforced force of better argument". In war, parties exchange brute force, not words or minds. Objective reason faces particularly severe challenge for those participating directly in war. Chapters 6 and 7 elaborate on how military institution and the environment of war erode moral judgment and behavioural capacities of perpetrators of war crimes.

In sum, war poses philosophical and empirical challenges to cosmopolitan morality. The philosophical challenge is that there may be goods which compete with and should be pursued at the cost of cosmopolitan goods. The practical challenge lies in adhering to any cosmopolitan values or beliefs consistently in war. As we shall see in the rest of the book, the struggle between war and cosmopolitanism has direct consequences for the conception and application of war crimes law.

[118] See Luban's characterization of mass violence addressed by international criminal law, in David Luban, "Fairness to Rightness: Jurisdiction, Legality, and the Legitimacy of International Criminal Law", in Samantha Besson and John Tasioulas (eds.), *The Philosophy of International Law*, Oxford University Press, 2010, p. 578.

3

Social Foundations of War Crimes Law: Conceptions of a Cosmopolitan Community

A formalist understanding of war crimes as international crimes is closely linked to the idea of a cosmopolitan moral community. A cosmopolitan war crimes law does not see its direct application to individuals as an accident, but as a necessary consequence of a universal order. This chapter first describes criminal law as a kind of social relation between the community and its members. The intra-community bond provides standing for criminal law to identify public wrongs and impose public punishment. Such a relational understanding of a cosmopolitan war crimes law requires, as I argue in this chapter, a cohesive and concerted cosmopolitan community primarily consisted of individuals. I illustrate possible moral and political models of a cosmopolitan community as the social foundation of the cosmopolitan law. Chapter 4 continues with the substantive wrongs prohibited by war crimes law and their relationship with cosmopolitan values.

3.1. Public Wrongs and Public Response: The Role of Community in Criminal Law

Criminal law is a social practice which is carried out in most modern States. It is one of the regulatory mechanisms used to achieve certain social goals. There are numerous conceptions of criminal law and practices vary greatly. What can be the "common defining features" of criminal law?[1] That is, what are the elements that any practice must display if it is to be regarded as a system of criminal law?[2] A comprehensive overview of the concept of criminal law is beyond the scope of this chapter. Rather, I focus on criminal law's distinct substance and form as they are pertinent to a cosmopolitan approach to war crimes law. That is, I describe the kind of wrongs the law seeks to prohibit and the nature of law's response. A relational account sees criminal law as an embodiment of a

1 R.A. Duff and Stuart P. Green, "Introduction: Searching for Foundations", in R.A. Duff and Stuart P. Green (eds.), *Philosophical Foundations of Criminal Law*, Oxford University Press, 2011, p. 5. For more on theoretical studies of domestic criminal law, see, for example, R.A. Duff *et al.* (eds.), *The Boundaries of the Criminal Law*, Oxford University Press, 2010; R.A. Duff *et al.* (eds.), *The Structures of the Criminal Law*, Oxford University Press, 2011; R.A. Duff *et al.* (eds.), *The Constitution of the Criminal Law*, Oxford University Press, 2013; R.A. Duff *et al.* (eds.), *Criminalization: The Political Morality of the Criminal Law*, Oxford University Press, 2014.

2 Duff and Green, 2011, p. 5, see *supra* note 1.

particular kind of relationship between the community and the individual, and among individuals within the community. Community-wide interactions help define important common values and produce common responses. The presence of an integrated community is key to the system of criminal law. The remaining of this chapter examines the publicness of the wrongs and response, with a focus on the role of community in a cosmopolitan war crimes law. An inquiry into these issues will also shed light on the intrinsic appropriateness of the characterization and response of criminal law when it comes to war crimes.

3.1.1. Publicness of Wrongs Proscribed by Criminal Law

Criminal law defines a type of wrongs as serious and public. A crime is not just any conduct which is inconsistent with shared values of the community.[3] As a subset of "law-breaching" conducts, crimes cross the threshold of seriousness required to justify the characterization of criminal law.[4] Criminal wrongs are not only serious but also public in that they are of special concern to the whole community. The community declares a certain kind of conduct criminal because it is a matter on which the collective must claim normative authority.[5] A crime is a "socially proscribed wrongdoing".[6] The community takes a proper interest in such public wrongs. The publicness of crimes lies in the violation of a kind of Durkheimian "collective consciousness", something that is beyond the individual victim and is "transcendent".[7] In what manner is the wrong done to an individual related to the community? Marshall and Duff provide a useful theory of relationship between the individual and the community in criminal law. According to them, individual interests or goods protected under criminal law are important to the identity and self-understanding of the community.[8] In this way, the group "share" the wrongs done to its members. Attack on the individual equals attack on the community.[9] The community is not wronged *instead* of the individual, but it is wronged *because* the individual is wronged.[10] The common and shared values of the community are vested in every member. There is simultaneously collective and individual ownership of these fundamental values.

---

3. S.E. Marshall and R.A. Duff, "Criminalization and Sharing Wrongs", in *Canadian Journal of Law and Jurisprudence*, 1998, vol. 11, no. 1, p. 13.
4. Massimo Renzo, "Responsibility and Answerability in the Criminal Law", in R.A. Duff *et al.* (eds.), 2013, p. 215, see *supra* note 1.
5. Marshall and Duff, 1998, p. 13, see *supra* note 3.
6. *Ibid.*
7. Cited in Kjersti Lohne, *Advocates of Humanity: Human Rights NGOs in International Criminal Justice*, Oxford University Press, 2019, p. 188.
8. Marshall and Duff, 1998, p. 20, see *supra* note 3.
9. *Ibid.*
10. *Ibid.*

A theory of criminal law must presume some version of political theory which determines the relationship between the individual and the community. The legitimacy of criminal law ultimately depends on the quality of the intra-communal bond. Criminal law stands to express and valorise collective identity and morality,[11] not to control or oppress the population at the behest of sheer power. This means the intra-communal solidarity should be sufficiently coherent and stable at least concerning issues falling under the realm of criminal law.[12] Marshall and Duff's theory of shared wrongs, for example, is premised on the conception of a community "united by mutual concern, by genuinely shared (as distinct from contingently coincident) values and interests, and by the shared recognition that its members' goods (and their identity) are bound up with their membership of the community".[13] Such is a *constitutive* conception of the self. It reflects a kind of inter-subjective relation where the political community is perceived as a constituent part of the self. The individual and the community are mutually constitutive in their identity and interests. It is true that all individuals have an interest in being protected against certain kinds of wrongs. Yet criminal law does not proceed from "an aggregate of individual interests" such as that of security, but from collective interests which members would identify as "our interests".[14] A collective interest derives from a proper collectivity such as the State where people see themselves as members of a common enterprise; it cannot be derived from a random set of individuals who only share habitat, not values.[15] In other words, the community is one of "shared fate",[16] not coincided interests. The collective must be sufficiently involved in characterizing criminal wrongs. Hence, the publicness of criminal wrongs. Only when the individual and community are bound so closely as inseparable in certain important life areas, public wrongs can be meaningfully distinguished from private wrongs, and criminal law from civil law. As such the wrongs done to the individual "properly

[11] Mark Goodale, "After International Law: Anthropology Beyond the 'Age of Human Rights'", in *AJIL Unbound*, 2021, vol. 115, p. 289.

[12] If citizens do not share "a commitment to a substantial set of values that define a civic enterprise in which they see themselves as mutually engaged", according to Duff, "the legitimacy of criminal law is radically undermined, as is the legitimacy of much else about the state". What Duff presents as a genuine or ideal political community can be seen as aspirational for real polities. See R.A. Duff, "Responsibility, Citizenship and Criminal Law", in Duff and Green, 2011, p. 141, *supra* note 1.

[13] Marshall and Duff, 1998, p. 20, see *supra* note 3.

[14] Duff, 2011, p. 137, see *supra* note 12.

[15] *Ibid.*

[16] Cited in *ibid.*, p. 21. Marshall and Duff relate their argument to Charles Taylor's distinction between "convergent" and "common" goods.

concern" the community, and the community has the right (or duty) to take collective action towards the wrongdoer.[17]

Extended to the cosmopolitan level, the wrongs singled out by war crimes law are public in that they properly concern the whole human community. The common and shared values of humanity are vested in every human being. The entire human community is wronged in virtue of the victim's membership in humanity. The values are simultaneously individual and universal. As domestic criminal law is concerned with important values shared by members of the State, international criminal law is concerned with the most important values shared by the human species. In particular, the wrongs which concern international criminal law demonstrate "a lack of respect and concern that we owe to our fellow human beings qua human beings".[18] The wrongness of international crimes is not contingent upon any laws adopted by particular polities. The cosmopolitan law professes norms of justice governing the relation among all human beings, not just within States or other collectivities.[19]

A cosmopolitan war crimes law prioritizes the relationship between the human person and the cosmopolitan community over other relationships in issues falling under its concern. The universal obligation remains even if one finds oneself in a social or political community where such crimes are permitted or even enforced. Because even if such conducts are not considered as crimes in a particular community, they are crimes in the wider community consisted of human beings. Suppose targeting enemy civilians of State A is not criminalized by State B, it is still a crime in the cosmopolitan community encompassing both States. Such wrongs may be called violations of "basic human rights",[20] of a "reasonable set of self-defining values",[21] of important shared values of humanity, or of laws of humanity, depending on one's reference system. We can see why a wider community is needed in establishing war crimes law. War crimes are typically committed by individuals from one State or group against those from another State or group. In such a context, the criminal law cannot be justified by the pre-existing political or moral relationship within the same national community. The wrong has to be linked to a community encompassing both the

[17] *Ibid.*, p. 137.

[18] Renzo, 2013, p. 219, see *supra* note 4.

[19] Samuel Scheffler, *Boundaries and Allegiances: Problems of Justice and Responsibility in Liberal Thought*, Oxford University Press, 2002, p. 4.

[20] Renzo, 2013, p. 214, see *supra* note 4.

[21] Ryan Long, "Responsibility, Authority, and the Community of Moral Agents in Domestic and International Criminal Law", in *International Criminal Law Review*, 2014, vol. 14, nos. 4–5, p. 838.

perpetrator and victim. Such is the community of humanity or a cosmopolitan community.

The public – and universal – nature of wrongs conceived as such resonates with some practices and theories of war crimes law. An imagined cosmopolitan community is often invoked in theory and practice. The following examples serve to illustrate how the idea of a cosmopolitan community is a familiar justification in the field, rather than to argue such practices in themselves validate the cosmopolitan approach. The 1899 *Hague Convention on the Laws and Customs of War on Land* already identifies the "interests of humanity" as its purpose and "laws of humanity" as supplementary to its text. Robert H. Jackson refers to "the common sense of mankind" in his opening address before the Nuremberg Tribunal.[22] The Nuremberg Judgment states that torture and murder of prisoners of war not only violate international law, but also contravene "elementary dictates of humanity".[23] The Rome Statute of the ICC declares, in its Preamble, that international crimes "shock the conscience of humanity" and are of "concern to the international community as a whole". Margaret deGuzman points out that the ICC presupposes "a global community with values and goals" in its legitimacy narrative.[24] International criminal jurisdictions have repeatedly confirmed species-wide concern caused by international crimes. Wrongs done to individuals and groups are linked to humanity: as an attack on humanity itself,[25] harm

[22] Robert H. Jackson, "Opening Statement Before the International Military Criminal Tribunal", in *Trial of Major War Criminals Before the International Military Tribunal, Nuremberg, 14 November – 1 October 1946*, Volume 2: Proceedings, International Military Tribunal ('IMT'), Nuremberg, 1947, pp. 98–102 (https://www.legal-tools.org/doc/3c08b1/).

[23] IMT, "Judgment of 1 October 1946", in *The Trial of German Major War Criminals before the International Military Tribunal*, Volume 22, 27 August 1946–1 October 1946, p. 451 (https://www.legal-tools.org/doc/d1427b/).

[24] Margaret M. DeGuzman, "Mission Uncertain: What Communities Does the ICC Serve?", in Margaret M. deGuzman and Valerie Oosterveld (eds.), *The Elgar Companion to the International Criminal Court*, Edward Elgar Publishing, Cheltenham, 2020, p. 389. See also, Margaret M. deGuzman, *Shocking the Conscience of Humanity: Gravity and the Legitimacy of International Criminal Law*, Oxford University Press, 2020, pp. 18–32 ("The institutions, norms, and doctrines of international criminal law point to the existence of a global justice community.").

[25] International Criminal Tribunal for the former Yugoslavia ('ICTY'), *Prosecutor v. Biljana Plavšić*, Trial Chamber, Sentencing Judgment, 27 February 2003, IT-00-39&40/1-S, para. 122 (https://www.legal-tools.org/doc/f60082/):

> The Prosecution said that the Trial Chamber's task was to determine a sentence which addresses the conduct of the accused, not only towards the immediate victims but also towards the whole of mankind, in a campaign of persecution which destroyed countless lives and communities: the extent and gravity of such inhumane acts led humanity itself to come under attack and be negated.

felt not only by specific victims but by all of humanity,[26] "a matter of concern to the international community as a whole",[27] injuring all of humanity,[28] violating the interests of the world community,[29] *et cetera.*

Protection of cultural property in armed conflict illustrates the cosmopolitan ethos in conceiving the publicness of wrongs of war crimes.[30] Francesco Francioni, for example, sees cultural heritage as "part of the shared interest of humanity".[31] The concept of "cultural property internationalism" proposes that "everyone has an interest in the preservation and enjoyment of cultural property, wherever it is situated, from whatever cultural or geographic source it derives".[32] This cultural property internationalism is an inspiration for key international conventions on cultural heritage. The 1954 Convention for the Protection of Cultural Property in the Event of Armed Conflict states, in its Preamble, that "damage to cultural property belonging to any people whatsoever means damage to the cultural heritage of all mankind", since "each people makes its contribution to the culture of the world".[33] It further underlines that "the preservation of the cultural heritage is of great importance for all peoples of the world".

---

[26] ICTY, *Prosecutor v. Radislav Krstić*, Appeals Chamber, Judgment, 19 April 2004, IT-98-33-A, para. 36 (https://www.legal-tools.org/doc/86a108/):

> Those who devise and implement genocide seek to deprive humanity of the manifold richness its nationalities, races, ethnicities and religions provide. This is a crime against all of humankind, its harm being felt not only by the group targeted for destruction, but by all of humanity.

[27] ICTY, *Prosecutor v. Dragan Nikolić*, Appeals Chamber, Decision on Interlocutory Appeal Concerning Legality of Arrest, 5 June 2003, IT-94-2-AR73, paras. 24, 25 (https://www.legal-tools.org/doc/61711b/).

[28] The *Kordić and Čerkez* judgment states that "all of humanity is […] injured by the destruction of a unique religious culture and its concomitant cultural objects". See ICTY, *Prosecutor v. Dario Kordić and Mario Čerkez*, Trial Chamber, Judgment, 26 February 2001, IT-95-14/2-T, para. 207 (https://www.legal-tools.org/doc/d4fedd/).

[29] ICC, *Prosecutor v. Thomas Lubanga Dyilo*, Appeals Chamber, Judgment on the Appeal of Mr. Thomas Lubanga Dyilo against the Decision on the Defence Challenge to the Jurisdiction of the Court pursuant to article 19(2)(a) of the Statute of 3 October 2006, 14 December 2006, ICC-01/04-01/06-772, para. 39 (https://www.legal-tools.org/doc/1505f7/).

[30] For more details, see Janine Natalya Clark, "The Destruction of Cultural Heritage in Armed Conflict: The 'Human Element' and the Jurisprudence of the ICTY", in *International Criminal Law Review*, 2018, vol. 18, no. 1, p. 42.

[31] Francesco Francioni, "Beyond State Sovereignty: The Protection of Cultural Heritage as a Shared Interest of Humanity", *Michigan Journal of International Law*, 2004, vol. 25, no. 4, p. 1210.

[32] John H. Merryman, "Cultural Property Internationalism", in *International Journal of Cultural Property*, 2005, vol. 12, no. 1, p. 11.

[33] Convention for the Protection of Cultural Property in the Event of Armed Conflict, 14 May 1954, Preamble (https://www.legal-tools.org/doc/oddjooab/).

The 1972 *Convention Concerning the Protection of the World Cultural and Natural Heritage* states, in its Preamble, that "deterioration or disappearance of any item of the cultural or natural heritage constitutes a harmful impoverishment of the heritage of all the nations of the world".[34] It recognizes "the importance, for all the peoples of the world, of safeguarding this unique and irreplaceable property, to whatever people it may belong"; and that "parts of the cultural or natural heritage are of outstanding interest and therefore need to be preserved as part of the world heritage of mankind as a whole". The planet-wide interest of cultural property is confirmed in the judgment of the ICC in the *Al Mahdi* case, where it was held that the destruction of World Heritage sites affects not only the direct victims and the local communities, but the international community as a whole.[35]

3.1.2. Community's Response to Public Wrongs

The community plays a key role not only in defining public wrongs, but also in responding to such wrongs. Criminal law gives an appropriate response to the kind of wrongs discussed above. In a formal and solemn manner, criminal law pronounces "the moral condemnation of the community".[36] The formal response is collective and grave in both symbolic and material terms. Criminalization signifies strong social and moral disapproval of certain wrongs. The label 'crime' carries symbolic importance in that it expresses "the community's hatred, fear, or contempt".[37] Accompanying serious moral condemnation is the feeling that "something ought to be done", which means a collective response from the whole community.[38] The community not just provides institutions through which victims can pursue their offenders, as civil law does, but calls the offender to account on its own initiative.[39] The community seeks to clarify its "moral

[34] Convention Concerning the Protection of the World Cultural and Natural Heritage, 16 November 1972, Preamble (https://www.legal-tools.org/doc/a5y5k2/).

[35] ICC, *Prosecutor v. Ahmad Al Faqi Al Mahdi*, Trial Chamber, Judgment and Sentence, 27 September 2016, ICC-01/12-01/15-171, para. 80 ('*Al Mahdi* Judgment') (https://www.legal-tools.org/doc/042397/). The Prosecutor says that the war crime of attacking religious and historic buildings "impoverishes us all and damages universal values we are bound to protect". ICC, "Statement of the Prosecutor of the International Criminal Court, Fatou Bensouda, at the opening of Trial in the case against Mr Ahmad Al-Faqi Al Mahdi", Press Release, 22 August 2016 (https://www.legal-tools.org/doc/1rmzb50v/).

[36] Henry M. Hart Jr., "The Aims of the Criminal Law", in *Law and Contemporary Problems*, 1958, vol. 23, no. 3, p. 405.

[37] George K. Gardner, "Bailey v. Richardson and the Constitution of the United States", in *Boston University Law Review*, 1953, vol. 33, no. 2, p. 193.

[38] Marshall and Duff, 1998, p. 7, see *supra* note 3.

[39] Duff, 2011, p. 130, see *supra* note 12.

boundaries"[40] and preserve its norms and solidarity through criminal law. The calling to account performs a communicative function, constructing "a formal confrontation"[41] between the alleged perpetrator and the community as a whole. Duff sees criminal trials not just as "attempts to identify the guilty, or to express norms", but also occasions "to engage the defendant in a communicative enterprise".[42] Norm expression is a one-way activity which treats the defendant as a passive object or pedagogical instrument. Communication is a two-way process where the defendant is engaged as a responsible agent and assigned an active role.[43] The community, or the public, speaks "in a moral voice" to define public wrongs and condemn those who commit them,[44] while the accused speaks as a moral agent and citizen in providing explanation, refutation, defence or admission of the accusations.

Criminal law's response entails the community's close relationship not only with the victim, but also with the perpetrator. Like the public nature of criminal wrongs, criminal responsibility is to be understood in relational terms. Normative relationship precedes normative claim over the perpetrator. Within a domestic community, members have "normatively laden" relationships with each other in virtue of their membership.[45] People, for instance, have special duties towards fellow members which they do not have towards non-members. Consequently, the intra-community bond gives members the standing to call each other to account when important duties are breached.[46] Responsibility arises from "interdependence of individuals" and their commitment to the community.[47]

Criminal law also dispenses the community's punishment. Punishment "is an independently significant dimension" of the community's formal response.[48] Criminal punishment is not personal, but social vengeance towards the

---

40 Moshe Hirsch, "Core Sociological Theories and International Law", in Moshe Hirsch and Andrew Lang (eds.), *Research Handbook on the Sociology of International Law*, Edward Elgar Publishing, Cheltenham, 2018, p. 393.

41 *Ibid.*

42 Duff, 2010, p. 593, see *supra* note 18.

43 *Ibid.*, pp. 593–594.

44 R.A. Duff *et al.*, "Introduction: Towards a Theory of Criminalization?", in Duff *et al.* (eds.), 2014, p. 27, see *supra* note 1.

45 Renzo, 2013, p. 214, see *supra* note 4.

46 *Ibid.*

47 Roger Cotterrell, *Law's Community: Legal Theory in Sociological Perspective*, Clarendon Press, Oxford, 1995, p. 202.

48 Duff, 2011, p. 130, see *supra* note 12.

perpetrator.[49] An important difference between moral and criminal responsibility is that moral responsibility justifies punishment, and criminal responsibility authorizes some people to punish others.[50] Punishment is carried out by designated personnel on behalf of the community. The penal response is different from other responses of the community. For instance, it is different from restorative responses such as professional discipline, government inspections, civil compensation (tort law and contract law), *et cetera*. While criminal justice response features punishment, restorative justice focuses on mediating conflicts and repairing harms.[51]

As in domestic criminal law, the standing of a cosmopolitan community to call an individual to account is generated by a certain conception of the community's relationship with the victim and the perpetrator. Criminal law is a serious way in which the cosmopolitan community claims normative authority over its members regarding important shared values. The perpetrator has to answer to humanity as a whole, not just to the direct victim or any specific local community. Resort to criminal law symbolizes a minimum cohesion, solidarity and interdependence among members of humanity.

The cosmopolitan "penal imaginary"[52] transpires through legal texts, judicial decisions and academic writings in the field of international criminal law. Humanity can provide "*telos*" and legitimacy to law's response to grave wrongs.[53] In *Češić*, an ICTY Trial Chamber held that the sentencing of the defendant "conveys the indignation of humanity for the serious violations of international humanitarian law".[54] A certain cosmopolitan community or its equivalent is often invoked to justify a cosmopolitan right to summon and to punish. For example, the Preamble of the Rome Statute refers to a kind of cosmopolitan solidarity, unity and cultural pluralism among all peoples. It recognizes that "all peoples are united by common bonds", whose "cultures [are] pieced together in a shared heritage".[55] In the *Al Mahdi* case, the ICC noted that the function of

[49] Lohne, 2019, p. 188, see *supra* note 7.

[50] John Hasnas, "Once More Unto the Breach: The Inherent Liberalism of the Criminal Law and Liability for Attempting the Impossible", in *Hastings Law Journal*, 2002–2003, vol. 54, no. 1, p. 50.

[51] Duff *et al.*, 2014, pp. 28–29, see *supra* note 1.

[52] Lohne, 2019, p. 187, see *supra* note 7.

[53] Luigi D.A. Corrias and Geoffrey M. Gordon, "Judging in the Name of Humanity: International Criminal Tribunals and the Representation of a Global Public", in *Journal of International Criminal Justice*, 2015, vol. 13, no. 1, p. 103.

[54] ICTY, *Prosecutor v. Ranko Češić et al.*, Trial Chamber, Sentencing Judgment, 11 March 2004, IT-95-10/1-S, para. 23 (https://www.legal-tools.org/doc/c86c07/).

[55] See Rome Statute of the International Criminal Court, 17 July 1998, Preamble (https://www.legal-tools.org/doc/7b9af9/).

international criminal law is to express "the international community's condemnation of the crimes".[56] The cosmopolitan ethos is further manifest in Claus Kreß' argument that international criminal courts exercise jurisdiction over core international crimes on behalf of the international community as a whole.[57] According to Kreß, the jurisdiction of international criminal courts is not delegated from relevant national criminal jurisdictions, but is derived from the international community's *ius puniendi*.[58] Similarly, Kai Ambos suggests that the collective response to international crimes through criminal law is premised on a "valued-based world order" and a cosmopolitan society composed of world citizens.[59]

Criminal law as a normative frame is built on necessary factual fictions of the individual and the society. A relational theory of criminal law conceives of a substantive relationship between the individual and the community which affirms a set of important values and authorizes public response. In the domestic context, the political organization of the State can more or less satisfy the required relationship. For war crimes law, however, despite frequent invocation of a cosmopolitan community in theory and in practice, specific components and structure of such a community are unclear. The quality of the cosmopolitan community's relationship with its members is posited, not substantiated. The function of the cosmopolitan community remains largely "ideological".[60]

What then can be the social foundations of a cosmopolitan war crimes law? What is required of the cosmopolitan community to give social valence and moral legitimacy to its criminal law? Should it be a political or moral community? With these questions in mind, the next sections turn to moral and political philosophy to illustrate possible forms of a cosmopolitan community.

3.2. A Thin Cosmopolitan Moral Community for Avoiding the Worst Sufferings in War

A cosmopolitan moral community is premised on a universal human identity, as described in Chapter 2. It is not a community of collective entities such as States,

56 *Al Mahdi* Judgment, para. 67, see *supra* note 35.

57 Claus Kreß, "Preliminary Observations on the ICC Appeals Chamber's Judgment of 6 May 2019 in the Jordan Referral re Al-Bashir Appeal", Occasional Paper Series No. 8, Torkel Opsahl Academic EPublisher, Brussels, 2019, p. 19 (https://www.toaep.org/ops-pdf/8-kress/).

58 *Ibid.*

59 Kai Ambos, "Punishment Without a Sovereign? The *Ius Puniendi* Issue of International Criminal Law: A First Contribution Towards a Consistent Theory of International Criminal Law", in *Oxford Journal of Legal Studies*, 2013, vol. 33, no. 2, p. 23.

60 Bruno Simma, "From Bilateralism to Community Interest in International Law", in *Collected Courses of the Hague Academy of International Law*, Volume 250, Brill/Martinus Nijhoff, 1994, p. 248.

but of individual persons. Its primary unit or component is the individual human being. The cosmopolitan view holds that human beings can and must share a common moral life. This means a universal moral community "bound together by a spirit of mutual concern, common interests, and a shared fate".[61] Humanity endows us with the ability to imagine that a stranger is not an enemy, and that a stranger can be like us and fit for moral relations. In a species-wide community, we can conduct "respectful exchanges of goods, services, information, and emotions" with strangers.[62] Cosmopolitan moral principles promote positive human features such as autonomy, rationality, empathy and compassion. Human disunity, sufferings and propensity to commit evils should be avoided as much as possible. Cosmopolitan morality has multifaceted concerns about human life, including the redistribution of wealth across the world and the eradication of structural inequality between the Global North and Global South.

War crimes is a subset of cosmopolitan moral concerns. A cosmopolitan war crimes law is emblematic of the species-wide moral unity. The cosmopolitan solidarity, for the purposes of criminal law, can be restricted to "the moral universalism of human rights alone".[63] It is a kind of 'thin' cosmopolitan community which only addresses some of the worst human sufferings. It appeals to a minimalist cosmopolitan solidarity which puts cruelty first and is preoccupied with the "universal human capacity to inflict and suffer harm".[64] It prioritizes the negative task of avoiding pain, not a utopian vision of inevitable moral progress.[65] The concern is thus human survival, not human perfectibility.[66] As humans, we are all mortal, vulnerable to physical pain and mental torment. Such is part of the permanent, unalterable human condition.

Philosophers have reflected on the effect of pain on human existence. According to Arne Johan Vetlesen, pain reduces a person to a pure physical-biological being, stripping all human abilities, dispositions and dimensions that are above "elementary physical existence". [67] It reduces one's experience to

---

[61] Bhikhu Parekh, "Cosmopolitanism and Global Citizenship", in *Review of International Studies*, 2003, vol. 29, no. 1, p. 11.

[62] David Berreby, *Us and Them: The Science of Identity*, University of Chicago Press, 2018, pp. 220–221.

[63] Jürgen Habermas, *The Postnational Constellation: Political Essays*, ed. and trans. by Max Pensky, MIT Press, Cambridge, Massachusetts, 2001, pp. 107–112.

[64] Catherine Lu, "The One and Many Faces of Cosmopolitanism", in *The Journal of Political Philosophy*, 2000, vol. 8, no. 2, p. 254.

[65] *Ibid.*

[66] *Ibid.*

[67] Arne Johan Vetlesen, *A Philosophy of Pain*, trans. by John Irons, Reaktion Books, London, 2010, p. 14.

"sentience" and nothing else.[68] Pain effects a "transformation from human to merely animal existence".[69] One is forced to withdraw from "a common human universe"[70] where one is a social and moral being. Pain is agency-denying. Pain is utterly disempowering. It is the most primitive and direct form of dehumanization.

Empirical research has found that all cultures share a common concern for others' suffering. There is a kind of moral intuition which is averse to seeing others suffer.[71] This may be a result of evolutionary adaptation which drives human beings to aid their distressed children.[72] The human body's "physiological homogeneity" serves as "a scientific basis" for common experience and aversion of pain.[73] We are "transparent to each other" in our sensation of physical pain, regardless of cultures and historical epochs.[74] Catherine Lu notes that among the earliest cosmopolitans are medical writers like Hippocrates. Physicians' work enables them to see the unity of humankind in "a wretched, feeble and pitiable existence" which lacks certainty and eventually ends with death.[75] Human vulnerability is a natural equalizer.[76] Reflecting on Auschwitz, Theodor W. Adorno calls for a return to human vulnerabilities. He observes that identifying what is bad is rather less difficult than agreeing on what is the good life.[77] Hannah Arendt reminds us of the "animal pity" which affects all human beings who witness physical suffering.[78] "Repugnance",[79] "revulsion",[80] "moral

[68] *Ibid.*, p. 24.

[69] *Ibid.*, p. 15.

[70] *Ibid.*, p. 28.

[71] Jonathan Haidt and Craig Joseph, "Intuitive Ethics: How Innately Prepared Intuitions Generate Culturally Variable Virtues", in *Daedalus*, 2004, vol. 133, no. 4, p. 58.

[72] *Ibid.*, p. 59.

[73] *Ibid.*, p. 28.

[74] *Ibid.*, p. 27.

[75] Lu, 2000, p. 254, see *supra* note 64.

[76] *Ibid.*

[77] Cited in Andrew Linklater, "Distant Suffering and Cosmopolitan Obligations", in *International Politics*, 2007, vol. 44, p. 22.

[78] Cited in Arne Johan Vetlesen, *Evil and Human Agency: Understanding Collective Evildoing*, Cambridge University Press, 2009, p. 28.

[79] Daniel Chernilo, *The Natural Law Foundations of Modern Social Theory*, Cambridge University Press, 2013, p. 113.

[80] Cited in Vetlesen, 2009, p. 28, see *supra* note 78.

outrage",[81] and "feeling of indignation"[82] are natural and universal reactions toward egregious human sufferings.

Cosmopolitanism has always been concerned about "the predicament of the stranger".[83] Cosmopolitan solidarity is a kind of enlarged compassion, which goes beyond the face-to-face, eye-witness situation, beyond one's immediate community, and reaches the remote and abstract other as if they are present right here and now.[84] The empathetic capacity of "feeling into", of gaining moral perception of others "sensitizes" us to our shared vulnerability with other human beings.[85] It brings "other-directedness" which is needed to overcome the distance between the feeling subject and suffering others.[86] Richard Rorty argues that common experiences of pain and humiliation enable us to transcend traditional social and political boundaries and form a species-wide solidarity.[87] Every human being can identify with another's need to avoid pain and humiliation. Every human being has an interest in the integrity of shared moral life concerned with avoiding cruelty.[88] Such cosmopolitan solidarity is believed to be "slender but robust".[89]

Criminal law represents a response from the cosmopolitan community to avoid "passive injustice"[90] in face of suffering. It is believed that the kind of acute, serious physical sufferings present more urgency than other more implicit, chronic sufferings caused by social economic conditions. War-time atrocities have direct perpetrators, intermediate instigators, and behind-the-scene masterminds, to whom moral indignation can be effectively channelled through criminal law. The solidarity for avoiding such sufferings is supposed to be more readily available than for other cosmopolitan projects.

Chapter 4 will show, in light of criminalization, that what war crimes law tries to avoid is even less than mass cruelty and sufferings. This is because war itself causes deaths and destructions which are comparable to other international

---

81 Jürgen Habermas, *The Divided West*, ed. and trans. by Ciaran Cronin, Polity, Cambridge, 2006, p. 143; Habermas, 2001, pp. 107–112, see *supra* note 63.

82 *Ibid.*

83 Noah Feldman, "Cosmopolitan Law?", in *The Yale Law Journal*, 2007, vol. 116, no. 1022, p. 2007.

84 Arne Johan Vetlesen, *Perception, Empathy, and Judgment: An Inquiry into the Preconditions of Moral Performance*, Penn State University Press, Pennsylvania, 1994, p. 333.

85 *Ibid.*

86 *Ibid.*

87 Richard Rorty, *Contingency, Irony and Solidarity*, Cambridge University Press, 1989, p. 192.

88 Vetlesen, 1994, p. 324, see *supra* note 84.

89 Habermas, 2001, pp. 107–112, see *supra* note 63.

90 Lu, 2000, p. 264, see *supra* note 64.

crimes. In war, human vulnerabilities are exploited, rather than protected, to succumb the enemy. The decision to go to war means that the consensus to avoid grave human sufferings has been breached in the first place. War crimes law does not seek to avoid all serious sufferings in war, which equals eliminating war itself. Rather, the law seeks to criminalize certain harms which are considered unnecessary during the war, such as excessive harms to civilians and certain sufferings of military personnel. It has conceded that mass violence and sufferings are unavoidable in war. In other words, the kind of cosmopolitan solidarity supporting criminalization and punishment of war crimes is not absolute aversion to grave sufferings, but opposition to excessive and unnecessary sufferings amid organized mass violence. Such a cosmopolitan community is more particular and even thinner than the above-mentioned general solidarity to avoid serious pain.

3.3. Theoretical Models of a Cosmopolitan Political Community

Another position is that political organization is necessary to define and respond to public wrongs within the system of criminal law. At least in the domestic context, it is argued that the nature and scope of criminal law, that is, the character and extent of the polity's claims on citizens' lives, is a matter for political deliberation.[91] What is required in domestic criminal law does not have to be automatically transplanted to a cosmopolitan criminal law. Nevertheless, political theorists have come up with theoretical models of a cosmopolitan political community which can provide social foundations for a cosmopolitan criminal law. Political cosmopolitanism focuses on the creation of a cosmopolitan political order, or a "*cosmopolis*".[92] Political cosmopolitanism is inseparable from moral cosmopolitanism. Cosmopolitan morality is the ideological inspiration and legitimating force behind political cosmopolitanism. The latter seeks to provide institutional vehicles to realize the cosmopolitan moral vision. If the cosmopolitan project were to replace the nation-State project, Ulrich Beck poses the critical question: How can we image post-national political communities?[93] Advocates of political, legal cosmopolitanism believe that profound institutional transformations are necessary to achieve cosmopolitan ideals. Their discussions centre on institutional arrangements for defending peace and human rights,

---

[91] See Duff, 2011, p. 138, *supra* note 12.

[92] Angela Taraborrelli, *Contemporary Cosmopolitanism*, trans. by Ian McGilvray, Bloomsbury, London, 2015, p. 47.

[93] Ulrich Beck, "The Cosmopolitan Perspective: Sociology of the Second Age of Modernity", in *British Journal of Sociology*, 2000, vol. 51, no. 1, p. 90.

materializing the ever-increasing sense of cosmopolitan membership, and guaranteeing equal participation of all world citizens.[94]

Political theorists have put forward models of cosmopolitan polity which can largely accommodate existing forms of political organization and treat the individual as the primary unit of concern. A cosmopolitan polity for the purposes of criminal law need not be a world State with a central government ruling all of humanity. While some theories envision a cosmopolitan political order based on sovereign-restricting principles, others hold that political organization and democracy should be the source of legitimacy. All of them seek to depart from a State-centric international law. With the "political and constitutional loss of power of the nation-state"[95] in a cosmopolitan order, the consent of the State no longer counts as the sole source of legitimacy for law. The cosmopolitan perspective challenges both the normative privilege of the nation-State and the accompanying Westphalian inter-State order.

In terms of substance, European Union ('EU') laws have occupied and stimulated much of political theorists' cosmopolitan imagination.[96] Notably, all the theorists examined in this chapter refer to the EU as an inspiration for their conception of a cosmopolitan polity: it is one with "a binding constitution, the rule of law, a bill of rights for all citizens, [and] a vibrant civil society".[97] Kant's vision of cosmopolitan law is also frequently referred to as a basis, or rather, a starting point for many contemporary cosmopolitan political theories. These theories draw on Kant's tripartite system of national, international and cosmopolitan law and often expand the scope of cosmopolitan law to fit contemporary needs. Kantian cosmopolitan law originally concerns the relationship between the individual person and the foreign State, in particular, the individual's right to hospitality in a foreign nation. It is supposed to be neither international law nor domestic law, but a new kind of law. Building on Kantian cosmopolitan law, many contemporary cosmopolitan theorists argue that international law should be either transformed into, or supplemented by cosmopolitan law. On the other hand, a cosmopolitan legal theory does not have to be traced back to Kant. With these theoretical underpinnings in mind, I illustrate two ways of organizing a cosmopolitan political community: cosmopolitan constitutionalism and cosmopolitan democracy.

---

[94] Taraborrelli, 2015, p. 47, see *supra* note 92.

[95] Beck, 2000, p. 84, see *supra* note 93.

[96] For example, Pavlos Eleftheriadis argues that EU law can be seen as a type of cosmopolitan law, see Pavlos Eleftheriadis, "Cosmopolitan Law", in *European Law Journal*, 2003, vol. 9, no. 2, pp. 241–263.

[97] See Robert Fine and Will Smith, "Jürgen Habermas's Theory of Cosmopolitanism", in *Constellations*, 2003, vol. 10, no. 4, p. 478.

3.3.1. Cosmopolitan Constitutionalism

Cosmopolitan constitutionalism, or the "constitutionalization of international law",[98] presents a political alternative between a world government and the Westphalian order. Cosmopolitan constitutionalism is conceived in reaction to failings of the nation-State to realize the freedom of its citizens in the face of global capitalism and "irrational manifestations of national sovereignty" such as mass atrocities.[99] It envisions a global political order based on sovereign-restricting principles and the rule of law, but without a world State. A State-centred world should be transformed into "the post-national constellation of a global society".[100] International law is taken to be "constituted from, and constrained by" certain normative principles recognizing the worth and dignity of individual human beings.[101] In other words, it is a political order formed around the State, but ultimately concerned with individual human beings.

Within such a global order, a cosmopolitan criminal law is derived from constitutional principles which express public values of humanity.[102] Cosmopolitan constitutional principles derive their substance from cosmopolitan morality. I draw on four different but related conceptions of a constitution-based cosmopolitan order, namely, Habermas' global society of States and citizens, Eleftheriadis' "principled federation" of States, Brown's constitutional federation of States, and Kumm's "world of cosmopolitan states".

Jürgen Habermas elaborates on the possibility and legitimacy of cosmopolitan constitutionalism. He believes that the Kantian cosmopolitan condition can be realized through the "constitutionalization of international law". While Kantian cosmopolitan law co-exists with national and international law, Habermas envisions a "transition" from classical international law into cosmopolitan law, that is, from a State-centred international law to a rights-centred cosmopolitan law.[103] In *The Divided West*, Habermas describes a kind of cosmopolitan constitution that can normatively transform power relations between States, not merely reflecting them.[104] Habermas believes such a legally binding constitution

---

[98] See Habermas, 2006, p. 120, *supra* note 81; see also Jürgen Habermas, "The Constitutionalization of International Law and the Legitimation Problems of a Constitution for World Society", in *Constellations*, 2008, vol. 15, no. 4, pp. 444–455.

[99] Fine and Smith, 2003, p. 482, see *supra* note 97.

[100] Habermas, 2006, p. 115, see *supra* note 81.

[101] Garrett Wallace Brown, "Moving from Cosmopolitan Legal Theory to Legal Practice: Models of Cosmopolitan Law", in *Legal Studies*, 2008, vol. 28, no. 3, p. 438.

[102] Long, 2014, p. 854, see *supra* note 21. Long takes candidate values to include reciprocity, respect, bodily integrity, freedom of conscience, and autonomy.

[103] Habermas, 2006, p. 120, see *supra* note 81.

[104] *Ibid.*

is key to maintaining the permanent union of States, which is not specified by Kant himself.[105] Such a politically constituted global society consists of States and citizens.[106] This is somewhere between classical international law and a world republic State of individuals. States remain prominent actors in such a legal order, while individuals are actual bearers of rights. At both the supranational and regional levels, States participate in institutions and procedures of global governance. A world organization, such as a reformed UN, can perform vital but limited functions of maintaining peace and protecting human rights "in an effective and non-selective manner".[107] Habermas' cosmopolitan constitutional order attempts to provide an alternative means for citizens to realize their freedom.

The constitutionalization of international law envisions a legal order without a State or democratic legislation. Habermas relies on Brun-Otto Bryde's separation of a "constitutional order" from the State:

> Although a constitutional state [*Verfassungsstaat*] cannot exist at the international level, constitutionalism can; likewise, there cannot be a [global] *Rechtsstaat* but there can be a [worldwide] rule of law, there cannot be an international welfare state but there can be [global social justice].[108]

Habermas admits that such a supranational constitution cannot conform to the standards of a republican constitution of a State. This reflects certain "asymmetry" between the evolution of State law and cosmopolitan law. According to Habermas, the constitutional principles of international law are more like pre-modern forms of law.[109] While a national constitution can determine its own political competences, a cosmopolitan constitution is restricted to vital and circumscribed functions.[110]

In his article "Cosmopolitan Law", Pavlos Eleftheriadis presents what he calls a "principled federation" – a federation of States based on sovereignty-limiting principles – as a third way besides a federal world State and classical international law.[111] International human rights protection, the prohibition of crimes against humanity and torture are examples of these constitutional

[105] *Ibid.*, p. 121.

[106] *Ibid.*, p. 135. Habermas refers to the Brussels Convention's draft of the European constitution in the name of "the citizens and the States of Europe".

[107] *Ibid.*, p. 136.

[108] *Ibid.*, p. 139.

[109] Robert Fine, *Cosmopolitanism*, Routledge, Abingdon, 2007, p. 71.

[110] Habermas, 2006, p. 134, see *supra* note 81.

[111] Eleftheriadis, 2003, p. 242, see *supra* note 96.

principles.[112] Eleftheriadis argues that these principles fall under the spirit of Kantian cosmopolitan law. Kant conceives cosmopolitan law as based on a cosmopolitan right to hospitality which is a relation between an individual and a foreign State within the peaceful federation. In the same spirit, contemporary States are accountable for their human rights performance to external mechanisms and organizations. Eleftheriadis believes that these are "relations between the state and outside institutions or groups of citizens in a broad sense" which Kant could not have foreseen. In this way, Eleftheriadis links Kant's cosmopolitan law to the idea of international accountability.[113] Eleftheriadis argues that there is an emergent Kantian cosmopolitan law in existing human rights law and EU law.[114]

Garrett Wallace Brown elaborates a Kantian cosmopolitan constitution voluntarily entered into by States. Member States undertake obligations to advance conditions of public rights included in such a constitution.[115] Brown argues that "international law should be constituted from, and constrained by, moral and normative principles of universal human worth, human respect and global justice".[116] Some kind of cosmopolitan law, which is a higher-level law than national and international law, is necessary "to place greater limits on the *law of nations*, the Treaty of Westphalia, and the injustices legitimated by claims to state sovereignty made under these legal regimes".[117]

While the above-mentioned Kant-inspired cosmopolitan theories seek to constitutionalize cosmopolitan law, Mattias Kumm's theory seeks to cosmopolitanize domestic constitutions. They are essentially two sides of the same coin, both seeking to limit State sovereignty with supra-national principles. Kumm's cosmopolitanization of constitutionalism requires "a world of cosmopolitan states".[118] Kumm notices that nowadays many State activities can have significant impact outside their jurisdiction. The authority of national constitution, if conceived in isolation and absoluteness, is thus problematic.[119] According to Kumm, a State can only claim legitimate authority regarding issues that do not have serious extraterritorial impact. Unilaterally exercising State authority to

[112] *Ibid.*, p. 242.

[113] *Ibid.*, p. 255.

[114] *Ibid.*, pp. 260–262.

[115] Garrett Wallace Brown, "Kantian Cosmopolitan Law and the Idea of a Cosmopolitan Constitution", in *History of Political Thought*, 2006, vol. 27, no. 4, pp. 673–676.

[116] Brown, 2008, p. 438, see *supra* note 101.

[117] *Ibid.*, p. 434.

[118] Mattias Kumm, "Constituent Power, Cosmopolitan Constitutionalism, and Post-Positivist Law", in *International Journal of Constitutional Law*, 2006, vol. 14, no. 3, pp. 703–709.

[119] *Ibid.*

resolve "justice-sensitive externalities" is an act of domination.[120] Kumm argues that the constituent power not only includes "We the People" within a State, but also "the international community" of States.[121] The national constitutional legitimacy cannot be assessed in a vacuum. It should be viewed in light of its relationship with the external world.

Kumm characterizes his constitutionalism as "post-national" and "post-positivist". Post-national because States should submit matters of common interest to an impartial, stable mechanism – an international constitutional order, an international law which delimitates and arbitrates authority among sovereign States.[122] The establishment of the UN system should be regarded as "an international community acting as a global constituent power, by way of sovereign states signing and ratifying a treaty". States are bound by some fundamental principles of this new constitutional order including sovereign equality, prohibition of the use of force, self-determination of peoples, and respect for human rights.[123] Kumm's cosmopolitan constitutionalism sets out conditions for the legitimate exercise of State sovereignty. National and international constitutions are neither derived nor autonomous from each other, but are interdependent. Kumm's constitutionalism is also post-positivist because the constituent power is circumscribed. The concept of constituent power can appear voluntarist in that the authority of the constitution ultimately comes from the will of "We the People". The law is accordingly understood as source-based. Yet, a legitimate constitutional authority has to follow certain fundamental norms which precede the constituent will. Kumm identifies three limiting principles to the constituent will, which he calls "the Trinitarian constitutionalist formula of human rights, democracy, and the rule of law". These principles cannot be changed by the constituent power, whose authority is limited to giving meaning and interpreting them. They are essential for a justifiable constitutionalism. They should be integrated into standards imposed by international law on States, which brings about the cosmopolitanization of constitutionalism.[124]

While the voluntary contractual arrangement successfully avoids the risk of despotism of a world State, the question remains "how to create quasi-legally binding obligations through voluntary commitments [...] in the absence of an overwhelming sovereign power with the ultimate right of enforcement".[125] Brown adopts Kant's argument about realization of universal rights and

[120] *Ibid.*

[121] *Ibid.*

[122] *Ibid.*

[123] *Ibid.*

[124] *Ibid.*, pp. 709–711.

[125] Cited in Brown, 2008, p. 445, see *supra* note 101.

concludes that a cosmopolitan constitution is dictated by human reason.[126] Eleftheriadis also posits that the legitimacy of cosmopolitan law principles has to come from their own substance.[127] According to Eleftheriadis, cosmopolitan law resembles "a *common law* of fundamental political justice" which "does not follow strict legislative or other procedural models of sources".[128] Similarly, Kumm argues that just as natural persons have a duty to establish just relations among each other by forming a constitutional system, States have a "standing duty" to participate in an international legal system that can resolve disagreements through a fair procedure. Such an international legal system is established by the international community as a "global *pouvoir constituant*".[129]

Habermas is more subtle in his reliance on human reason to realize the constitutionalization of international law. He invokes the potential of domestic public opinion to push States, especially the powerful ones, to participate in a global constitution. There needs to be a change of perspective on the side of the State from "national interest" to "global governance".[130] Only by transforming the normative self-understanding of the State, can the constitutionalization of international law be realized. Habermas draws on the somewhat self-legitimating nature of law to mitigate a perceived democratic deficit in cosmopolitan law. He maintains that the legitimacy of law comes from the "deliberative and representative character of the procedures of democratic opinion- and will-formation which are institutionalized in law".[131] It means that law itself, if created and practiced in the right way, has democratic qualities. Given his position on the inseparability of democracy and the State, he further justifies the legitimacy of a cosmopolitan constitution with its limited function on the one hand, and indirect and supplementary forms of democracy on the other. In other words, for the limited function of a cosmopolitan constitution, *indirect* democratic legitimation from constitutional States and *supplementary* legitimation from the global public opinion are sufficient.

First, supranational constitutions can obtain indirect legitimation from democratic processes within constitutional States. This is crucial to avoid instrumentalization of constitutional law as "a hegemonic legal façade".[132] Supranational constitutions draw on "*basic rights*, *legal principles*, and *criminal codes*"

[126] Brown, 2006, p. 684, see *supra* note 115.

[127] Eleftheriadis, 2003, p. 254, see *supra* note 96.

[128] *Ibid.*

[129] Kumm, 2006, pp. 703–709, see *supra* note 118.

[130] Habermas, 2001, pp. 111, see *supra* note 63.

[131] Habermas, 2006, p. 140, see *supra* note 81.

[132] *Ibid.*

which have been practiced within democratic States.[133] In other words, their substance comes from universal constitutional principles developed in the domestic context. This is what Habermas calls "a derivative status" of the constitutionalization of international law – its legitimacy is derived from that of the democratic constitutional State, or what he calls "universalistic principles of a democratic constitutional state".[134] At a deeper level, Habermas believes there cannot be the same civic solidarity in the international arena as in a nation-State. Compared to the familiar kind of thick solidarity among compatriots, a thin cosmopolitan solidarity can only support a constitution that is limited to maintaining peace and protecting human rights.[135] It is a *negative* solidarity expressed in "moral outrage toward egregious human rights violations and manifest acts of aggression".[136] A cosmopolitan constitution is therefore built on the "negative duties of a universalistic morality of justice".[137]

The second prong of democratic legitimation comes from the supplementary role of global communication in an informal public sphere. According to Habermas, the democratic procedure no longer derives its legitimacy solely from "the general accessibility of a deliberative process" which can be expected to produce "rationally acceptable results".[138] He takes participation of civil society in international deliberations and negotiations as a legitimating factor in global governance. According to Habermas, a "functioning public sphere, the quality of discussion, accessibility, and the discursive structure of opinion- and will-formation" should be balanced with, although not replacing, conventional procedures of decision-making and political participation.[139] A mature and active global civil society therefore may affirm the legitimacy of cosmopolitan law.

Under cosmopolitan constitutionalism, the cosmopolitan polity confers authority to its criminal law not through direct democratic participation, but through a set of constitutional principles and values. The above-mentioned authors agree that supranational constitutional principles should include protection of human rights, in particular, prohibition of mass atrocities committed by the State. The constitutional principles define wrongs which are not subject to the discretion of particular States. The wrongness of international crimes does not

---

[133] *Ibid.*

[134] *Ibid.*, pp. 107, 140.

[135] *Ibid.*, p. 143.

[136] *Ibid.*, p. 143.

[137] *Ibid.*, p. 143.

[138] Habermas, 2001, pp. 110, see *supra* note 63.

[139] *Ibid.*, p. 111.

depend on the national legislation of any State or the place or victim of the crimes.

3.3.2. Cosmopolitan Democracy

Alternatively, the authority of criminal law can be derived from a cosmopolitan democratic order comprised of States and other democratic bodies and organized under the overarching framework of a cosmopolitan democratic law. Such a cosmopolitan democratic community can include local, national, inter-State, regional and global institutions, transnational communities and non-government bodies.[140] A cosmopolitan democratic law is designed to guarantee rights and freedoms of global citizens.[141] While cosmopolitan constitutionalism focuses on substantive issues of the global order, cosmopolitan democracy emphasizes individual participation in decision-making. Criminal law is established by some kind of cosmopolitan legislation respecting democratic principles. Cosmopolitan democracy is more radical than the reformative attempts of cosmopolitan constitutionalism in that it extends democratic practices beyond State borders. The project of deterritorialization of democracy subjects "institutional boundaries and limitations to radical critique" and pursues "greater freedom and communication between radically different subjectivities".[142]

3.3.2.1. Cosmopolitan Democratic Principles

Cosmopolitan democracy seeks to maximize, or even optimize, inter-subjective communication at a species level. It starts from the belief that a discursive community where everyone can participate and "everything is decided through words and persuasion" is best suited for human emancipation.[143] Emancipation is understood as freedom from unjustifiable forms of exclusion.[144] In particular, every human being should be free to speak and to be heard – everyone should be allowed to participate in the communication.[145] A person's social relations such as those with family, friends and fellow countrymen are morally contingent. Before belonging to a nation, an ethnicity or a class, a human being belongs to humanity.[146] While a particular identity can be transient and relative, the human

140 Daniele Archibugi, "Cosmopolitan Democracy: A Restatement", in *Cambridge Journal of Education*, 2012, vol. 42, no. 1, p. 12.

141 *Ibid.*

142 Richard Shapcott, *Justice, Community and Dialogue in International Relations*, Cambridge University Press, 2001, p. 72.

143 *Ibid.*, pp. 82, 86.

144 *Ibid.*, p. 86.

145 *Ibid.*, p. 71.

146 David Held, "Principles of Cosmopolitan Order", in Gillian Brock and Harry Brighouse (eds.), *The Political Philosophy of Cosmopolitanism*, Cambridge University Press, 2005, p. 10.

identity is permanent and unconditional. On the other hand, the social contingency of one's self-perception and worldviews means one should respect different responses to "mysteries of existence".[147] Certain procedural rules should be followed in order to allow "the unforced force of the better argument" to prevail. David Held, for example, proposes eight principles for cosmopolitan democracy. These eight principles are:

- equal worth and dignity;
- active agency;
- personal responsibility and accountability;
- consent;
- reflexive deliberation and collective decision-making through voting procedures;
- inclusiveness and subsidiarity;
- avoidance of serious harm and the amelioration of urgent need; and
- sustainability.[148]

These principles form the basis of equal consideration of each person's interest in institutional decision-making.[149] The first three principles valorise egalitarian individualism, rational capacity and self-accountability. They explicate conditions of human agency on which principles of collective decision-making are built. As we will see in greater detail, active and rational human agency is the cornerstone of the project of cosmopolitan democracy. Principles 4–6 require democratic legitimation of public authority. The remaining two principles guide public decision-making to prioritize urgent need and preserve long-term sustainability.[150] The eight cosmopolitan principles embody two "metaprinciples" of personal autonomy and impartialist reasoning. In particular, impartialist reasoning:

> is a moral frame of reference for specifying rules and principles that can be universally shared; and, concomitantly, it rejects as unjust all those practices, rules, and institutions anchored in principles not all could adopt. […] This social, open-ended, moral perspective is a device for focusing our thoughts and testing the intersubjective validity of our conceptions of the good. It offers a way

[147] Cited in Shapcott, 2001, p. 72, see *supra* note 142.

[148] Held, 2005, pp. 12–15, see *supra* note 146.

[149] David Held, "Law of States, Law of Peoples: Three Models of Sovereignty", in *Legal Theory*, 2002, vol. 8, p. 24.

[150] Held, 2005, p. 15, see *supra* note 146.

> of exploring principles, norms, and rules that might reasonably command agreement.[151]

Impartialist reasoning performs a critical function towards established conventions and exclusivist practices; it detaches individuals from power relations by focusing on their active agency. Structural obstacles such as inequality, oppression should be exposed and eliminated to ensure free and open dialogue.[152] These two "metaprinciples" correspond to cosmopolitan individualism and rationalism described in Chapter 2.

The cosmopolitan democratic principles constitute the basis of cosmopolitan law and institutions. They apply at various levels, ranging from universal to local communities, where nation-State is one form of governance. This means political authority and organization are "diffused 'below,' 'above,' and 'alongside' the nation-state".[153] These cosmopolitan principles provide a certain procedural framework for establishing common moral codes. Unlike the veil of ignorance or categorical imperative, which determine universal principles in monological thinking,[154] cosmopolitan democratic principles require dialogical processes to arrive at normative validity.

3.3.2.2. Cosmopolitan Democratic Community

The project of a cosmopolitan democracy envisions a cosmopolitan order comprised of plural actors coming from various levels of governance and communities. A cosmopolitan democracy is diverse in its goals and visions, and I will draw on its two leading proponents – David Held and Daniele Archibugi – to illustrate elements of a legal order based on multi-layered democratic governance.[155] Proposals of cosmopolitan democracy typically insist on the exclusive legitimating force of democracy. In the words of Daniele Archibugi, democracy has become "the sole source of legitimate authority and power".[156] Projects of cosmopolitan democracy generally seek to protect human rights and guarantee greater political participation worldwide. These objectives require democracy to go beyond the nation-State and territorial boundaries. De-nationalizing democracy requires initiation of democratic processes within and above the State.[157]

---

151 *Ibid.*, p. 22.

152 Shapcott, 2001, p. 90, see *supra* note 142.

153 Held, 2002, p. 38, see *supra* note 149.

154 Shapcott, 2001, p. 65, see *supra* note 142.

155 For a comprehensive introduction of the cosmopolitan democracy proposals, see Taraborrelli, 2015, pp. 47–85, *supra* note 92.

156 Archibugi, 2012, p. 9, see *supra* note 140.

157 David Held, *Democracy and the Global Order: From the Modern State to Cosmopolitan Governance*, Polity Press, Oxford, 1995, pp. 276–277.

At different governance levels, legislative and executive bodies operate according to principles of democratic law.[158] The State remains a key actor in the cosmopolitan order, but not the *sole* actor. Proponents of cosmopolitan democracy seek to find a middle place between a confederation of States where the sole legitimate actor is State, and a federalist world State that subsumes individual States. Cosmopolitan democracy is built on "a voluntary and revocable union of government and meta-government institutions".[159] The power of State is shared with a "parallel series of democratic institutions" elected and organized under principles of democratic law.[160] These democratically organized institutions are what differentiate cosmopolitan democracy from other global governance projects because they "enable the voice of individuals to be heard in global affairs irrespective of their resonance at home".[161] Cosmopolitan democracy aims to change the reality of international decision-making which is "dominated by *raison d'etat*" and subject to the "relative strengths and interests of the various players".[162]

A cosmopolitan democratic order therefore envisions a kind of synergy between States and other democratic bodies organized under cosmopolitan democratic law. David Held proposes a cosmopolitan democratic law which recognizes rights and obligations of groups and associations following the principle of self-determination.[163] Legal principles are adopted to regulate individual and collective action at all levels.[164] Held relates his conception of cosmopolitan democratic law to Kant's cosmopolitan law. Following Kant, Held describes cosmopolitan law as "a domain of law different in kind from the law of states and the law made between one state and another".[165] It is the basis for articulating the equal moral standing of every human being in the "universal community", and a "necessary complement to the codes of national and international law".[166] While Kantian cosmopolitan law only concerns the right to hospitality, Held gives cosmopolitan law a broader meaning: it guarantees "the equal moral standing of all human beings", and recognizes the individual right to liberty and consent-based governance.[167] In particular, cosmopolitan law should articulate

[158] *Ibid.*

[159] Taraborrelli, 2015, p. 70, see *supra* note 92.

[160] Daniele Archibugi, "Cosmopolitical Democracy", in *New Left Review*, 2000, vol. 4, p. 144.

[161] *Ibid.*

[162] Archibugi, 2012, p. 9, see *supra* note 140.

[163] Held, 1995, p. 271, see *supra* note 157.

[164] *Ibid.*

[165] Held, 2005, p. 25, see *supra* note 146.

[166] *Ibid.*

[167] *Ibid.*, p. 26.

Held's eight cosmopolitan democratic principles cited above.[168] Following these eight principles, Held proposes (1) entrenchment of cosmopolitan democratic law through a new 'charter of rights and obligations' which extends to different sectors of political, social and economic power; (2) an interconnected global legal system of criminal and civil law; and (3) the establishment of an international criminal court.[169] He emphasizes that governance at all levels – regional, national and local – should be subordinated to this overarching framework of cosmopolitan law.[170]

Similarly, Daniele Archibugi proposes a multi-level governance structure within which institutions are related functionally, not hierarchically. Conflicts among these levels of laws can be resolved within the framework of global constitutionalism and with possible involvement of jurisdictional bodies.[171] Archibugi argues that the concept of sovereignty should be replaced with that of constitutionalism, both within States and in inter-State relations.[172] Three principles apply at all levels of democracy: "non-violence among the various factions or political parties, political equality among the members of the community, and popular control over decisions and decision-makers".[173]

Both Held and Archibugi assign judicial institutions an important role in guaranteeing individual rights. Cosmopolitan democracy proposals include complex and comprehensive institutional arrangements, which cannot be detailed here. This strand of political cosmopolitanism illustrates an audacious attempt to address the perceived democratic deficit of a State-centred international order. It expands democratic participation beyond the nation-State while trying to preserve self-determination of local and transnational communities and institutions. Political legitimacy is freed from territorial boundaries and imagined in new contexts.[174] A war crimes law so conceived has its social foundation in the democratic expression of solidarity on avoiding excessive human sufferings in war.

The project of cosmopolitan democracy has been critically engaged from realist, Marxist and communitarian perspectives, and for its lack of a global

[168] *Ibid.*, p. 13; Held, 2002, see *supra* note 149.

[169] Held, 1995, p. 279, see *supra* note 157.

[170] *Ibid.*

[171] Archibugi, 2012, p. 16, see *supra* note 140.

[172] *Ibid.*

[173] *Ibid.*, p. 14.

[174] Held, 2002, p. 38, see *supra* note 149.

demos and rule of law failings.[175] Habermas, for example, identifies democracy with limited boundaries:

> Any political community that wants to understand itself as a democracy must at least distinguish between members and non-members. The self-referential concept of collective self-determination demarcates a logical space for democratically united citizens who are members of a particular community. Even if such a community is grounded in the universalistic principles of a democratic constitutional state, it still forms a collective identity, in the sense that it interprets and realizes these principles in light of its own history and in the context of its own particular form of life. This ethical-political self-understanding of citizens of a particular democratic life is missing in the inclusive community of world citizens.[176]

The political theories reviewed above are inspirational and even imaginative in some instances. Conscious of risks of both hegemony and anarchy, these theories all seem to rely on individual and/or collective enlightenment in forging a cosmopolitan solidarity for change. They have varying degrees of theoretical maturity and practical feasibility. No human community, or its theoretical account, is infallible. Nevertheless, these theories can inform us of possible moral and social conditions prerequisite for an effective and legitimate cosmopolitan criminal law.

3.4. The Role of Local Communities

3.4.1. The Necessity and Good of Local Communities

Cosmopolitan moral principles suggest a kind of unmediated relationship between the individual and humankind, between one and all. There exist intermediate categories of human groups. Human sociability and fellowship do not necessarily result in a species-wide community. Sociability can be expressed through smaller communities whose members possess particular commonalities in addition to human universals. Common features across the species are therefore a necessary but not sufficient condition for a cosmopolitan community. In fact, limited communities have been the norm throughout history. A universal community, on the other hand, has been an inspiration, an image, a proposal for change, but never reality. Cosmopolitan imagination alone, a "one-size-fit-all label Homo sapiens",[177] cannot satisfy human beings' need for close social

[175] See Daniele Archibugi, "Cosmopolitan Democracy and its Critics: A Review", in *European Consortium for Political Research*, 2004, vol. 10, no. 3, pp. 437–473; and Taraborrelli, 2015, pp. 81–85, see *supra* note 92.

[176] Habermas, 2001, p. 107, see *supra* note 63.

[177] Berreby, 2018, p. 15, see *supra* note 62.

relations. Particular societies and cultures are instrumental for the well-being of the cosmopolitan individual.

The existence of human groups is necessary, not accidental – "human kinds exist because of human minds".[178] A distinct mental code tells us when certain people should be seen as belonging together in a group, not as separate individuals.[179] This innate metal code operates in an "automatic" manner, independent from our will and outside our consciousness.[180] "Kind-seeing, kind-feeling, kind-promoting behavior" makes a person feel good.[181] It is part of human nature and "an absolute requirement for being human".[182] A person not belonging to any human group cannot live a fully human life. As Aristotle says: "He who is unable to live in society, or who has no need because he is sufficient for himself, must be either a beast or a god".[183] History or anthropology knows no people who lack a distinction between 'Us' and 'Them'.[184] Human groups exist because of human need – the "fundamental human need to belong", which comes from the desire for social association, co-operation and normative guidance.[185] Human groups provide vital emotional and practical support to their members. David Luban, for example, sees human beings as "political animals" who must live a social life to survive and flourish.[186] An individual needs to live in human groups to feel secure and nourished. The mind links social security to physical security. Social rejection, on the other hand, is coded as a *physical* threat.[187] If the emotions of belonging are nourishing, the emotions of not-belonging can be toxic.[188] Mind and body are closely connected in this respect. Moreover, belonging to a group produces the feeling of being part of something that is larger than oneself, something that is eternal and immortal. The individual person perishes, but communities can last forever. Group membership can be "reassuring" and "ennobling".[189] The group is often described as a living being with thoughts,

---

178 *Ibid.*, p. 331.

179 *Ibid.*, p. 129.

180 *Ibid.*, p. xiii (Preface).

181 *Ibid.*, p. xv.

182 *Ibid.*, p. 16.

183 *Ibid.*, p. 236.

184 *Ibid.*, p. 43.

185 Philip Zimbardo, *The Lucifer Effect: Understanding How Good People Turn Evil*, Random House Trade Paperbacks, New York, 2007, p. 230.

186 David Luban, "A Theory of Crimes Against Humanity", in *Yale Journal of International Law*, 2004, vol. 29, p. 90.

187 Berreby, 2018, p. 260, see *supra* note 62.

188 *Ibid.*, p. 257.

189 *Ibid.*, p. xiii.

moods, spirits and even a soul. One French writer describes France as "the same soul which spans the generations, constantly rejuvenating but always the same".[190]

Like all categories, human categories help explain the world and guide human actions. Human groups impart knowledge and insights. One does not have to figure out the world from scratch.[191] The group preselects perceptions and options in life and excludes experiences or lifestyles which do not fit its standards. It helps situate the self and others in the world. With group references, we understand people we do not know personally. It provides a stable and comprehensive map of the world which informs our self-understanding, other-understanding and problem-solving. This saves time, provides mental clarity, avoids confusion and fragmentation.[192] Socially and culturally anchored, one is not bewildered and overwhelmed by the enormity of information in the world, nor does one feel clueless with uncertain interpersonal interactions. Social structures help human beings achieve goals which the individual brain alone cannot achieve.[193] It is as if the group connected individual physical and mental capacities and transformed them into something infinite.

3.4.2. A Functional Approach to State

With all the emotional and practical benefits provided by local groups, the collective culture and wisdom also restrict a person's perspective and freedom to choose. It becomes difficult for an embedded member of a group to learn new lessons or to appreciate other ways of life outside the group's experience. It makes most people susceptible to 'ethnocentrism' which takes one's own group as "the center of everything" and measures all others with one's own standards.[194] Contrary to cosmopolitan thinking, tribal thinking is more emotional, concrete than rational and abstract.[195] The cosmopolitan law itself is a reaction to experiences of State harming instead of protecting individual human beings. Nevertheless, a cosmopolitan community for the purposes of war crimes law seeks to limit, not eliminate local communities in general, and the State in particular. The nation-State is still a necessary moral and political community for

[190] *Ibid.*, p. 31.

[191] *Ibid.*, p. 184.

[192] *Ibid.*, p. 136.

[193] *Ibid.*, p. 184, citing Naomi Quinn, "Universals of Child Rearing", in *Anthropological Theory*, 2005, vol. 5, p. 479: "Cultural models of this kind evolve because culture and brain together can achieve shared solution to human tasks that the individual brain alone is ill-suited to perform".

[194] Cited in *ibid.*, p. 211.

[195] *Ibid.*, p. 43.

the purposes of cosmopolitan ideals. A literal realization of the cosmopolitan political ideal would be a world government.[196] Its viability is often cast in doubt. Duff concedes that humanity as a moral community is sufficient for a cosmopolitan criminal law, considering it is impossible to have species-wide political organization in a literal sense.[197] Duff is, of course, not alone in thinking humanity can never form a unitary political enterprise. Luban, for example, also argues that humanity as a whole cannot be seen as a single people for the purposes of a polity. So-called 'laws of humanity' therefore cannot be regarded as an expression of the political will of one people.[198] The relationship among human beings in general is simply not strong enough to provide sufficient political solidarity.[199] Humanity lacks the "centripetal forces of shared customs, languages, experiences, and projects" which bind a community together, and is divided by "the centrifugal forces of diversity".[200] Most advocates for cosmopolitan institutions seek to circumvent a centralized "planetary Leviathan".[201] Cosmopolitan democracy seeks to inaugurate supra-State decision-making at a global level without requiring a world-State.[202]

Models for cosmopolitan polity introduced in this chapter all include the State as a necessary component. A functional approach to the State is taken: the State is seen as a necessary and effective means to promote human well-being. There are principled and practical reasons for the State to exist. The State can provide emotional comfort and co-ordinate social and political affairs for the benefit of its citizens. Habermas, for example, argues that only the State can guarantee individual rights and equal participation in democratic processes through "institutionalized publics, elections, parliaments, and other forms of participation" and "administrative mechanisms".[203] On the other hand, the State must perform essential functions for the well-being of its citizens. The State has an obligation to follow certain important moral and political principles as discussed above. The idea of a State duty is not unique in Western cosmopolitan thinking. For example, sovereign duty to its people is also emphasized in the Confucian tradition. Mencius argues that if people commit crimes because the

[196] See, for example, Luis Cabrera, *Political Theory and Global Justice: A Cosmopolitan Case for the World State*, Routledge, Abingdon, 2004.

[197] Duff, 2010, p. 600, see *supra* note 18.

[198] Luban, 2004, p. 126, see *supra* note 186.

[199] *Ibid.*, p. 126.

[200] *Ibid.*

[201] William E. Scheuerman, "Cosmopolitan Democracy and the Rule of Law", in *Ratio Juris*, 2002, vol. 15, no. 4, p. 444.

[202] *Ibid.*

[203] Habermas, 2001, pp. 107, see *supra* note 63.

sovereign is unable to sustain their livelihood, this is entrapment.[204] To gain legitimacy, the State must meet certain minimum standards.

For any cosmopolitan theory, it is very difficult, if not impossible, to avoid including the State as the primary form of political and moral organization. A cosmopolitan political community is to co-exist, not replace the national community. There is competition and mutual dependence between the cosmopolitan and local communities, both making identity and normative claims over the individual human being. Cosmopolitan morality questions the absolute authority of the nation-State; on the other hand, cosmopolitan human agency cannot be realized directly through a world State, but has to be fulfilled in a reasonably well-organized political community. Individuals are linked to the cosmopolitan community through the State and other entities. The morality of the State comes from the human person, who is the ultimate scale of value measurement.

[204] Cited in Xiang Shuchen, *Chinese Cosmopolitanism: The History and Philosophy of an Idea*, Princeton University Press, 2023, pp. 55, 58.

4

Cosmopolitan Values and Criminalization in the Context of War

Criminal law does not have to conform to certain pre-legal, pre-institutional or pre-political categories of moral wrongs.[1] Nevertheless, criminal law typically has a moral constitution. "The criminal law", Duff argues, "does not (cannot) turn conduct that was not already wrongful into a moral wrong".[2] The conduct in question is already a moral wrong before criminal law characterizes it as a crime. Criminal law singles out certain pre-existing moral wrongs and subjects them to its particular characterization and response. That is to say, even without criminal law, one already has good reason to refrain from committing the wrongs in question. Criminal law, of course, has its own methods to select appropriate wrongs. These methods generate extensive philosophical and doctrinal studies of criminalization.[3] This chapter examines whether and to what extent it is possible to build cosmopolitan morality into criminalization of excessive violence in war.

4.1. Criminalization in a Cosmopolitan Community: War Crimes Law as Confirming Universal Human Values

A cosmopolitan war crimes law should identify wrongs which violate important values of the cosmopolitan community. It should reflect the kind of beings we are and what we value in our humanity. Universal human rationality is expected to ultimately guarantee consensus on and solidarity over the selection of wrongful conducts for criminalization in war.

First, the individual person should be regarded as the primary source of values. A cosmopolitan war crimes law seeks to protect individual interests and

1 R.A. Duff *et al.*, "Introduction: Towards a Theory of Criminalisation?", in R.A. Duff *et al.* (eds.), *Criminalization: The Political Morality of the Criminal Law*, Oxford University Press, 2014, p. 21.

2 R.A. Duff, "Responsibility, Citizenship and Criminal Law", in R.A. Duff and Stuart P. Green (eds.), *Philosophical Foundations of Criminal Law*, Oxford University Press, 2011, p. 127.

3 Among others, the *Rechtsgut* theory and the harm principle are well-known methods. For use of the legal goods theory in international criminal law, see Ioanna N. Anastasopoulou, "Legal Goods in International Criminal Law", in Morten Bergsmo, Emiliano J. Buis and Song Tianying (eds.), *Philosophical Foundations of International Criminal Law: Legally-Protected Interests*, Torkel Opsahl Academic EPublisher, Brussels, 2022, pp. 117–138 (https://www.toaep.org/ps-pdf/36-bergsmo-buis-song).

rights, not material objects or collective rights as they are. Collective interests and material goods are justified by their function to advance human interests. The human person is the ultimate "referent object"[4] in value assignment. Larry May, for example, argues that the main justification for prosecuting war crimes is the duty to treat certain individuals humanely during the war, rather than the duty of a State to protect its citizens.[5] Attack on objects or communities are seen as a violation of material and social needs of individual persons. Properties are protected in so far as they are important to the survival and well-being of the population or, in the case of cultural property, for their symbolic significance for the existence and continuity of human societies.[6]

The universalist orientation of the law means some values should attach to all of humanity in virtue of the common human nature. Universal values are grounded in universal human features and can be defended by "interculturally shareable good reasons".[7] Marcus Aurelius, the Roman Emperor and Stoic philosopher, invokes human identity as the ground to recognize and treat the enemy as a fellow human being. He says that another person who treats me with hostility must be met with the recognition of his common humanity.[8] This other person, according to Aurelius, "is from one of the same stock, and a kinsman and partner" who should be treated "according to the natural law of fellowship with benevolence and justice".[9] The non-relational characterization of values serves to dissolve established boundaries which are typically present in war. Human identity precedes all other collective identities. Values attached to the human identity are absolute, not relative. An individual's particular social identity or circumstances should not affect the protection of these values. The State is considered morally arbitrary and historically contingent in comparison to the eternal and universal human interests. Ethics and community should not be limited to the prevalent form of political organization and should be de-territorialized and universalized, even in war. A cosmopolitan war crimes law

4 Janine Natalya Clark, "The Destruction of Cultural Heritage in Armed Conflict: The 'Human Element' and the Jurisprudence of the ICTY", in *International Criminal Law Review*, 2018, vol. 18, no. 1, p. 41.

5 Larry May, *War Crimes and Just War*, Cambridge University Press, 2007, p. 15.

6 See Clark, 2018, p. 46, *supra* note 4.

7 Bhikhu Parekh, "Non-Ethnocentric Universalism", in Tim Dunne and Nicholas J. Wheeler (eds.), *Human Rights in Global Politics*, 2012, Cambridge University Press, p. 150. For more on universality of human identity, see Chapter 1 in the present book.

8 Cited in Noah Feldman, "Cosmopolitan Law?", in *The Yale Law Journal*, 2007, vol. 116, no. 1022, p. 1057.

9 *Ibid.*

communicates humanity's determination to protect "the right to have rights, or the right of every individual to belong to humanity".[10]

The moral salience of universalist and individualist values is taken seriously in judicial reasoning, sometimes even more seriously than the law itself. That is, cosmopolitan morality is invoked to not only justify and enrich the law, but to also evaluate and remedy the law in some instances. The following examples of judicial and treaty practices are intended to illustrate, rather than validate, cosmopolitan conceptions of values in war crimes trials. They show that the cosmopolitan approach is not alien to the practice of war crimes law.

The Nuremberg Judgment makes sure to say that torture and murder of prisoners of war are "in complete disregard of the elementary dictates of humanity", in addition to violating positive international law.[11] The *Kupreškić* Trial Chamber of the ICTY prioritizes universal moral dictates of humanity over legal dogmatism. The Trial Chamber, in finding a customary-law prohibition of belligerent reprisals against civilians, holds that "law may emerge through a customary process under the pressure of the demands of humanity or the dictates of public conscience, even where State practice is scant or inconsistent".[12]

The extension of individual criminal responsibility from international armed conflict to non-international armed conflict is another case in point. It is argued that the same act, if criminalized in international armed conflict, or in domestic legal systems in general, should also be criminalized in non-international armed conflict.[13] The criteria of criminalization should centre on human interests, not the circumstances of their violations. For the sake of moral consistency, comparable acts should be criminalized regardless of the type of armed conflict. The criminalization gap between international and non-international armed conflicts follows the logic that State violence is naturally more legitimate than non-State violence,[14] which is indefensible considering the contingent value of the State and absolute value of persons. Such cosmopolitan morality is

---

10 Hannah Arendt, *The Origins of Totalitarianism*, Harcourt Brace Jovanovich Publishers, New York, 1979, p. 298.

11 IMT, "Judgment of 1 October 1946", in *The Trial of German Major War Criminals before the International Military Tribunal*, Volume 22, 27 August 1946–1 October 1946, p. 451 (https://www.legal-tools.org/doc/d1427b/).

12 ICTY, *Prosecutor v. Kupreškić et al.*, Trial Chamber, Judgment, 14 January 2000, IT-95-16-T, paras. 527, 530 (https://www.legal-tools.org/doc/5c6a53/).

13 *Ibid.*, para. 313. See also Theodor Meron, "International Criminalisation of Internal Atrocities", in *American Journal of International Law*, 1995, vol. 89, no. 3, p. 561.

14 Nathaniel Berman, "Privileging Combat? Contemporary Conflict and the Legal Construction of War", in *Columbia Journal of Transnational Law*, 2004, vol. 43, no. 1, p. 21.

first promoted by the *Tadić* Appeals Chamber's famous statement extending individual criminal responsibility to non-international armed conflict:

> A State-sovereignty-oriented approach has been gradually supplanted by a human-being-oriented approach. [...] It follows that in the area of armed conflict the distinction between interstate wars and civil wars is losing its value as far as human beings are concerned. Why protect civilians from belligerent violence, or ban rape, torture or the wanton destruction of hospitals, churches, museums or private property, as well as proscribe weapons causing unnecessary suffering when two sovereign States are engaged in war, and yet refrain from enacting the same bans or providing the same protection when armed violence has erupted 'only' within the territory of a sovereign State? If international law, while of course duly safeguarding the legitimate interests of States, must gradually turn to the protection of human beings, it is only natural that the aforementioned dichotomy should gradually lose its weight.[15]

The Appeals Chamber highlights that the universality and primacy of human values is required by "elementary considerations of humanity and common sense".[16] It means protection of these important and primary values by criminal law is equally important in all circumstances, whether it is peacetime or during any kind of armed conflict. From a legal technical perspective, the Appeals Chamber's decision to close the criminalization gap between the two types of armed conflicts was without statutory or customary law support at the time. As Corrias and Gordon put it, "the tribunal took as a basis for its decision not strictly 'what states believed as a matter of law' but also or instead 'what was deemed necessary for humanity as a matter of exigency'".[17] Cosmopolitan individualism and universalism provide powerful moral justification for this "legal leap of faith".[18] The gap in protecting the most important human interests is narrowed at the cost of State sovereignty. Apparently, the more important the values in question, the more reason there should not be any gap in their protection in different types of armed conflicts. Common Article 3 of the 1949 Geneva Conventions is deemed to enshrine the most fundamental human interests. Those who

---

15 ICTY, *Prosecutor v. Duško Tadić*, Appeals Chamber, Decision on the Defence Motion for Interlocutory Appeal on Jurisdiction, 2 October 1995, IT-94-1, para. 97 ('*Tadić*') (https://www.legal-tools.org/doc/866e17/).

16 *Ibid.*, para. 119.

17 Luigi D.A. Corrias and Geoffrey M. Gordon, "Judging in the Name of Humanity: International Criminal Tribunals and the Representation of a Global Public", in *Journal of International Criminal Justice*, 2015, vol. 13, no. 1, p. 101.

18 Robert Cryer, "War Crimes", in Nigel D. White and Christian Henderson (eds.), *Research Handbook on International Conflict and Security Law: Jus ad Bellum, Jus in Bello, and Jus Post Bellum*, Edward Elgar Publishing, Cheltenham, 2013, p. 490.

commit violations of Common Article 3 in internal conflicts should not, according to the ICTY Trial Chamber, "on any level of reasoning, be treated more leniently" than perpetrators of the same acts in international armed conflicts.[19] This is because the "nature" of prohibitions contained in Common Article 3 dictates that they should have equally serious consequences in both types of armed conflicts.[20] According to the *Tadić* Appeals Chamber, other rules which clearly concern very important human interests may include prohibitions of attacks on civilians, indiscriminate attacks, the protection of those not taking part in hostilities, the general principles of Additional Protocol II, the prohibition of perfidy, and of the use of gas weapons.[21]

I now turn to specific provisions of positive war crimes law to illustrate, in a more systematic manner, the kind of cosmopolitan human values which can be read into war crimes law. I use as an example the definition of war crimes in the Rome Statute of the ICC, which is relatively comprehensive and contemporary. The ICC's list of war crimes is, of course, neither definitive nor perfect. However, any conception of war crimes cannot depart completely from the positive law. A theory of war crimes law is at least informed by past and current practices to be a theory of this particular law, not other laws or any other human practices such as philosophy or religion. A cosmopolitan war crimes law is, after all, seeking to orient the development of positive law, not chasing a fantastic ghost which is conjured up from imagination. The table below shows categories of cosmopolitan human values which can be considered as protected by war crimes law under the Rome Statute.

<table>
<tr><th>International armed conflict</th><th>Non-international armed conflict</th><th>Specific human values</th></tr>
<tr><td colspan="2">1. Human person: life, physical/mental integrity</td><td></td></tr>
<tr><td>(2)(a)(i) "Wilful killing";</td><td rowspan="2">(2)(c)(i) "Violence to life and person, in particular murder of all kinds, mutilation, cruel treatment and torture";</td><td rowspan="2">Life, physical, mental integrity of protected persons</td></tr>
<tr><td>(2)(a)(ii) "Torture or inhuman treatment, including biological experiments";</td></tr>
</table>

[19] ICTY, *Prosecutor v. Zdravko Mucić et al.*, Trial Chamber, Judgment, 16 November 1998, IT-96-21-T, paras. 300–301 ('*Mucić et al.*') (https://www.legal-tools.org/doc/6b4a33/). In the *Stakić* case, the ICTY Trial Chamber expanded the reach of the crime of civilian deportation to non-international armed conflicts. See ICTY, *Prosecutor v. Stakić*, Trial Chamber, Judgment, 31 July 2003, IT-97-24-T, paras. 671–684 (https://www.legal-tools.org/doc/1hwcgbxv/). The ruling was not upheld by the Appeals Chamber, see ICTY, *Prosecutor v. Stakić*, Appeal Chamber, Judgment, 22 March 2006, paras. 288–303 (https://www.legal-tools.org/doc/09f75f/).

[20] *Mucić et al.*, 16 November 1998, paras. 300–301, see *supra* note 19.

[21] *Tadić*, 2 October 1995, paras. 100–124, see *supra* note 15.

(2)(a)(iii) "Wilfully causing great suffering, or serious injury to body or health";		
(2)(b)(x) "Subjecting persons who are in the power of an adverse party to physical mutilation or to medical or scientific experiments of any kind which are neither justified by the medical, dental or hospital treatment of the person concerned nor carried out in his or her interest, and which cause death to or seriously endanger the health of such person or persons";	(2)(e)(xi) "Subjecting persons who are in the power of another party to the conflict to physical mutilation or to medical or scientific experiments of any kind which are neither justified by the medical, dental or hospital treatment of the person concerned nor carried out in his or her interest, and which cause death to or seriously endanger the health of such person or persons";	
(2)(b)(xxi) "Committing outrages upon personal dignity, in particular humiliating and degrading treatment";	(2)(c)(ii) "Committing outrages upon personal dignity, in particular humiliating and degrading treatment";	Dignity, mental integrity of persons
(2)(b)(xxii) "Committing rape, sexual slavery, enforced prostitution, forced pregnancy, as defined in article 7, paragraph 2 (f), enforced sterilization, or any other form of sexual violence also constituting a grave breach of the Geneva Conventions";	(2)(e)(vi) "Committing rape, sexual slavery, enforced prostitution, forced pregnancy, as defined in article 7, paragraph 2 (f), enforced sterilization, and any other form of sexual violence also constituting a serious violation of article 3 common to the four Geneva Conventions";	Physical integrity of persons
(2)(a)(viii) "Taking of hostages";	(2)(c)(iii) "Taking of hostages";	Life, physical integrity, freedom of movement of individual civilians and protected persons
(2)(b)(xxiii) "Utilizing the presence of a civilian or other protected person to render certain points, areas or military forces immune from military operations";		
(2)(b)(vi) "Killing or wounding a combatant who, having laid down his arms or having no longer means of defence, has surrendered at discretion";		Life, physical integrity of persons *hors de combat*
(2)(b)(xii) "Declaring that no quarter will be given";	(2)(e)(x) "Declaring that no quarter will be given";	
(2)(b)(i)-2 "Intentionally directing attacks against individual civilians	(2)(e)(i)-2 "Intentionally directing attacks against individual	Life, physical integrity of special-

not taking direct part in hostilities";	civilians not taking direct part in hostilities";	status civilians, including United Nations personnel, medical personnel
(2)(b)(iii) "Intentionally directing attacks against personnel, installations, material, units or vehicles involved in a humanitarian assistance or peacekeeping mission in accordance with the Charter of the United Nations, as long as they are entitled to the protection given to civilians under the international law of armed conflict";	(2)(e)(iii) "Intentionally directing attacks against personnel, installations, material, units or vehicles involved in a humanitarian assistance or peacekeeping mission in accordance with the Charter of the United Nations, as long as they are entitled to the protection given to civilians or civilian objects under the international law of armed conflict";	
(2)(b)(xxiv) "Intentionally directing attacks against personnel using the distinctive emblems of the Geneva Conventions in conformity with international law";	(2)(e)(ii) "Intentionally directing attacks against personnel using the distinctive emblems of the Geneva Conventions in conformity with international law";	
(2)(b)(xvii) "Employing poison or poisoned weapons";	(2)(e)(xiii) "Employing poison or poisoned weapons";	Physical well-being of military personnel and civilians
(2)(b)(xviii) "Employing asphyxiating, poisonous or other gases, and all analogous liquids, materials or devices";	(2)(e)(xiv) "Employing asphyxiating, poisonous or other gases, and all analogous liquids, materials or devices";	
(2)(b)(xix) "Employing bullets which expand or flatten easily in the human body, such as bullets with a hard envelope which does not entirely cover the core or is pierced with incisions";	(2)(e)(xv) "Employing bullets which expand or flatten easily in the human body, such as bullets with a hard envelope which does not entirely cover the core or is pierced with incisions";	Physical well-being of military personnel
(2)(b)(xx)-1 "Employing weapons, projectiles and material and methods of warfare which are of a nature to cause superfluous injury or unnecessary suffering in violation of the international law of armed conflict, provided that such weapons, projectiles and material and methods of warfare are the subject of a comprehensive prohibition and are included in an annex to this Statute, by an amendment in accordance with the relevant provisions set forth in articles 121 and 123";		

(2)(b)(xxvi) "Conscripting or enlisting children under the age of fifteen years into the national armed forces or using them to participate actively in hostilities".	(2)(e)(vii) "Conscripting or enlisting children under the age of fifteen years into armed forces or groups or using them to participate actively in hostilities";	Life and well-being of children
2. Civilian population – survival, security, well-being		
(2)(a)(vii) "Unlawful deportation or transfer or unlawful confinement";	(2)(e)(viii) "Ordering the displacement of the civilian population for reasons related to the conflict, unless the security of the civilians involved or imperative military reasons so demand";	Security, demographic composition, peaceful life, integrity of communities
(2)(b)(viii) "The transfer, directly or indirectly, by the Occupying Power of parts of its own civilian population into the territory it occupies, or the deportation or transfer of all or parts of the population of the occupied territory within or outside this territory";		
(2)(b)(i)-1 "Intentionally directing attacks against the civilian population as such";	(2)(e)(i)-1 "Intentionally directing attacks against the civilian population as such";	Survival, security, well-being of civilian persons
(2)(b)(iv) "Intentionally launching an attack in the knowledge that such attack will cause incidental loss of life or injury to civilians which would be clearly excessive in relation to the concrete and direct overall military advantage anticipated";		Life, security, well-being of civilian persons
(2)(b)(xx)-2 "Employing weapons, projectiles and material and methods of warfare which are inherently indiscriminate in violation of the international law of armed conflict, provided that such weapons, projectiles and material and methods of warfare are the subject of a comprehensive prohibition and are included in an annex to this Statute, by an amendment in accordance with the relevant provisions set forth in articles 121 and 123";		

(2)(b)(v) "Attacking or bombarding, by whatever means, towns, villages, dwellings or buildings which are undefended and which are not military objectives";		
(2)(b)(xxv) "Intentionally using starvation of civilians as a method of warfare by depriving them of objects indispensable to their survival, including wilfully impeding relief supplies as provided for under the Geneva Conventions";		
3. Right to fair trial		
(2)(a)(vi) "Wilfully depriving a prisoner of war or other protected person of the rights of fair and regular trial";	(2)(c)(iv) "The passing of sentences and the carrying out of executions without previous judgement pronounced by a regularly constituted court, affording all judicial guarantees which are generally recognized as indispensable";	Right to fair trial
(2)(b)(xiv) "Declaring abolished, suspended or inadmissible in a court of law the rights and actions of the nationals of the hostile party";		
4. Conscience, national loyalty		
(2)(a)(v) "Compelling a prisoner of war or other protected person to serve in the forces of a hostile Power";		Moral conscience
(2)(b)(xv) "Compelling the nationals of the hostile party to take part in the operations of war directed against their own country, even if they were in the belligerent's service before the commencement of the war";		
5. Property		
(2)(a)(iv) "Extensive destruction and appropriation of property, not justified by military necessity and carried out unlawfully and wantonly";		Survival, well-being of civilian persons

(2)(b)(xiii) "Destroying or seizing the enemy's property unless such destruction or seizure be imperatively demanded by the necessities of war";	(2)(e)(xii) "Destroying or seizing the property of an adversary unless such destruction or seizure be imperatively demanded by the necessities of the conflict";	
(2)(b)(xvi) "Pillaging a town or place, even when taken by assault";	(2)(e)(v) "Pillaging a town or place, even when taken by assault";	
(2)(b)(ii) "Intentionally directing attacks against civilian objects, that is, objects which are not military objectives";		
(2)(b)(iv) "Intentionally launching an attack in the knowledge that such attack will cause incidental damage to civilian objects which would be clearly excessive in relation to the concrete and direct overall military advantage anticipated";		
(2)(b)(v) "Attacking or bombarding, by whatever means, towns, villages, dwellings or buildings which are undefended and which are not military objectives";		
(2)(b)(ix)-1 "Intentionally directing attacks against buildings dedicated to religion, education, art, science or charitable purposes, historic monuments, provided they are not military objectives";	(2)(e)(iv)-1 "Intentionally directing attacks against buildings dedicated to religion, education, art, science or charitable purposes, historic monuments, provided they are not military objectives";	Objects needed for human beings to create meaning and purpose in life
(2)(b)(ix)-2 "Intentionally directing attacks against hospitals and places where the sick and wounded are collected, provided they are not military objectives";	(2)(e)(iv)-2 "Intentionally directing attacks against hospitals and places where the sick and wounded are collected, provided they are not military objectives";	Medical objects needed to save life and remedy health problems of persons
(2)(b)(xxiv) "Intentionally directing attacks against buildings, material, medical units and transport using the distinctive emblems of the Geneva Conventions in conformity with international law";	(2)(e)(ii) "Intentionally directing attacks against buildings, material, medical units and transport using the distinctive emblems of the Geneva Conventions in conformity with international law";	

6. Environment		
(2)(b)(iv) "Intentionally launching an attack in the knowledge that such attack will cause widespread, long-term and severe damage to the natural environment which would be clearly excessive in relation to the concrete and direct overall military advantage anticipated";		Natural environment which is important for long-term survival and well-being of humankind
7. (Confidence in) Identification system in the battlefield		
(2)(b)(vii) "Making improper use of a flag of truce, of the flag or of the military insignia and uniform of the enemy or of the United Nations, as well as of the distinctive emblems of the Geneva Conventions, resulting in death or serious personal injury";		Life and security of protected persons
(2)(b)(xi) "Killing or wounding treacherously individuals belonging to the hostile nation or army".	(2)(e)(ix) "Killing or wounding treacherously a combatant adversary".	

Table 1: Perceived cosmopolitan values underlying the ICC's list of war crimes.

The voluminous and diverse human values listed in this table can be reorganized into three categories. These categories are interconnected, and can even be overlapping. To view them separately is to provide an analytical frame, not to assert rigid difference. Prohibition of certain acts in a single article can straddle multiple types of human interests, and the same human interest can be protected under several war crimes.

The first category of human interests include life, and physical and mental integrity of persons. They represent basic biological conditions for human existence and exercise of agency. The corresponding prohibitions are mainly concerned with preserving human life and avoiding the worst human sufferings. This category directly reflects human fragility, considering the "universal human capacity to inflict and suffer harm".[22] Prohibitions include killing, acts which result in physical or mental damage of persons, all kinds of ill-treatment and torture, using human beings for medical experiments or as a shield, starvation of civilian population, *et cetera.*

[22] Catherine Lu, "The One and Many Faces of Cosmopolitanism", in *The Journal of Political Philosophy*, 2000, vol. 8, no. 2, p. 245.

The second category of human interests concern basic material and social needs for survival. Human existence requires not only lack of negative harm but also minimum positive conditions. To sustain human survival and dignity, people should be allowed to reside in their homes and belong to their own community (hence the prohibition of deportation and forcible transfer of population), to have minimum freedom of movement, to own property, to have access to medical care, to live in relative security and stability, to be free from arbitrary exercise of power, to have some privacy and control over their lives, to live in long-term harmony with the natural environment, *et cetera*. The prohibition of compelling prisoners of war and enemy civilians to fight against their own nation also falls into this category. It recognizes national allegiance, or a need to belong, as an important kind of moral conscience for an individual person, especially considering the context of war.

The third category of human interests concern human achievements which signify human worth, that is, achievements which "reflect creativity, energy, search for meaning and significance, depth of emotion, and capacity for co-operation and altruism, and add to the beauty of the world".[23] This consideration underlies protection of buildings dedicated to religion, education, art, science or charitable purposes, historic monuments, *et cetera*. These objects serve symbolic, emotional and practical functions for their local constituency and, in some instances, for all of humankind. In other words, the value of these special-status objects is derived from their function and meaning for human beings.[24] Cultural objects and buildings not only generate group identity through representation of history and culture, but also attest to humanity's general cultural capacity.[25] They can contribute to "identity generation" and "communication".[26] In the *Al Hassan* case before the ICC, the trial judgment affirmed that demolition of historical mausoleums and the door of a mosque in Timbuktu is "a serious attack on the identity of Timbuktu", "an act of aggression against their faith, and a crime against their cultural and traditional symbols".[27] It takes away the people's "respect" and "augustness".[28] It also causes emotional trauma, according to the

[23] Parekh, 2012, p. 147, see *supra* note 7.

[24] Clark, 2018, p. 41, *supra* note 4.

[25] Markus M. Muller, "Cultural Heritage Protection: Legitimacy, Property, and Functionalism", in *International Journal of Cultural Property*, 1998, vol. 7, no. 2, p. 399.

[26] *Ibid.*

[27] ICC, *Prosecutor v. Al Hassan Ag Abdoul Aziz Ag Mohamed Ag Mahmoud*, Trial Chamber X, Trial Judgment, 26 June 2024, ICC-01/12-01/18, para. 1045 (footnote omitted) (https://www.legal-tools.org/doc/o613gxre/).

[28] *Ibid.*

judgment, creating "fear, sadness, frustration and anger" among the population.[29]

Overall, the values listed above concern preservation and promotion of basic human agency and dignity, although unevenly and inconsistently. This is because what is included in the list of war crimes is based on past experiences of war. Normative questions can always be raised about the inclusion of some values and not others as universal, or the fact that conducts violating the same values are not consistently criminalized.[30] Questions of comprehensiveness and consistency of the value system represented by the current list are important for the evolution of the law. However, this chapter continues with a greater concern about the interactions between cosmopolitan values and the logic of war. That is, how the protection of these values is relativized in the context of war, and what this means for a cosmopolitan approach to war crimes law. This is because reading cosmopolitan values out of war crimes law is only a job half done. The question is not whether these core human values are *generally* important; rather, it is whether and how important they are in the context of war. Put another way, how can cosmopolitan morality and war be compatible within the system of war crimes law? Dictates of war, not just humanity, need to be accounted for. From the table above, we can see the system of legal protection is graded and selective. Recognition and protection of human values differ according to the persons' role and the circumstances they find themselves in. Placed in the context of war, these values are no longer absolute, nor common-sensical. War inhabits its own common sense. Cosmopolitan rationality has to adapt to the unique reality of war. Although compromises over the universality and absoluteness of human interests are often taken for granted in the regime of war crimes law, I would like to re-examine these compromises as part of the strategy of criminalization and find out to what extent such inevitable compromises affect a cosmopolitan approach to war crimes law.

4.2. Criminalization in the Context of War: Between Misfortune and Inhuman

Criminal law is a peace-time means of social control. Applied to conducts in war, it needs to reinvent its strategies of criminalization. Context is important. In particular, war crimes law needs to find a way to re-characterize conducts which are regarded criminal in peace-time. Murder, assault, mass destruction of property, these obvious candidates for criminalization in peace-time have to be

[29] *Ibid.*, para. 1046.

[30] See, for example, Claus Kreß, "Crimes de Guerre", in Olivier Beauvallet (ed.), *Dictionnaire Encyclopédique de la Justice Pénale Internationale*, Berger-Levrault, Boulogne-Billancourt, 2017; and discussion in May, 2007, see *supra* note 5.

re-assessed in war. If peace-time criminalization requires more than a general feeling of outrage,[31] war-time criminalization requires more than a general understanding of crimes. Serious moral wrongfulness is a good reason, but not a conclusive one, for criminalization in the context of war. The law has to exempt certain forms of violence and criminalize others.

Pursuant to the need to distinguish between lesser and grave evils, rationalizations are developed to make the distinction appear principled and legitimate. Certain sufferings are seen as unfortunate but *necessary*, and others as unnecessary and inhuman. Jean-Jacques Rousseau reasons that the nature of war prohibits inflicting "any more destruction than is necessary for victory".[32] Louis Renault, in his 1918 article, provides a more elaborate justification for the criminalization of certain conducts in war. According to Renault, while the loss of thousands of lives during a battle causes feelings of *misery*, excessive violence such as killing a surrendering enemy soldier incurs real *indignation*. This is because excessive violence is unnecessary and against the law of humanity.[33] Necessary violence is unfortunate but just; excessive violence is malicious and unjust.[34] Misfortunes are like natural disasters; they are to be suffered in silence. Injustice, on the other hand, is a human error and must be rectified. Misfortunes are inevitable and unpunishable, while injustice is avoidable and punishable. Acknowledging necessary violence in war is to recognize war as part of the human condition. One cannot eliminate, but only mitigate, the inevitable miseries in the human condition. A prominent pacifist during the Second World War urges that a pacifist who has failed to prevent war should still seek to "mitigate war's worst excesses".[35] The starting point of regulating warfare is the failure to prevent war.

If, in peace-time, criminal law serves to entrench the existing social order, in war, it tends to legitimate the social reality of war. In war, legitimation and criminalization of violence are two sides of the same coin. Legitimation of certain acts of combat, as Peter H. Wilson points out, serves an ideological purpose in eliminating the deeply-rooted social stigma of killing.[36] In other words, law

31 S.E. Marshall and R.A. Duff, "Criminalisation and Sharing Wrongs", in *Canadian Journal of Law and Jurisprudence*, 1998, vol. 11, no. 1, p. 7.

32 Cited in Chris af Jochnick and Roger Normand, "The Legitimation of Violence: Critical Analysis of the Gulf War", in *Harvard International Law Journal*, 1994, vol. 35, no. 2, p. 400.

33 Louis Renault, "De L'Application Du Droit Penal aux Faits de Guerre", in *Revue Générale de Droit International Public*, 1918, vol. 25, pp. 6–7.

34 *Ibid.*

35 Cited in Richard Norman, *Ethics, Killing, and War*, Cambridge University Press, 1995, p. 162.

36 Peter H. Wilson, "Defining Military Culture", in *The Journal of Military History*, 2008, vol. 72, no. 1, p. 34.

lends its own credibility to military practices which can otherwise be condemned or disapproved.[37] By criminalizing only certain 'excesses' of violence in war, the law of war crimes acknowledges the necessity of killing and destruction. This is a notable difference between war crimes and other identity-based crimes. War crimes law's binary characterization of violence *requires* identity-based violence – attacks must be directed only against military personnel and objects; while laws of genocide and crimes against humanity criminalize the very act of identity-based attack. One way to see this is that criminal responsibility is compartmentalized in crimes of aggression and war crimes, meaning the part of legitimate killing and destruction in war actually falls under the responsibility of aggression. I will elaborate on this dimension of criminalization in Chapter 8.

Here, I illustrate two concrete strategies in the construction of lawful and unlawful violence. The first one is to channel violence primarily to a specific group of persons and to try to spare the rest. This means that persons are assigned different moral worth. On the basis of such distinction, the second strategy is to restrict means and methods of violence towards the designated group. These two strategies are presented below in a skeletal manner without considering the nuances which might incur in the actual application of the law. Such a structural overview shows clearly the nature and scope of compromises on cosmopolitan values.

The principle of distinction has been developed over centuries as a progressive cannon of the law of war, parting from total wars. An Enlightenment scholar already argues for the need to distinguish between enemy civilians and combatants in war: "the right against persons in war is not the right of the promiscuous slaughter of those who are in the category of enemies".[38] There must be some kind of civilian-military distinction among the enemy. A nineteenth-century international declaration pronounces that "the only legitimate object which States should endeavour to accomplish during war is to weaken the military forces of the enemy".[39] Ideally, with such a distinction clearly marked, the troops alone carry out the war, while the rest of the population remain undisturbed.[40]

---

[37] Jochnick and Normand, 1994, p. 394, see *supra* note 32.

[38] Cited in Pablo Kalmanovitz, *The Laws of War in International Thought*, Oxford University Press, 2020, p. 104.

[39] Declaration Renouncing the Use, in Time of War, of Explosive Projectiles Under 400 Grammes Weight, 29 November 1868 (https://www.legal-tools.org/doc/c951bc/).

[40] Kalmanovitz, 2020, p. 111, see *supra* note 38. Kalmanovitz quotes Vattel's evocation of this ideal as follows:

The doctrine of combatants' privilege provides legal immunity for "certain kinds of large-scale violence".[41] It enables different criteria of criminalization to apply to the same actor and the same action. Armies are thus distinguished from criminal gangs when they carry out their war-fighting mission. Such is, according to Nathanial Berman, the function of "the legal construction of war".[42] The sense of order in war comes from identity-based, organized mass violence. Indiscriminate, senseless violence must be avoided. Identity-based violence enables identity-based protection for the rest of the population. Those who enjoy the privilege to kill can be killed or detained for the duration of the conflict. Physical attack and deprivation of liberty do not depend on an individual's behaviour but his or her identity as a combatant. Soldiers are treated as members of the enemy force, not as unique human beings with independent worth. Or rather, the legal form abstracts soldiers from their wider reality of life and reduces them to mere specimen of the enemy force.[43] Upon surrender, though, soldiers are partly and temporarily re-humanized. They should re-enter the moral universe of their enemy and be treated with dignity and respect. Recognition of and respect for the human status is discriminatory and conditional under the law.

The second strategy is to criminalize certain means and methods of warfare and allow others. The kind and degree of force against legitimate military targets is regulated. Although soldiers can be killed, they should not be subjected to unnecessary suffering. Killing is inevitable and therefore necessary, but certain sufferings are so inhuman that they are regarded as unjust. The law tends to prohibit use of weapons which are "designed to maim or disfigure or torture"[44] or make the death of the enemy inevitable. Poison or poison weapons, bullets which expand or flatten easily in the human body, blinding-laser weapons, for example, fall into this category.[45] Use of flamethrowers and napalm is considered "an atrocity in all circumstances" for they are "both extremely painful and

---

> at present, war is carried on by regular troops: the people, the peasants, the citizens, take no part in it, and generally have nothing to fear from the sword of the enemy. Provided the inhabitants submit to him who is master of the country, pay the contributions imposed, and refrain from all hostilities, they live in as perfect safety as if they were friends […] By protecting the unarmed inhabitants, keeping the soldiery under strict discipline, and preserving the country, a general procures an easy subsistence for his army, and avoids many evils and dangers.

[41] Berman, 2004, p. 3, see *supra* note 14.

[42] *Ibid*., p. 4 (footnote omitted).

[43] Norman, 1995, p. 180, see *supra* note 35.

[44] Cited in *ibid*.

[45] See Rome Statute of the International Criminal Court, 17 July 1998, Article 8 and its amendments (https://www.legal-tools.org/doc/7b9af9/).

extremely disfiguring".[46] The pain and disfiguring caused by prohibited weapons are grave and unnecessary, compared to a quick death by a bullet or bomb. Technological advances may bring about new weapons which cause sufferings no one could have expected. The law usually falls behind in criminalizing the use of such weapons. The spirit of this second criminalization strategy lies in limitations in harming even the legitimate target.

Regardless of the concrete strategies adopted, the law can be inevitably arbitrary in drawing the line between lawful and unlawful violence. It is *conceptually* inevitable because the law seeks to impose uniform regulation on a wide range of conducts in the extremely complex environment of war. Comparable conducts may not be regulated in a similar manner. Criminalization can be criticized as either overbroad or underinclusive. Arbitrariness is also caused by *historical* contingency. What is considered as war crimes has evolved throughout history. Legal prohibitions reflect past experiences and do not anticipate future threats. For example, many weapons of superior technological features were prohibited in war at different times and in different places in history;[47] they are no longer considered as taboos today. Larry May speculates that historically what was prohibited were simply new strategies or technologies of war which were acquired by some but not others. Law was used as a means to counter military disadvantages.[48] Conceptual and genealogical critiques can be directed to all laws. Indeed, any legal practice, including criminalization, can be criticized for being unfair in certain scenarios. Norms are accompanied and threatened by their necessary conceptual opposites: exceptions. And all law, including criminal law, can only be reactionary and contingent.

War crimes law's conceptual and genealogical contingencies are general compared to its particular *structural* arbitrariness. In the next section, I argue that the *structural* arbitrariness incurred in strategies of criminalization poses substantial threats to the cosmopolitan approach.

4.3. Unnatural Alliance of Cosmopolitanism and War

4.3.1. Structural Arbitrariness in Criminalization

The two strategies of criminalization necessarily result in *structural* arbitrariness in the way law draws a line in the continuum of violence. The structural arbitrariness is most obvious in the distinction between civilians and combatants. In 1944, George Orwell exclaims, in his newspaper column, that there is no point trying to distinguish between more and less "barbarous" or "legitimate"

---

[46] Cited in Norman, 1995, p. 180, see *supra* note 35.

[47] See Mark Osiel, "Obeying Orders: Atrocity, Military Discipline, and the Law of War", in *California Law Review*, 1998, vol. 86, no. 5, p. 995.

[48] May, 2007, p. 17, see *supra* note 5.

forms of warfare. After all, so-called "legitimate" warfare "picks out and slaughters all the healthiest and bravest of the young male population".[49] He poses the critical question: "Why is it worse to kill civilians than soldiers?".[50] Orwell's question is radical in that it challenges the legitimacy of distinguishing between civilians and combatants in war, which is often taken for granted in legal literature. Killing civilians is wrong, but it does not make killing combatants right. The attack against combatants is often "depersonalised".[51] Such identity-based violence does not treat individuals as unique humans being of worth and dignity or as "active beings with their own hopes and aspirations".[52] Soldiers have to submit themselves as mere means to an end, the end being the State or the group they are fighting for. They need to treat not only themselves, but also enemy soldiers and some civilians if necessary as means to an end. As Habermas puts it: "Even cabinet wars conducted with standing armies are incompatible 'with the right of humanity in our own person,' because a state that hires its citizens 'to kill or be killed' degrades them into 'mere machines'".[53] Turning soldiers into machines fits Arendt's characterization of "double dehumanisation", that is, dehumanization and denial of agency of the self and other.

Killing combatants is worse in some cases than others. A case in point is mass killings of enemy combatants before they could surrender. During the Gulf War, the United States-led coalition forces buried alive and killed from the air thousands of Iraqi troops attempting to flee.[54] These soldiers were not killed because of their conduct at the time. They were killed as mere specimen of the enemy forces. What makes their case more tragic, and a possible cause for moral indignation, is that they had no opportunity to surrender. Another central logic of the combatant-civilian distinction is to sacrifice some people for others. Soldiers are prepared to sacrifice their lives so that the larger part of the population can continue to live. If we see individuals as truly unique moral agents, the loss

---

49 Cited in Norman, 1995, p. 163, see *supra* note 35.

50 *Ibid.*

51 *Ibid.*, p. 188.

52 *Ibid.* Larry May similarly criticizes the just war theory today for not taking the individual rights of soldiers seriously, at least in part because these views continue to think of soldiers as a class rather than as individuals. See Larry May, "Human Rights, Proportionality, and the Lives of Soldiers", in Saba Bazargan and Samuel C. Rickless (eds.), *The Ethics of War: Essays*, Oxford University Press, 2017, pp. 55–56.

53 Jürgen Habermas, *The Divided West*, ed. and trans. by Ciaran Cronin, Polity, Cambridge, 2006, p. 120.

54 Jochnick and Normand, 1994, p. 396, see *supra* note 32.

of some lives cannot be compensated by the preservation of others.[55] A person is not a digit in mathematical calculations. Human lives are not interchangeable.

This is not to say that identity-based construction of lawful and unlawful violence does not have moral significance. It certainly has great moral significance, though in a relative sense. Killing is wrong, no matter who is the victim; only that killing civilians is morally worse than killing combatants. Norman rightly argues that the difference between killing innocent civilians and soldiers is one "in degree, not […] in kind".[56] "The contrast is not", as Norman puts it, "between the killing of non-combatants which is impermissible and the killing of combatants which is morally legitimate".[57] He describes "a continuum of degrees of depersonalisation" of victims of military attack, not "a simple moral dichotomy":

> What we have is a continuum, a progressive depersonalisation of those who are attacked. In the sequence from (a) to (e), the attack is less and less a response to what people are actually doing, and increasingly a response to them simply as belonging to a certain category of people.[58]

There is a relative, not categorical, difference in the continuum of violence and wrongs. What war crimes law seeks to criminalize is something morally worse than fighting the war itself. The aim is to mitigate, not optimize. While the law demands respect for human fellowship in the battlefield, it also allows cruelty and dehumanization.[59]

Structural arbitrariness is also inherent in the other strategy of criminalization introduced above: the prohibition of causing unnecessary sufferings. If soldiers are to be treated as mere means, why should the manner of harming matter?[60] And why is unnecessary suffering worse than death by legitimate killing?

---

55 For more on killing and the meaning of individual life, see Norman, 1995, p. 225, *supra* note 35.

56 *Ibid.*, p. 188.

57 *Ibid.*

58 *Ibid.*, p. 178.

59 The paradox is elaborated by May, 2007, pp. 15 ff., see *supra* note 5. Eric David also highlights "the basic contradiction" characteristic of the law of war in *Principes de Droit des Conflits Armés*, cited in Jean-Jacques Frésard, *The Roots of Behaviour in War: A Survey of the Literature*, International Committee of the Red Cross, Geneva, 2004, p. 27:

> It is possible to be even more succinct [...] in expressing the quintessence of the law of armed conflict: respect your fellow men even in the midst of fire and bloodshed! Quite an ambitious undertaking, and also quite a paradox! Is it possible to respect someone on whom you are dropping bombs, who you are lining up in the sights of your rifle, who is fighting you hand to hand? (pp. 731–732).

60 See May, 2017, p. 47, *supra* note 52.

Larry May poses the question from a human rights perspective: "why have soldiers forfeited their rights to life, but retained their rights not to suffer?".[61] Comparing extreme and often permanent sufferings caused by certain weapons and ultimate resignation from this world by death is almost an impossible task. But one cannot say that unnecessary sufferings, however terrible they are, are inhuman, and killing is not. The term unnecessary suffering is self-contradictory, just like the humanization of the laws of war, as Theodor Meron points out in his book *The Humanization of International Law*.[62]

4.3.2. Mutual Limitation Between Cosmopolitanism and War Within Criminal Law

Perhaps what is considered normatively arbitrary is desired of law. The function of law is to not only confirm certain values, but also manage moral disagreements.[63] Law provides an institutionalized response to multiple and sometimes competing values.[64] Integration of incompatible or even opposing values makes the law somewhat arbitrary. Richard Norman is certainly right to declare war as "one of the most deeply divisive of moral problems".[65] A cosmopolitan war crimes law has to accommodate both war and cosmopolitanism. The basic norms of war thoroughly contradict universalist and individualist values of cosmopolitan morality. From a cosmopolitan perspective, killing of any human being in war constitutes deprivation of humanity. Death does not just put an end to one's soldierly activities, but to all his or her life activities.[66] Law's depersonalization of combatants contradicts the cosmopolitan message – the message of humanity, respect and compassion. War and cosmopolitanism place on us two irreconcilable sets of moral responsibilities. War begins where cosmopolitanism cracks: a particular identity is prioritized over human identity, particular interests over universal interests, and exchange of brute force over rational

[61] *Ibid.*

[62] Theodor Meron, *The Humanization of International Law*, Martinus Nijhoff, 2006, p. 50.

[63] Peter Sutch, "The Slow Normalization of Normative Political Theory: Cosmopolitanism and Communitarianism Then and Now", in Chris Brown and Robyn Eckersley (eds.), *The Oxford Handbook of International Political Theory*, Oxford University Press, 2018, p. 45.

[64] James Griffin, "Human Rights and the Autonomy of International Law", in Samantha Besson and John Tasioulas (eds.), *The Philosophy of International Law*, Oxford University Press, 2010, p. 353. Non-moral philosophical reasons also influence criminalization. Pragmatic reasons including feasibility, efficacy and the costs of criminalizing a type of conduct can influence the decision-making. As Duff explains, in Duff *et al.*, 2014, p. 19, see *supra* note 1:

> Such pragmatic reasons are highly context sensitive, and no philosophical account of the criminal law can be expected by itself to yield determinate conclusions about what ought to be criminalised in a particular social, political, and historical context.

[65] Norman, 1995, p. 1, see *supra* note 35.

[66] *Ibid.*, p. 180.

communication. The logic that the individual's moral standing is not independently valid but relies entirely on his or her membership in a group cannot square with cosmopolitan moral claims. The cosmopolitan starting point is that all human beings have equal moral status in the same moral community. War is to assume the other group is so alien and dangerous that they must be defeated or eliminated by force. If in peace-time competing responsibilities from our own national community and humanity can be accommodated at varying degrees, war leads to dramatic clashes of these two sets of moral demands. It is universal human fellowship on the one hand, and, on the other, our specific community which gives us history, culture, identity and meaning of life. War makes tragic moral conflicts.[67] The conflicting moral demands of cosmopolitanism and war are reflected in conflicting policies in the creation and interpretation of the laws of war itself.

The writer Pablo Kalmanovitz holds the concept of civilized or humane war nonsense, and humanitarian neutrality in the face of war deeply troubling.[68] The faith in our common humanity, "illusory" as it may be, is the first victim of war.[69] What makes application of criminal law in war possible, that is, the construction of lawful and unlawful violence, remains "an objective anomaly within our moral thinking".[70] It is this anomaly which constitutes the defining feature of war crimes law. Any theoretical approach to the law, say, cosmopolitan or utilitarian, cannot completely eradicate its structural construct. This would amount to eradicating the law itself because the intrinsic structural arbitrariness is what distinguishes war crimes law from other criminal laws or legal practices.

The structure of war crimes law is permanent, but not petrified. There is room for ideological intervention. Different theoretical approaches have different rationalizations, assessments and suggestions of improvement for the law.[71]

---

67 See *ibid.*, p. 225. Norman refers to Hegel's observation that tragic conflicts arise because we are members of different social groups and institutions which sometimes make incompatible moral demands on us.

68 Kalmanovitz, 2020, p. 144, see *supra* note 38.

69 Cited in Steven R. Ratner, *The Thin Justice of International Law: A Moral Reckoning of the Law of Nations*, Oxford University Press, 2015, p. 67.

70 Norman, 1995, p. 251, see *supra* note 35.

71 For example, a utilitarian approach can promote economy of violence and other resources. A utilitarian critique of the law of war can be that the protection accorded to prisoners of war may harm military security, prolong the war and waste resources. See May, 2007, p. 18, *supra* note 5. Another instance of a utilitarian critique is that the combatant-civilian distinction may not align with the individual's actual contribution to the war effort. Civilians can make significant political, material and technological contributions which exceed the impact of many combatants. See, for example, Helen Frowe, "Non-Combatant Liability in War", in Helen Frowe and Gerald Lang (eds.), *How We Fight: Ethics in War*, Oxford University Press, 2014, p. 174.

A cosmopolitan approach offers justifications of universal human values and seeks to guide the development and application of war crimes law towards a more human-centred direction, to the extent possible. A cosmopolitan ideology can influence the law, but not derail it off the track of war. This is because for the law to be applied in the context of war, and to be able to guide military practice, not cosmopolitan fantasy, it has to *internalize*, not *externalize*, the logic of war. A cosmopolitan war crimes law cannot succumb to "an excess of sentimentality" or indulge in "utopianism" and "misguided philanthropy".[72] As long as war exists, there is always the inner tension between the requirement of fighting a war and that of recognizing the common humanity of the enemy. One has to turn on and off these two ideological appeals at different moments.

The enterprise of law does not indulge in tomorrow's possibilities, but occupies itself with today's struggles.[73] Mutual limitation between cosmopolitanism and war constitutes the unique dynamic within a cosmopolitan war crimes law which seeks to maximize, not fully realize, cosmopolitan moral principles. Section 4.1. in this chapter illustrates some of the efforts in practice to expand the scope of the protection of human values in war. The strategies of criminalization determine that the law can only protect some cosmopolitan values partially and conditionally. The reinvention of criminality in war, as it is guided by cosmopolitan ideology, is Janus-faced: it confirms cosmopolitan values of human life, dignity, fellowship, and, at the same time, legitimates killing and destruction. It promotes co-operation and common human identity in some cases and allows hostility and mutual dehumanization in others. Cosmopolitan morality has to live with its ideological opposite within the structure of war crimes law. A war crimes law conceived in the cosmopolitan spirit should be seen as part of the moral tragedies created by war, not as a triumph of cosmopolitanism. The moral message of a cosmopolitan war crimes law is destined to be ambivalent rather than consistent, partial rather than comprehensive, relative rather than absolute.

---

72 Kalmanovitz, 2020, p. 147, see *supra* note 38.

73 Jochnick and Normand, 1994, p. 78, see *supra* note 32.

5

From Cosmopolitan Law to Social Psychology: The Individual as Source of Value and Evil

Together, Chapters 3 and 4 show that criminal law requires and embodies a particular kind of relationship between the individual and the community. They extend the application of criminal law to a cosmopolitan community which provides social support and a value system for criminalization and condemnation of war crimes. A war-crimes law so conceived is universalist in its reach, individualist in its value-orientation, and rationalist in its moral psychology. Despite its substantive ambivalence which is necessitated by war, the moral message of a cosmopolitan war crimes law is firm in its tone and confident of its assumptions about the moral nature of human beings.

Is cosmopolitanism out of sync with the reality of war? Empirical questions can be raised regarding the faith placed in human rationality and its motivating force for human action. The cosmopolitan law is normatively top-down, but sociologically bottom-up – it must evoke support from local communities and concrete persons to succeed. The normative claim of a cosmopolitan war crimes law is grounded in certain sociological and psychological assumptions. A commentator questions the uniting force of human reason: "Reason could demonstrate the absurdity of the international anarchy; and with increasing knowledge, enough people would be rationally convinced of its absurdity to put an end to it".[1] While we do not need to share the sarcasm of this comment, it challenges us to examine social conditions of a cosmopolitan war crimes law in a more empirically informed way. The quality of moral psychology underlying the cosmopolitan community and its value system has implications for the quality of cosmopolitan law's normative claim. Cosmopolitan norms can be undermined by misguided notions of human agency. Moral reasoning's stability and impartiality can be overrated, as is its uniting and regulative force. A cosmopolitan war crimes law cannot supersede sociological particularities and contingencies by sheer normative supremacy.

This chapter turns to the moral psychology behind the individual as source of cosmopolitan law and perpetrator of war crimes. I examine the influence of local communities and immediate social circumstances on the relationship

1 Cited in Catherine Lu, "The One and Many Faces of Cosmopolitanism", in *The Journal of Political Philosophy*, 2000, vol. 8, no. 2, p. 248.

between the cosmopolitan community and its members. In particular, I look at how empirical evidence can potentially challenge a cosmopolitan war crimes law's normative claim.

5.1. A Top-Down Cosmopolitan Law, the Disempowered State, and the Empowered Individual

5.1.1. Top-Down Universalism

A cosmopolitan community and its value system give war crimes law a universalist orientation. This top-down normative framework is directed towards local communities in general, and nation-States in particular. The cosmopolitan war crimes law imposes restrictions on State sovereignty during organized armed hostilities. Mutual engagement among individuals worldwide can be organized through cosmopolitan constitutional principles or democratic arrangements. Individuals are reminded that they are not only citizens of a State, but also citizens of the world. Chapter 3 shows that cosmopolitan moral and political models assign a functional role to the State. The State should only be an instrument, and not an obstacle, to realizing fundamental human goods. The cosmopolitan community is thin in terms of issues falling into its realm. It concerns fundamental matters of human life which are constitutive of every member of the human species. In particular, it is preoccupied with the individual as possible victim of unjust violence of the State or other exclusive human communities. In these matters, the State does not have the sole discretion. Dichotomies and exclusions dictated by the principle of State sovereignty, such as the criminalization gap between international and non-international armed conflicts, are seen as morally arbitrary. The universalist orientation of cosmopolitan morality provides a powerful normative reference for war crimes law to counter particularist interests of the State. It can motivate a kind of "post-Westphalian shift"[2] in the law. Chapters 3 and 4 above illustrate examples of international criminal tribunals and academics invoking cosmopolitan universalism to rationalize war crimes law and sometimes its progressive development.

5.1.2. The Individual as Source of Norms and Crimes

The marginalization of the State is inevitable within a "homocentric"[3] scale of valorisation. Human worth and agency are promoted through cosmopolitan

---

2 See Claus Kreß, "Major Post-Westphalian Shifts and Some Important Neo-Westphalian Hesitations in the State Practice on the International Law on the Use of Force", in *Journal on the Use of Force and International Law*, 2014, vol. 1, no. 1, pp. 11 ff.

3 Moshe Hirsch, "The Sociological Perspective on International Law", in Jeffrey L. Dunoff and Mark A. Pollack (eds.), *International Legal Theory: Foundations and Frontiers*, Cambridge University Press, 2022, p. 293.

individualism and rationalism. "Normative individualism"[4] guides the creation and interpretation of war crimes law. The individual person is taken to be the origin of values and ultimate reference point. The worth of the person is fundamental, and that of the collective and objects derivative. Promoting and protecting individual agency against established structures should be at the centre of the cosmopolitan agenda. For example, David Held and Daniele Archibugi propose a World Parliament Assembly consisted of individuals to give individuals a voice and representation in global affairs, separate and independent from the voice and representation of their governments.[5]

Individuals are not only creators and supporters of the cosmopolitan community and its war crimes law, but also potential perpetrators of war crimes. Primacy of persons means they are sources of both good and evil. The individual is "the coin of the operating realm" in modern criminal law and many disciplines such as medicine and psychiatry.[6] All these areas focus on the individual person as "the sole causal agent".[7] The individual is regarded as a "more or less integrated motivational and cognitive universe".[8] In this sense, breaking the law is entirely a personal choice, coming directly from individual agency. Stanton-Ife says: "Criminal law, unlike natural disasters, is [...] concerned with harms and wrongs resulting from human agency".[9] Crimes are not just "undesirable occurrences"[10] which are out of human control. Criminal law focuses on the individual soul rather than its social environment. It interprets internal, intra-psychic factors in isolation rather than in context. This means the defect can only or mainly lie in individual disposition or normative faculties. It is therefore a failure of individual judgment, not lack of social nourishment and regulation, that leads to crimes.

Criminal law's conception of human agency is congruent with its attributional logic – autonomy corresponds to responsibility. Criminal law holds

---

4 Roland Pierik and Wouter Werner, "Cosmopolitanism in Context: An Introduction", in Pierik and Werner (eds.), *Cosmopolitanism in Context: Perspectives from International Law and Political Theory*, Cambridge University Press, 2010, p. 2.

5 David Held and Daniele Archibugi, "Cosmopolitan Democracy: Paths and Agents", in *Ethics & International Affairs*, 2011, vol. 25, no. 4, pp. 446–447.

6 Philip Zimbardo, *The Lucifer Effect: Understanding How Good People Turn Evil*, Random House Trade Paperbacks, London, 2007, p. 298.

7 *Ibid.*, p. 445.

8 Cited in John M. Doris, *Lack of Character: Personality and Moral Behavior*, Cambridge University Press, 2005, p. 105.

9 John Stanton-Ife, "Horrific Crime", in R.A. Duff *et al.* (eds.), *The Boundaries of the Criminal Law*, Oxford University Press, 2010, p. 141.

10 S.E. Marshall and R.A. Duff, "Criminalization and Sharing Wrongs", in *Canadian Journal of Law and Jurisprudence*, 1998, vol. 11, no. 1, p. 14.

human agents, not collective entities or social conditions, responsible. It does so by individuating human behaviour and responsibility with great sophistication. A cosmopolitan war crimes law seeks to limit collective actions by regulating individual behaviours. Human beings cannot be victims of the State but only of other human beings. The centrality of the individual is illustrated by the Nuremberg Tribunal's famous declaration that crimes are committed by persons, not "abstract entities".[11] A cosmopolitan criminal law which recognizes all human beings as autonomous agents simultaneously protects and *coerces* personal autonomy.[12] It extends the individualistic foundation of modern Western law to the entire human community. Criminal law's response to violations of laws of war is in sharp contrast to its predecessor – belligerent reprisal. For reprisal as an enforcement mechanism invokes collective, not individual punishment.[13] Responsibility is attributed vicariously, not directly. The collective nature of reprisal ultimately denies human agency and dignity as it instrumentalizes human beings to enforce the law.

Operating in the context of war, criminal justice focuses on motivational and dispositional[14] causes of war crimes. If a person has difficulty to see the necessity of the prohibitions under war crimes law, he clearly has a problem and is to blame. As such, there is a high degree of equation between direct causation and responsibility, with the exception of some obvious peace-time excusing conditions. The frame of criminal justice does not allow for more subtle yet powerful situational determinants. The fact that certain individuals are caught up in unfavourable situations for legal and ethical behaviour is a question of moral luck.[15] Soldiers, for example, are extremely unlucky to undergo moral challenges which ordinary citizens do not face. However, bad moral luck, according

---

11 IMT, "Judgment of 1 October 1946", in *The Trial of German Major War Criminals before the International Military Tribunal*, Volume 22, 27 August 1946–1 October 1946, p. 223 (https://www.legal-tools.org/doc/d1427b/).

12 Danilo Zolo, "A Cosmopolitan Philosophy of International Law: A Realist Approach", in *Ratio Juris*, 1999, vol. 12, no. 4, p. 433.

13 For more on historical transition from reprisal to individual responsibility, see Patryk I. Labuda, "The Lieber Code, Retaliation and the Origins of International Criminal Law", in Morten Bergsmo *et al.* (eds.), *Historical Origins of International Criminal Law: Volume 3*, Torkel Opsahl Academic EPublisher, Brussels, 2015, pp. 299 ff. (https://www.toaep.org/ps-pdf/22-bergsmo-cheah-song-yi).

14 Zimbardo, 2007, p. 298, see *supra* note 6.

15 For more discussion on moral luck and war crimes, see Matthew Talbert and Jessica Wolfendale, *War Crimes, Causes, Excuses, and Blame*, Oxford University Press, 2018, pp. 103–104.

to the logic of criminal law, does not affect the agent's responsibility.[16] Intentionality leads to responsibility: an agent is responsible for crimes he commits on purpose. Perhaps the fear is that any hesitation in pronouncing criminal condemnation may amount to denying or diminishing the wrongfulness of the act itself. In this sense, the frame of criminal law can be attributing responsibility and dispensing punishment out of moral "expediency".[17]

The attributional logic of criminal law, as it is applied in war crimes, can be morally resonant among its audience.[18] It activates receptive moral reasoning and emotion. It aligns well with pre-existing sentiments and beliefs of the population and as such is able to arouse supportive responses. It is common assumption that war crimes predominantly result from *individual* failures – lack of self-control and rational judgment.[19] Such assumption is intuitively appealing because our brain tends to spontaneously code behaviours as results of personal traits, even without conscious thinking.[20] Attribution of behaviour to persons and persons alone, is the "default setting" in our causal interpretation.[21] It appears "natural and familiar".[22] Criminal law's emphasis on personal causality provides collective catharsis and satisfaction of just retribution. As such, the frame of criminal law capitalizes on our automatic and most natural reactions towards morally repellent behaviours. It can effectively shape the perception of causes, consequences and potential solutions to atrocities.[23] It minimizes or disregards systemic and situational determinants that "shape behavioral outcomes and transform actors".[24] The retributive and purifying functions partly explain the appeal of the project of criminal law in the context of war.

Hannah Arendt already points to criminal law's focus on individual conduct and guilt in her report on the Eichmann trial. Arendt highlights that on trial

---

16 David Luban discusses the issue of criminal responsibility under trying circumstances in David Luban, *Legal Ethics and Human Dignity*, Cambridge University Press, 2009, pp. 237 ff.

17 John M. Doris and Dominic Murphy, "From My Lai to Abu Ghraib: The Moral Psychology of Atrocity", in *Midwest Studies in Philosophy*, 2007, vol. 31, no. 1, p. 54.

18 The term "moral resonance" draws from the concept "cultural resonance" in Charles M. Rowling, Penelope Sheets and Timothy M. Jones, "American Atrocity Revisited: National Identity, Cascading Frames, and the My Lai Massacre", in *Political Communication*, 2015, vol. 32, no. 2, p. 312.

19 Talbert and Wolfendale, 2018, pp. 139 ff., see *supra* note 15.

20 Doris, 2005, p. 101, see *supra* note 8.

21 *Ibid.*

22 Charles M. Rowling, Timothy M. Jones and Penelope Sheets, "Some Dared Call It Torture: Cultural Resonance, Abu Ghraib, and a Selectively Echoing Press", in *Journal of Communication*, 2011, vol. 61, no. 1, p. 1046.

23 Rowling, Sheets and Jones, 2015, p. 312, see *supra* note 18.

24 Zimbardo, 2007, p. 445, see *supra* note 6.

was Eichmann's deeds, "not the German people or mankind, not even anti-Semitism and racism".[25] By re-opening what is made natural within the frame of criminal law, Arendt gives new insights into the function and meaning of criminal law. Criminal law perhaps helps us avoid facing the universal ability to commit atrocity under certain circumstances:

> all the general questions we involuntarily raise as soon as we begin to speak of these matters – why did it have to be the Germans? Why did it have to be the Jews? What is the nature of totalitarian rule? – are far more important than the question of the kind of crime for which a man is being tried, and the nature of the defendant upon whom justice must be pronounced; more important, too, than the question of how well our present system of justice is capable of dealing with this special type of crime and criminal. […] It can be held that the issue is no longer a particular human being, a single distinct individual in the dock.[26]

Coming from a different cultural and historical context, Confucian philosophy also teaches a pertinent lesson here. In *Analects*, it is said that 'when you see someone who is unworthy, use this as an opportunity to look within yourself'. That is, one should see the failings of others as an opportunity for self-reflection.[27] War crimes trials should be an occasion for self-reflection for observers, but they are often not taken as such.

In sum, a cosmopolitan war crimes law tends to perceive virtuous human acts as universal and solidarity-generating, and evil acts as entirely individual and exceptional. The project of criminal justice separates the wider community from the evil and evildoers. Evil is not transgressed to the rest of humanity. When we use words such as 'unthinkable', 'unimaginable' or 'senseless', we mean that as 'normal' human beings, we simply cannot imagine, or make sense of most war crimes and would never do the same if we were put in the same situation. Our common humanity is displayed in our concern for grave human suffering, not in our ability to commit evil.

5.1.3. The Individual as Rational Agent

Underlying the value primacy of the individual is the rationalist glorification of human agency. The value of the human person partly comes from his/her immanent rationality. Chapter 2 above describes the assumption that species-wide normative unity can be made possible by objective and impartial reasoning in

[25] Hannah Arendt, *Eichmann in Jerusalem: A Report on the Banality of Evil*, The Viking Press, New York, 1964, p. 5.

[26] *Ibid.*, p. 286.

[27] Cited in Xiang Shuchen, *Chinese Cosmopolitanism: The History and Philosophy of an Idea*, Princeton University Press, 2023, p. 168. In Chinese: 见贤思齐焉，见不贤而内自省也.

accordance with elementary principles of theoretical rationality. It is assumed that the rational human agency is universal, invariable and independent from social structure and circumstances. The rational cosmopolitan community should impose restrictions on the irrational State. With intrinsic capacities for moral judgment and experiencing pain, all rational human beings can agree on the cosmopolitan imperative to avoid unnecessary sufferings in war. It is followed by construction of lawful and unlawful violence in war which can be seen as the rational way to maximize protection of fundamental human values. There is strong identification of most war crimes with objective moral wrongs. This confirms Duff's claim that criminal law does not and cannot invent moral wrongs from scratch.[28] As Chapter 4 already points out, criminal law typically singles out certain pre-existing moral wrongs and subjects them to its particular characterization and response. Given the deep integration of moral and criminal wrongs in war crimes, the cosmopolitan law can count on immanent and objective moral reasoning for its success.

Human rationality is not only a force for normative unity, but also a prerequisite to the functioning of criminal law. Criminal law can only communicate normative reasons for action to rational and relatively free persons. People need appropriate psychological states and capacities, including cognitive, motivational and affective capacities, to live up to normative demands.[29] The legal fiction of the perpetrator's agency is stable and consistent. Criminal law simplifies and represents war crimes as arising from "the interaction of atomized individuals",[30] following rational and conscious decision-making. Between the rational individual and the irrational State, a cosmopolitan criminal law must intervene with the rational human agent, not the irrational State or its institutions.

Although criminal law's legal fiction is derived from the domestic context and peace-time circumstances, it shares with cosmopolitanism the same assumptions of abstract and rational human agency. This is perhaps a key reason why international criminal law can easily integrate cosmopolitan morality. Here, I highlight two main rationalist assumptions of human agency in a cosmopolitan war crimes law: immanent moral judgment and conscious control over one's action.

First, it is assumed that participants in war can discern the wrongfulness of the acts underlying war crimes. Especially for acts which are expected to cause serious bodily or mental harm in other human beings, it is assumed that an

---

28 R.A. Duff, "Responsibility, Citizenship and Criminal Law", in R.A. Duff and Stuart P. Green (eds.), *Philosophical Foundations of Criminal Law*, Oxford University Press, 2011, p. 127.

29 Doris, 2005, p. 3, see *supra* note 8.

30 Mark Kelman, "Law and Behavioral Science: Conceptual Overviews", in *Northwestern University Law Review*, 2002, vol. 97, no. 3, p. 1388.

individual in his or her right mind would be able to tell that such acts constituting war crimes are serious moral – not just legal – wrongs. The perpetrator as a rational human being can make the right normative judgment simply by using the reflective faculties. This innate capacity for moral judgment is not dependant on one's social environment or relations with others, which are external to the agent. The unwavering faith in such "moral constitution of our species" makes the wrongfulness of most war crimes – mainly violations of life and physical integrity of human beings – appear "axiomatic".[31] Mistake of law, for example, is typically not accepted as an excusing condition in international criminal jurisprudence, as discussed in greater detail in Chapter 8.

Lawyers and politicians confidently assert the self-evidence of such wrongs, in the spirit of cosmopolitan rationalism. The Eichmann judgment pronounced on the requirement of "manifest unlawfulness" of an order which one has a legal duty to disobey. The Court was convinced that the wrongfulness of certain acts is so obvious and flagrant that it "pierces the eye and revolts the heart", unless "the eye is blind" and the heart stony and corrupt.[32] An inquiry report on the My Lai atrocities stated that "there were some things a soldier did not have to be told were wrong – such as rounding up women and children and then mowing them down, shooting babies out of mothers' arms, and raping".[33] Similarly, in the aftermath of the Abu Ghraib prisoner abuses, a high-ranking United States political leader said that if one does not know those acts are "wrong, cruel, brutal, indecent", no training or education can impart to this person the right moral judgment.[34] Every human being, in virtue of his humanity, should know certain acts are immoral *and* illegal.

All the above expressions of faith in human conscience imply that it is easy and natural for any human being, including the perpetrator, to agree with the underlying moral values of war crimes law. The individual, unless mentally ill, can and should recognize the criminality and, above all, immorality of most war crimes regardless of the social environment.

Second, the individual is assumed to be always in control of his conduct. As fully rational and autonomous human beings, soldiers are able to act independently from influences of the military institution and circumstances of war.

---

31 Mark Osiel, "Obeying Orders: Atrocity, Military Discipline, and the Law of War", in *California Law Review*, 1998, vol. 86, no. 5, p. 1010.

32 Israel, District Court of Jerusalem, *Attorney General v. Adolf Eichmann*, Judgment, 11 December 1961, Criminal Case No. 40/61, para. 21 (https://www.legal-tools.org/doc/aceae7/).

33 Cited in Osiel, 1998, p. 975, see *supra* note 31.

34 Full quote: "if someone doesn't know that doing what is shown in those photos is wrong, cruel, brutal, indecent, and against American values, I am at a loss as to what kind of training could be provided to teach them", cited in Zimbardo, 2007, p. 321, see *supra* note 6.

They should have "the inner strength and will power"[35] to resist any environment and honour their original moral judgment as a member of humanity. The action of ordinary soldiers is determined by their inner qualities, not their social environment. The actor as the sole causal agent should be invulnerable to the environment.

5.2. Individual and Social Contingencies in Expressing Species-Wide Solidarity

Can everyone adopt the cosmopolitans' rationality? Or rather, can everyone see the world as the cosmopolitans do? Certainly not. The conception of a cosmopolitan community concerning mitigation of sufferings in war rests heavily on a certain belief in the moral psychology of human beings. However, the imagined cosmopolitan solidarity, as modest as it is, can be contingent and unstable. Human capacities for compassion, empathy and solidarity may not be able to guarantee the kind of coherent and permanent cosmopolitan community required by criminal law. Cosmopolitanism is not an uncaused cause in human thinking. It does not come naturally or easily.

Capacity does not automatically translate into action. The expression of human universals is not pre-determined and uniform, but unpredictable and differentiated. True, a minimalist cosmopolitan community is more likely to be realized than an all-encompassing one. But even a minimalist cosmopolitanism is only one possible course of action for human agents possessing necessary capacities. The kind of cosmopolitan solidarity over pain and suffering can be short-lived and superficial. Reflecting on the effects of war images, Susan Sontag attempts a social-psychological explanation of the unreliable "negative solidarity" with remote strangers. People turn on and off compassion all the time. Being indifferent, numb, bored, cynical or apathetic are all familiar human emotions.[36] Due to the speed and intensity of information dissemination in contemporary life, we are easily "corrupted" and can "gradually become habituated" to "a diet of horrors".[37] The "discriminating powers of the mind" is blunted by "overstimulation".[38] Moral indignation in the face of distant suffering wears off in mundane daily routines. People tend to develop defensive mechanisms to cope with difficult reality.[39]

---

[35] *Ibid.*, p. 298.

[36] Susan Sontag, *Regarding the Pain of Others*, Farrar, Straus and Giroux, New York, 2003, p. 95.

[37] *Ibid.*

[38] *Ibid.*, p. 95.

[39] *Ibid.*, p. 73.

Sontag argues that moral indignation and aversion to suffering are insufficient to guarantee action.[40] Images of distant sufferings may be used to "steel oneself against weakness", to "make oneself more numb" or to "acknowledge the existence of the incorrigible".[41] Compassion for "abstract and absent others with whom we have never interacted"[42] may not be channelled into greater solidarity, but displaced by more immediate concerns in one's life. Solidarity with remote others has to compete with other values and preoccupations at the local level. If standing up to radical evil makes cosmopolitan ideal heroic, grappling with the fleeting human mind makes it trivial.

Compared to individual contingencies, social contingencies in the expression of cosmopolitan solidarity are even greater and more complex. Boaventura de Sousa Santos proclaims "the right to be equal whenever difference diminishes us", as quoted in Chapter 2 of this book. He continues to say that "we have the right to be different whenever equality decharacterizes us".[43] The cosmopolitan approach tends to under-socialize the human person.[44] Individuals are assimilated: they are abstract and rational, therefore similar. This "homogenizing assumption" detaches individuals from "ideational factors" existing in the immediate culture and society.[45] Social structure and immediate circumstances constitute contingent factors in the expression of universal human features. The expression of "human universals"[46] may be particular rather than universal.

Roberto M. Unger says that the biological brain is individual, but "the mind as consciousness" is social. Unger observes that the "means by which we develop a subjective life, from language to discourse, from ideas to practice, are all a common possession and shared construction".[47] Bhikhu Parekh similarly reminds us that the individual is not a "naturally given and biologically

---

40 *Ibid.*, p. 105.

41 *Ibid.*, p. 88.

42 Arne Johan Vetlesen, *Perception, Empathy, and Judgment: An Inquiry into the Preconditions of Moral Performance*, Pennsylvania State University Press, 1994, pp. 324–325.

43 Boaventura de Sousa Santos, "Nuestra America", in *Theory, Culture & Society*, 2001, vol. 18, nos. 2–3, p. 193.

44 Sungjoon Cho, "Social Constructivism and the Social Construction of World Economic Reality", in Moshe Hirsch and Andrew Lang (eds.), *Research Handbook on the Sociology of International Law*, Edward Elgar Publishing, Cheltenham, 2018, p. 374.

45 *Ibid.*, p. 369.

46 Bhikhu Parekh, "Non-Ethnocentric Universalism", in Tim Dunne and Nicholas J. Wheeler (eds.), *Human Rights in Global Politics*, 2012, Cambridge University Press, p. 142. For more on human universals, see Chapter 1 in the present book.

47 Roberto Mangabeira Unger, *The Religion of the Future*, Harvard University Press, Cambridge, Massachusetts, 2021, p. 98.

encapsulated" being but "a social construction".[48] The observations of Unger and Parekh concern fundamental human needs and social reality. If our genetic composition is like "hardware", the "cultural software" determines how this hardware functions. This cultural software is socially acquired, not "inherited".[49] In the process of life, a person learns from society means to understand the world and guidelines for action. To imagine the human person solely in certain natural features is to imagine an individual without context, without a history, a "naked" human being. Such a "self-contained, singular and internally unified moral agent" does not exist in real life.[50]

Human identity is not just universal and abstract, but also embedded and contextual. Individuals develop their identity within a community where they are seen as competent and responsible speakers and actors.[51] Personal integrity depends on the integrity of "the interpersonal relations of reciprocal recognition".[52] Selfhood is relative to the environment.[53] It is indeed a matter of "social practice" to draw the boundary between the individual and other human beings.[54] An insight often lost in conceptualizing cosmopolitan human agency. Social identity theory, for example, emphasizes the important role of social groups in shaping personal identity.[55] Society and culture provide not only identity, but also comfort, security and "symbolic resources"[56] to create meaning of life. Vetlesen notices a kind of "psychological 'exchange' between individual and group" where "individuals invest themselves, by way of projection, in collectivities, and that they, by way of introjection, let themselves be invested in by the 'psychic' attributes of the collectivity with which they identify themselves".[57] The State therefore is not a mere passive instrument for the cosmopolitan agenda. It also has important normative and practical functions for its members.

[48] Bhikhu Parekh, *Ethnocentric Political Theory: The Pursuit of Flawed Universals*, Springer, Cham, 2019, p. 12.

[49] Carmel O'Sullivan, *Killing on Command: The Defence of Superior Orders in Modern Combat*, Palgrave Macmillan, London, 2016, p. 188.

[50] Parekh, 2019, p. 12, see *supra* note 48.

[51] Vetlesen, 1994, p. 319, see *supra* note 42.

[52] *Ibid.*

[53] Richard Shapcott, *Justice, Community and Dialogue in International Relations*, Cambridge University Press, 2001, p. 5.

[54] Parekh, 2019, p. 12, see *supra* note 48.

[55] Rowling, Sheets and Jones, 2015, p. 313, see *supra* note 18.

[56] Arne Johan Vetlesen, *Evil and Human Agency: Understanding Collective Evildoing*, Cambridge University Press, 2009, p. 40.

[57] *Ibid.*, p, 49.

The social constitution of human beings is emphasized in certain cultures and times more than others. Iranian scholar Abdulaziz Sachedina highlights "the community and relational aspects of human existence" in the Islámic tradition, which does not support "the autonomy of the individual with an independent moral standard that transcends religious and cultural differences".[58] For the Confucians, self is culturally constituted: embodying culture and following social norms are essential to self-formation.[59] Historical Chinese cosmopolitanism makes explicit the normative dimension in the epistemology of universality. It emphasizes the role of education and acculturation in conceiving oneness of humankind.[60] Its preoccupation with moral agency serves as a useful and timely reminder for the purposes of this book: cosmopolitan morality is an insight that needs to be actively cultivated. Cosmopolitanism is a vision, a commitment that requires great agency on the part of the individual thinker.

The top-down cosmopolitanism tends to neglect the *mutuality* in the relationship between the collective and the individual: the individual can gain emotional and material benefits from the collective, as suggested in Chapter 3; the collective also shapes individual identity, attitude and behaviour. The sociological perspective distances agency from pure "subjectivity", "absolute freedom" and recognizes "structurally defined limits".[61] Individuals carry out "purposive action" under physical and social constraints.[62] Choosing from "structurally provided alternatives", the actor may have "a more or less transformative impact" on social structures.[63] Psychologist Philip Zimbardo observes that we are "shaped by the broad systems that govern our lives – wealth and poverty, geography and climate, historical epoch, cultural, political and religious dominance – and by the specific situations we deal with daily".[64] "Forces larger than ourselves" shape our mind and behaviour.[65] How we do and think about things are context- and path-dependent. Culture and society predispose people to certain interpretations of situations and choices. Zimbardo even claims that our social

58 Abdulaziz Sachedina, *Islam and the Challenge of Human Rights*, Oxford University Press, 2010, p. 7.

59 Xiang, 2023, p. 54, see *supra* note 27.

60 *Ibid.*, pp. 24–25.

61 Sharon Hays, "Structure and Agency and the Sticky Problem of Culture", in *Sociological Theory*, 1994, vol. 12, no. 1, p. 65.

62 Moshe Hirsch, "Core Sociological Theories and International Law", in Hirsch and Lang (eds.), 2018, p. 394, see *supra* note 44.

63 Hays, 1994, p. 65, see *supra* note 61.

64 Zimbardo, 2007, p. 298, see *supra* note 6.

65 *Ibid.*

conditions are more accurate indicators of our attitudes and behaviours than our personality trait.[66] There is perhaps truth in this somewhat radical claim.

Calling on citizens to pledge their "primary allegiance" to "the community of human beings in the entire world"[67] is normatively ambitious and practically challenging, no matter how modest the issue is. Philosophers and psychologists sometimes compare selflessness to a lightbulb, shining brightly on those close by and ever more dimly with increased distance.[68] Local communities are concrete not abstract, authentic not imagined, diverse not similar. The local community, such as the nation-State, has more intra-group loyalty and cohesion than the abstract "patriotism of rights"[69] derived from a general human identity. The cosmopolitan appeal may simply fail to penetrate thick local normative networks. Cosmopolitanism, with its methodological individualism, exaggerates bonds among strangers by prioritizing abstract individuals over concrete persons. Kjersti Lohne raises the question whether "the cult of the individual" can serve as a unifying moral force worldwide.[70] A cosmopolitan community consisted of abstract individuals may "have a hard time gripping the imagination".[71]

The relationship between the cosmopolitan community and local communities is multi-faceted and variegated. Local moral and political orders may compete with or conform to cosmopolitan ideals. In any event, the abstract cosmopolitan community needs to be mediated by specific societies and cultures. Cosmopolitan norms are not self-realizing. They must be given "a socially relevant interpretation" and applied by persons "with socially inculcated habits of moral perception".[72] This points to the importance of "social articulation of morality".[73] It means "contingent social factors" affect the application of abstract principles in concrete situations.[74] It is the function of a local moral community to impart what is morally relevant and how to interpret moral teachings in a particular situation. Our moral judgments of right and wrong do not arise in a social

---

66 *Ibid.*, p. 321.

67 Cited in Lu, 2000, p. 245, see *supra* note 1.

68 David Berreby, *Us and Them: The Science of Identity*, University of Chicago Press, 2018, p. 193.

69 Zolo, 1999, p. 440, see *supra* note 12.

70 Kjersti Lohne, *Advocates of Humanity: Human Rights NGOs in International Criminal Justice*, Oxford University Press, 2019, p. 189.

71 Lu, 2000, p. 249, see *supra* note 1.

72 Herlinde Pauer-Studer and J. David Velleman, "Distortions of Normativity", in *Ethical Theory and Moral Practice*, 2011, vol. 14, no. 3, p. 334.

73 *Ibid.*, p. 350.

74 *Ibid.*, p. 334.

vacuum.[75] They are "neither primordial nor reflexively primitive", but "end products of learning".[76] Moral intuitions are not "transhistorical" but culture-and-epoch specific.[77] Different cultures at different times produce different systems of morality and different understandings of abstract values and principles.[78]

Through mediation, the local moral and political order can compete with and pervert notions of cosmopolitan justice. Cosmopolitan principles such as respect for persons may well be used to justify war crimes.[79] Matthew Talbert and Jessica Wolfendale illustrate how virtues such as duty, self-restraint and empathy can be interpreted to facilitate, not prevent, State-sponsored torture and other atrocities.[80] Vetlesen points out that our faculty of empathy, which is vital in our perceiving of others as human and moral beings, is extremely vulnerable to societal manipulation.[81] Empathy can be selectively blocked towards certain groups of people. When emotional responses are suspended or impeded, the individual sees the other not as a relatable fellow human being, but as an abstract figure.[82] Moral intuition involves automatic, unconscious mental activities which are different from conscious reasoning. In fact, many have pointed out that moral reasoning is often "flagrantly illogical".[83] Rational faculties do not function alone; they operate in concert with other faculties. Cognitive competence and reflective self-control are greatly affected by emotions. Socialization may therefore prevent us from seeing "morally questionable" features of a certain situation.[84] Our moral judgment is so indispensable yet so precarious.[85] The next section introduces social influence on judgment and behaviour of perpetrators of war crimes and its implications for the attribution framework of a cosmopolitan criminal law.

5.3. Social Environment as Source of War Crimes

Alasdair MacIntyre reminds us of the extraordinary moral challenge posed by war: "only if we think seriously about ourselves in relation to war shall we be

[75] Vetlesen, 1994, p. 194, see *supra* note 42.

[76] Robert Sapolsky, *Behave: The Biology of Humans at Our Best and Worst*, Penguin Press, New York, 2017, p. 508.

[77] Kelman, 2002, p. 1389, see *supra* note 30.

[78] Sapolsky, 2017, p. 275, see *supra* note 76.

[79] Talbert and Wolfendale, 2018, p. 55, see *supra* note 15.

[80] *Ibid.*, p. 56.

[81] Vetlesen, 1994, p. 195, see *supra* note 42.

[82] *Ibid.*, p. 195.

[83] Sapolsky, 2017, p. 185, see *supra* note 76.

[84] Pauer-Studer and Velleman, 2011, p. 335, see *supra* note 72.

[85] Vetlesen, 1994, p. 195, see *supra* note 42.

able to think realistically about ourselves in other situations too".[86] Participation in war enhances general risks associated with social contingencies of cosmopolitan norms. National identity becomes one of the most salient forms of social identities in times of war. The nation carries "profound emotional legitimacy" for its citizens, who are routinely exposed to "cultural myths and embedded social narratives" entrenching the national identity.[87] This sense of national identity motivates citizens to protect the nation as an irreplaceable source of comfort and security.[88] A threat to the community is seen as a threat to the individual personally. Hence a community of common fate. War strengthens internal cohesion and weakens, if not eliminates, the already fragile cosmopolitan solidarity. Concerns for the national community are more immediate and urgent than for a cosmopolitan community. At least for the warring parties, war makes self-regarded and closed ideologies more attractive. Weaknesses of cosmopolitan solidarity are exacerbated in the case of typical perpetrators of war crimes. When the ordinary soldier inhabits normative frameworks which condone excessive sufferings of the enemy in war, it is difficult for a cosmopolitan war crimes law to win the normative competition. This is coupled with distorted interpretation and application of any cosmopolitan principles which still remain intact in their abstract form.

5.3.1. A Conducive Social Environment for Atrocities

The recent memory of the Holocaust reminds us of the social origins of "the unpunishable, unforgivable evil".[89] That is, radical evil which cannot be fully explained by sheer personal motives – "self-interests, greed, covetousness, resentment, lust for power, and cowardice"[90] – but has to be understood in its social, especially institutional, environment. In contrast to popular caricatures of "villainous"[91] characters, the perpetrators' seeming "ordinariness" has been a "persistent theme" in Holocaust studies.[92] The situationist assessment of atrocity crimes emphasizes the "sheer normality"[93] of perpetrators. Or in John Doris's

[86] Alasdair MacIntyre, "The Wrong Questions to Ask about War", in *The Hastings Center Report*, 1980, vol. 10, no. 6, p. 40.

[87] Rowling, Sheets and Jones, 2015, p. 313, see *supra* note 18.

[88] *Ibid.*

[89] Vetlesen, 1994, p. 87, see *supra* note 42.

[90] *Ibid.*

[91] Uğur Ümit Üngör and Kjell Anderson, "From Perpetrators to Perpetration Definitions, Typologies, and Processes", in Susanne C. Knittel and Zachary J. Goldberg (eds.), *The Routledge International Handbook of Perpetrator Studies*, Routledge, Abingdon, 2020, p. 9.

[92] Doris, 2005, p. 54, see *supra* note 8.

[93] Zimbardo, 2007, p. 293, see *supra* note 6.

words: "it does not take a monster to do monstrous things".[94] While some individuals commit crimes due to their personality traits, many more can commit extreme violence when necessary environmental conditions are met. When linking research on mechanisms of moral disengagement to the historical chronicle of human atrocities, Albert Bandura comments: "It requires conducive social conditions, rather than monstrous people, to produce heinous deeds. Given appropriate social conditions, decent, ordinary people can be led to do extraordinarily cruel things".[95] Another commentator argues that it is "the norm, not the exception" that evil "arises out of ordinary thinking and is committed by ordinary people".[96] Ordinary people can be led to commit atrocity through manipulation of natural psychological processes in motivations, thoughts and feelings.[97] Zygmunt Bauman presents the case for the social origins of evil in his seminal book *Modernity and Holocaust*. Bauman's thesis is that collective violence is caused by socialization, not human nature. He argues that atrocities have much more to do with "certain patterns of social interaction" than "personality features or other individual idiosyncrasies of the perpetrators".[98] According to Bauman, the origin of cruelty is "social" much more than "characterological".[99] Philip Zimbardo's Stanford prison experiment shows that the environment can transform moral standards of perfectly normal university students and cause them to mistreat their fellow students. Zimbardo observes that "[g]ood people can be induced, seduced, and initiated into behaving in evil ways".[100] According to Zimbardo, "total situations" can lead individuals to "act in irrational, stupid, self-destructive, antisocial, and mindless ways".[101] They challenge our sense of personal autonomy and ability to act autonomously. The stable and consistent *self* dissipates into the system and the environment.

It is a common assumption that war crimes are committed out of pure self-indulgence in primordial passions or sadistic inclinations. If this is true, atrocity is just an unfortunate consequence of "free-lance and self-seeking" behaviours of individual soldiers.[102] The natural disposition to cruelty at its extreme is found

---

[94] Doris, 2005, p. 54, see *supra* note 8.

[95] Albert Bandura, "Selective Activation and Disengagement of Moral Control", in *Journal of Social Issues*, 1990, vol. 46, no. 1, p. 39.

[96] Cited in O'Sullivan, 2016, p. 143, see *supra* note 49.

[97] *Ibid.*

[98] Zygmunt Bauman, *Modernity and the Holocaust*, Polity Press, Oxford, 2007, p. 166.

[99] *Ibid.*

[100] Zimbardo, 2007, p. 211, see *supra* note 6.

[101] *Ibid.*

[102] Osiel, 1998, p. 1030, see *supra* note 31.

in a psychopath, who "positively enjoys and seeks to hurt or kill others".[103] Psychopaths commit war crimes because of natural deficiencies in their moral competence. These cases fit our instinct about war crimes perpetrators but are rare in reality. While it is comforting to think perpetrators are "pathological or deranged",[104] the majority of atrocities in war are not committed by bloodthirsty psychopaths.[105] It is often ordinary persons, placed in extraordinary situations created by system and circumstances, who commit excesses in war.[106] Over-aggressive persons cannot be good soldiers because they are difficult to discipline and easily distracted by their own need to inflict pain. They cannot concentrate on their duty and may expose the group to greater risks. A commentator observes that "[m]ost soldiers are not criminals, and criminals have never made good soldiers".[107] Persons with moral and behavioural deficiencies are usually screened out in recruitment.[108] Arendt explains that participants in Nazi crimes were usually not "sadists or killers by nature" because "a systematic effort" was made to exclude those who enjoy violence or abuses.[109] Members of the notorious Reserve Police Battalion 101, who carried out mass murders in German-occupied Poland, represented the most ordinary segment of the population – "middle-aged, mostly working-class" people who were "least likely to be considered apt material out of which to mold future mass killers".[110] Zimbardo similarly concludes that torturers and death squad executioners are not particularly deviant or pathological in their behaviour before and after they take on their roles.[111] The roles and environment are designed to transform actors there and then. As Chapters 6

[103] Sara Mackmin, "Why do Professional Soldiers Commit Acts of Personal Violence that Contravene the Law of Armed Conflict?", in *Defence Studies*, 2007, vol. 7, no. 1, p. 78. Mackmin illustrates with Private Mark Northfield's account after the Falklands War, "some people act over the top, even in the context of war, with unnecessary waste of life [...] it was in some people anyway".

[104] Doris and Murphy, 2007, p. 30, see *supra* note 17.

[105] O'Sullivan, 2016, p. 144, see *supra* note 49.

[106] For example, studies show that only one per cent of the overall population in the United States are predisposed to excessive violence. See Paul Formosa, "Moral Responsibility and Evil", in Knittel and Goldberg (eds.), 2020, p. 250, *supra* note 91.

[107] Cited in Jean-Jacques Frésard, *The Roots of Behaviour in War: A Survey of the Literature*, International Committee of the Red Cross, Geneva, 2004, p. 25.

[108] See Mackmin, 2007, p. 79, *supra* note 103; see also Zimbardo on selection of torturers, Zimbardo, 2007, p. 290, *supra* note 6.

[109] Cited in Herbert C. Kelman, "Violence Without Moral Restraint: Reflections on the Dehumanization of Victims and Victimizers", in *Journal of Social Issues*, 1973, vol. 29, no. 4, p. 35.

[110] Cited in Frésard, 2004, p. 84, see *supra* note 107.

[111] Zimbardo, 2007, p. 290, see *supra* note 6.

and 7 below demonstrate in greater detail, there is a "cultural wisdom" to make soldiers kill in war.[112]

Instead of focusing on the individual character, the situationist approach reminds us that perpetrators do not operate in a social or cultural vacuum. Somewhere between complete and no free will, a military personnel's agency is mitigated by their social environment. Their choice is "pre-empted"[113] by their social structure's choice – only a limited number of normative frameworks are available to them. Without equally powerful alternative frameworks, ordinary members of the military structure cannot detach from or rise above the prevailing narratives in their relatively closed social environment.[114] Placed in the total institution, military personnel are more prone to obedience, group conformity, and to killing than ordinary people in peace-time social units (See Chapter 6). The conditions of war further corrupt soldiers' normative competence and induce antisocial behaviours (see Chapter 7). In fact, perpetrators of atrocities in war may be responding "quite normally" to the combat environment.[115] An ordinary soldier with normal moral principles and theoretical knowledge of laws of war can commit serious war crimes under the single or combined influence of military training, superior orders, group dynamics and the combat environment. As Stanley Milgram concludes from his experiments: "Ordinary people, simply doing their jobs, and without any particular hostility on their part, can become agents in a terrible destructive process".[116] The frequency of war crimes and representativeness of perpetrators – that they come from a normal cross-section of the society – confirm the powerful impact of the social environment on human behaviour in war.[117]

5.3.2. A Cosmopolitan Criminal Law's Attribution Bias in War

Criminal law's fiction of human agency is conceived in a domestic context and with peace-time conditions in mind. Cosmopolitanism confirms and exaggerates criminal law's assumptions of human rationality. Applied in the context of war, the framework of criminal law can display a particular kind of "dispositionist bias": an overestimation of the consistency and predictive power of individual

[112] *Ibid.*, pp. 303–304.

[113] Vetlesen, 1994, p. 194, see *supra* note 42.

[114] Talbert and Wolfendale, 2018, p. 152, see *supra* note 15.

[115] Doris and Murphy, 2007, p. 31, see *supra* note 17.

[116] Stanley Milgram, *Obedience to Authority: An Experimental View*, Harper & Row, New York, 1974, p. 6.

[117] Doris and Murphy, 2007, p. 32, see *supra* note 17.

disposition across situations.[118] It proceeds from a sense of deep "essentialism" which requires people be the same in all situations and at all times,[119] even when the situation is as extreme as war. Human beings aspire to be rational actors who can resist environmental pressures and appraise the situation with objectivity. We strive to be like God, always just and wise. When we judge others' behaviour after fact and declare it unthinkable, we take God's perspective. We erect a "seemingly impermeable boundary between Good and Evil", in great simplification of human experience.[120] We forget that decisions made under extreme external influence and pressure are inevitably confused.

Corresponding to the personal and environmental causes of behaviour, there are two kinds of attribution of responsibility: to the person and to the environment.[121] The situationist critique is that attributing war crimes to individual failure or character deficiency is based on common yet misguided moral psychology. According to social psychologists, such 'person-over-situation' essentialism is "pure ideology", not reality.[122] Social psychologists Lee Ross and Donna Shestowsky explain that our daily experience of predictability and stability of behaviour may be caused more by the stability of the environment rather than the stability of character.[123] Personality traits can only predict future behaviours based on "characteristic past reactions" in similar situations.[124] This is why novel settings make situational power more salient – previous guidelines for behaviour are no longer suitable, the usual reward system and expectations are no longer applicable.[125] When confronted with the all-powerful military structure and overwhelming combat conditions, a soldier's past civilian experience is not so helpful in informing behavioural options. Chapters 6 and 7 illustrate psychological studies which show that non-coercive situational factors, sometimes very subtle or insubstantial, can change the behaviour of a large percentage of subjects. While small and subtle environmental manipulations can have great impact on behaviour – much greater than common-sensical

---

[118] Lee Ross and Donna Shestowsky, "Contemporary Psychology's Challenges to Legal Theory and Practice", in *Northwestern University Law Review*, 2002, vol. 97, no. 3, p. 1093. An example is Adorno *et al.*'s attribution of Nazi crimes to an authoritarian personality. According to this theory, an authoritarian is consistently authoritarian in all times and situations. See Theodor W. Adorno *et al.*, *The Authoritarian Personality*, WW Norton & Co., New York, 1950.

[119] Berreby, 2018, p. 62, see *supra* note 68.

[120] Zimbardo, 2007, p. 211, see *supra* note 6.

[121] Herbert Kelman and V. Lee Hamilton, *Crimes of Obedience: Toward a Social Psychology of Authority and Responsibility*, Yale University Press, New Haven, 1989, p. 197.

[122] O'Sullivan, 2016, p. 192, see *supra* note 49.

[123] Ross and Shestowsky, 2002, p. 1095, see *supra* note 118.

[124] Zimbardo, 2007, p. 212, see *supra* note 6.

[125] *Ibid.*, p. 212.

expectations and predictions – in the case of soldiers, severe, unexpected environmental stressors can "swamp" individual differences in personality, values and prior experiences.[126] Chapters 6 and 7 describe how environmental factors are manipulated to adjust moral restraints against killing in war. In distorting the proportion of personal and environmental determinants of behaviour, the frame of criminal law risks a "fundamental attribution error" when it comes to the participants in war.[127]

5.3.3. Individual Differences in Reacting to Environment

Situational influence on normative competence and behaviour does not mean that all persons in the same situation think and act the same. Behaviour is not independent from the agent. Behavioural outcomes are results of complex interactions between the person and the situation.[128] People are shaped by the same social environment *differently*. Due to "internal psychological and affective processes",[129] agents may react to different stressors in the environment. The individual has a unique "network of cognitive and affective strategies" in their interpretation of and reaction to the world.[130] The environmental impact should be assessed in light of the actor's "personal and subjective" interpretations and reactions.[131] The strength of environmental stimuli, personal perception and coping ability (at the time) all affect one's reactions to obnoxious conditions and levels of aggression.[132] Moreover, soldiers are not pure instruments of the State nor are they "simply pawns in an omnipresent moral universe against which it was impossible to struggle".[133] They can be more "conscientious and self-directed" in performing their duties than automatons or mindless extensions of

---

[126] Ross and Shestowsky, 2002, p. 1095, see *supra* note 118.

[127] *Ibid*., p. 1092; Zimbardo, 2007, p. 212, see *supra* note 6. Zimbardo defines person, situation and system as follows:

> *Person*: an actor on the stage of life whose behavioral freedom is informed by his or her makeup – genetic, biological, physical, and psychological.
>
> *Situation*: is the behavioral context that has the power, through its reward and normative functions, to give meaning and identity to the actor's roles and status.
>
> *System*: consists of the agents and agencies whose ideology, values, and power create situations and dictate the roles and expectations for approved behaviors of actors within its sphere of influence.

[128] Doris, 2005, p. 25, see *supra* note 8.

[129] Talbert and Wolfendale, 2018, p. 60, see *supra* note 15.

[130] Cited in *ibid*., p. 61.

[131] *Ibid*.

[132] Mackmin, 2007, p. 80, see *supra* note 103.

[133] Joanna Bourke, *An Intimate History of Killing: Face-to-Face Killing in Twentieth-Century Warfare*, Basic Books, 1999, p. 229.

their superiors.[134] Kelman, for example, recognizes individual differences in conditions under which they are prepared to disobey an order.[135] People act differently within the possible range. In past wars, there have been soldiers trying to avoid participating in atrocities, even under considerable situational pressure.[136] They even engaged in self-harm to evade the anticipated slaughter.[137] Extreme circumstances create both evil and heroism.

As we will discuss further in Chapter 8, individuals should not be fully exonerated by situational pressures. Military personnel should assume personal responsibility for their acts to the extent they can think and act rationally. The influence of the war-time social environment seems to be more acute than other social environments. Although the same environment does not make everyone who is subject to its influence commit war crimes,[138] its general impact should not be ignored.

5.4. The Individual and the Dislocated Cosmopolitan Community

Roger Cotterrell reminds us that "the search for a morally meaningful legality will be unproductive without rigorous empirical study of the complex and varied conditions in which legality is to be sought".[139] This chapter contrasts the universalist, individualist and rationalist presuppositions of a cosmopolitan war crimes law with empirical observations of human agency. I situate the abstract cosmopolitan individual in concrete social environments and show weaknesses in moral psychological assumptions of the individual as the source of cosmopolitan norms and war crimes. The cosmopolitan approach tends to neglect or downplay social influence and personal weaknesses. Social integration, communication and interaction are important to the formation of and compliance with legal norms. The conception of a cosmopolitan community tends to exaggerate the bond among strangers and underestimate solidarity and cohesion within numerous local communities. Cosmopolitan normative expectations are consequently inflated.

From the perpetrator's perspective, the cosmopolitan community which exercises public authority to condemn and to punish is an *ex post facto*

---

[134] Bandura, 1990, p. 36, see *supra* note 95.

[135] Kelman, 1973, p. 39, see *supra* note 109.

[136] See examples from Vietnam War in Joanna Bourke, 1999, pp. 197–198, *supra* note 133.

[137] *Ibid.*, p. 231.

[138] Doris and Murphy provide justification for individual differences in the same environment. They point out that war crimes are more frequent and ubiquitous than people think. See Doris and Murphy, 2007, *supra* note 17.

[139] Roger Cotterrell, *Law's Community: Legal Theory in Sociological Perspective*, Clarendon Press, Oxford, 1995, p. 295.

community, a community which did not exist at the time of the commission of the crime. The cosmopolitan community represents a kind of top-down universalism which may be alien and cold for those at the bottom. This contrast takes us back to Danilo Zolo's observation that judgments of international criminal tribunals are passed from "outside and above the social, cultural and economic contexts within which those being tried acted".[140] Deviant behaviours are "de-contextualized" and punished.[141] That is, the cosmopolitan community can be imposing a criminal law without sufficient *prior relationship* with its target of regulation. A war crimes law so conceived tends to coerce individual agency and responsibility in war by providing a top-down normative framework which cannot reach the military personnel at the bottom. The "remoteness" of "normative expectations" from the top creates a kind of "moral distance" between the law and the agents it seeks to regulate.[142] As we will see in Chapters 6 and 7, the military institution and combat environment are incorrigibly hostile to 'normative individualism'. Promoting or coercing rational human agency in such a social environment can raise questions of fairness and legitimacy. A criminal law residing in a somewhat dislocated relationship between the community and the individual is bound to struggle in its reception and implementation.

[140] Danilo Zolo, "Peace Through Criminal Law?", in *Journal of International Criminal Justice*, 2004, vol. 2, no. 3, p. 729.

[141] *Ibid.*

[142] Cotterrell, 1995, pp. 304–305, see *supra* note 139.

6

Influence of the Military Institution on the Perpetrator*

Criminal law regulates by providing people with reasons and considerations for or against potential actions. As it makes normative demands on the individual person, criminal law inevitably relies on certain assumptions of human agency. Chapter 5 describes a cosmopolitan war crimes law's conception of rational agency which is abstract, universal and independent of social environment. The legal fiction of the rational agent and the sociological person are different concepts. Such difference is inherent to the criminal law as a normative system. Depending on its nature and degree, the difference between the legal fiction and social reality can have significant normative and practical implications. Drawing on social psychology, Chapters 6 and 7 describe the typical perpetrator of war crimes – the ordinary soldier – as a sociological person. Together, they illustrate how the military structure and combat environment create "moral distance"[1] to a cosmopolitan war crimes law through their influence on human agency.

6.1. Social Influence of Institutions

An ordinary soldier living in seventeenth-century China is unlikely to think using starvation as a method of warfare amounts to war crime – or its normative equivalent at the time. Every human being lives in a specific place in a specific time, and is bound by different relations. The human person is socially embedded. Socialization is done through social influence. Social influence links the individual to social structures.[2] Use of authority, for example, is a form of social influence. Social influence induces changes of behaviour, attitude or belief in the individual.[3] It happens either because the individual feels compelled to comply with certain social norms, identifies with certain social roles, or internalizes

* Part of this and the next two chapters are drawn upon in my article, "The Ordinary Soldier in Military Organization: Is International Criminal Law Delusional About Human Agency?", in *Journal of International Criminal Justice*, 2024, vol. 22, no. 3–4, pp. 479–497.

1 Roger Cotterrell, *Law's Community: Legal Theory in Sociological Perspective*, Clarendon Press, Oxford, 1995, pp. 304–305.

2 Herbert Kelman and V. Lee Hamilton, *Crimes of Obedience: Toward a Social Psychology of Authority and Responsibility*, Yale University Press, New Haven, 1989, pp. 77–78.

3 *Ibid.*, p. 87.

certain social values. These are three processes of social influence proposed by psychologist Herbert Kelman: compliance, identification and internalization.[4] By learning and adopting specific rules, role expectations and values of a society or group, the individual is socialized into the collective. "Rule-, role- and value-orientations" can co-exist and do not exclude one another.[5]

While even informal interactions between private individuals are minimally defined and structured by the larger society, social interactions within social units are more thoroughly regulated.[6] These social units, or so-called social systems, are governed by certain shared norms and expectations and have some identity, regularity and continuity beyond their members.[7] That is, a social unit is more than the sum of its individual members. Social institutions, a type of more formal social unit, can be seen as a kind of "established, significant, and recognised practice, relationship, or organisation in a society or culture".[8] Institutions need an explicit mission to justify their existence, and the self-worth, rewards and privileges of their members.[9] Institutions also need to renew themselves by recruiting members from society and "induct" them into the organization.[10] In their daily operation, institutions enact "processes of power, leadership, communication, and change".[11] The institutional structure formalizes the flow of information, resources and personnel through written regulations, centralizes decision-making of key matters, and delineates responsibilities throughout the lower levels.[12] A complex, formal, and centralized institution such as an armed force can exercise powerful influence and control over its members.

'Professionalization' often means taming. Modern institutions in their attempt to maximize efficiency tend to eliminate the individuality of their members. The bureaucratic machine can be so preoccupied with efficiency that it neglects the substance of its mission. This is a kind of separation of form and content, or rather, form overtaking content. The pursuit of technically superior methods of reaching a certain goal becomes more important than the goal itself. This represents, according to Bauman, bureaucracy's "double feat" as "the moralization of technology, coupled with the denial of the moral significance of non-

4 *Ibid.*, pp. 88–113.

5 *Ibid.*

6 *Ibid.*, p. 87.

7 *Ibid.*, p. 88.

8 Peter H. Wilson, "Defining Military Culture", in *The Journal of Military History*, 2008, vol. 72, no. 1, p. 16.

9 *Ibid.*, p. 18.

10 *Ibid.*, p. 28.

11 *Ibid.*, p. 31.

12 *Ibid.*, p. 32.

technical issues".[13] The quest for efficiency requires control over the members, for which obedience, conformity and predictability are important. The highly professionalized and depersonalized environment diminishes individuality and human agency. Division of labour causes "fragmentation" and "evaporation" of responsibility.[14] Individuals have no control over the ultimate outcome of the bureaucratic machine; they do not feel responsible for the outcome, be it charitable work or genocide. There is an implicit resignation from personal control and responsibility. A worker is physically at work, but has mentally or spiritually resigned. This results in a kind of "alienation" of "the subjective intentionality" of the participants from the output of their work.[15] Institutional agendas can therefore override the reason and will of its members.

6.2. "Total Institution": Collectivization of Agency in the Military

The primary mission of armed forces is quite different from other institutions. The stated mission and purpose of most military forces is to engage in collective armed violence, whether in defense or offence.[16] The military is required to take life and destroy property, that is, to break fundamental peace-time norms. The nature of military missions requires a high level of "institutional development and cohesion".[17] War is waged by entities, not by mobs or crowds. The military structure represents the pinnacle of "supremacy of society over the individual".[18] It glorifies and actively inculcates "the surrender of individuality".[19] Life in the military is highly communal and routinized. To achieve this, the military needs to eradicate individuality of soldiers – personal values, privacy, lifestyle – and assimilate them into the collective. The military institution emphasizes discipline and order, hierarchy and control. Soldiers eventually adopt the military's values, virtues and way of thinking, and become deeply embedded in the institution.[20] The closed institution creates its own normative order and reference system, which its members conform to, identify with and internalize. The

[13] Arne Johan Vetlesen, *Evil and Human Agency: Understanding Collective Evildoing*, Cambridge University Press, 2009, p. 19.

[14] *Ibid.*, p. 18.

[15] *Ibid.*, p. 46.

[16] Wilson, 2008, p. 20, see *supra* note 8.

[17] *Ibid.*

[18] Samuel P. Huntington, *The Soldier and the State: The Theory and Politics of Civil-Military Relations*, Harvard University Press, Cambridge, Massachusetts, 1957, p. 79.

[19] Karl Marlantes, *What It Is Like To Go To War*, Corvus, London, 2012, p. 143.

[20] Typical military virtues are, for example, "loyalty, duty, respect, selfless service, honor, integrity, and personal courage"; and an example of a typical military motto is, "obedience, discipline, survival, and sacrifice". See Carmel O'Sullivan, *Killing on Command: The Defence of Superior Orders in Modern Combat*, Palgrave Macmillan, London, 2016, p. 187.

extraordinary organization and mission of the military dictate the attitude, moral standards and behaviour of its members. It is "social engineering"[21] *par excellence*.

Not all military forces are the same, nor all soldiers. The institutional practices described in this chapter focus on what is common to most State armed forces, especially those of a relatively high degree of organization and complexity. The institutional experiences described below are characteristic of military life, but may not be shared by all members of the military.[22]

6.2.1. The 'Rite of Passage': From a Civilian to a Soldier

The military is characteristically "authoritarian, ritualistic, and isolated from the civilian world".[23] Soldiers do not have the same equality, freedom and autonomy as ordinary civilians. Military life is designed to transform the individual. Armies first "break down" the individual and then "rebuild" them according to institutional standards.[24] Leaving behind their past civilian world, recruits adopt military values and rules, develop an institutional mentality, and learn skills of war to become effective soldiers.[25] They go through "a rite of passage", in which they exchange one human identity for another – from ordinary civilians to combatants. The 'rite' convinces its participants that their new group is real, and that being a part of it is more important than any other identities.[26]

The rite has three phases: separation, transition and incorporation.[27] Recruits are first separated from civilian society and their former identities. They are situated in a culture that is "self-consciously alienated" from civilian life and values.[28] Lacking contact with the outside world, the recruits are in "moral and

---

21 David Berreby, *Us and Them: The Science of Identity*, University of Chicago Press, 2018, p. 184.

22 I focus on the experiences of frontline soldiers who are trained to go to the battlefield, not military personnel in logistical, educational and religious functions.

23 Matthew Talbert and Jessica Wolfendale, *War Crimes, Causes, Excuses, and Blame*, Oxford University Press, 2018, p. 152.

24 O'Sullivan, 2016, p. 79, see *supra* note 20.

25 *Ibid.*

26 Berreby, 2018, p. 272, see *supra* note 21.

27 O'Sullivan, 2016, p. 111, see *supra* note 20.

28 John M. Doris and Dominic Murphy, "From My Lai to Abu Ghraib: The Moral Psychology of Atrocity", in *Midwest Studies in Philosophy*, 2007, vol. 31, no. 1, p. 39. Culture can be understood as "a social, durable, layered pattern of cognitive and normative systems at once material and ideal, objective and subjective, embodied in artifacts and embedded in behavior, passed about in interaction, internalized in personalities, and externalized in institutions". See Sharon Hays, "Structure and Agency and the Sticky Problem of Culture", in *Sociological Theory*, 1994, vol. 12, no. 1, p. 65.

physical isolation".[29] They are removed from their previous "support networks"[30] and sources of social comfort such as friends and family. The transitional phase breaks down the new members and rebuilds them as soldiers.[31] "All-consuming" military training exhausts the body and the mind, builds cohesion, and instils self-discipline.[32] Brutalization and humiliation are common in training. One serviceman records:

> To be struck, to be threatened, to be called indecent names, to be drilled by yourself in front of a squad in order to make a fool of you, to do a tiring exercise and continue doing it whilst the rest of the squad does something else; to have your ears spat into, to be marched across parade-ground under escort, to be falsely accused before an officer and silenced when you try to speak in defence.[33]

A "perpetual state of shock and fear", another soldier recalls.[34] The harsh process and arbitrary treatment strip personal pride, diminish self-worth, and as such condition new recruits to be "amenable to any command" and willingly "accept the role of cannon-fodder on the battle-ground".[35]

The "total institution" has strict control over its members 24 hours a day.[36] It breaks down "the spheres of work, sleep, and play" which are fundamental to human existence.[37] Members are subjected to "a tightly controlled and regimented daily routine" which serves the military mission.[38] Every detail of military life is highly regulated. Exacting standards apply to room arrangement,

---

29 Philip Zimbardo, *The Lucifer Effect: Understanding How Good People Turn Evil*, Random House Trade Paperbacks, London, 2007, p. 422.

30 Wilson, 2008, p. 30, see *supra* note 8.

31 O'Sullivan, 2016, p. 111, see *supra* note 20. See also, Joanna Bourke, *An Intimate History of Killing: Face-to-Face Killing in Twentieth-Century Warfare*, Basic Books, 1999, p. 67. Richard Holmes similarly comments that "many training programmes are deliberately designed to break recruits down to a lowest common denominator before building them up again", cited in Jean-Jacques Frésard, *The Roots of Behaviour in War: A Survey of the Literature*, International Committee of the Red Cross, Geneva, 2004, p. 52.

32 O'Sullivan, 2016, p. 82, see *supra* note 20. Studies suggest that the level of psychological stress a new recruit undergoes is much higher than what is normally considered stressful, and is often comparable to a schizophrenic in incipient psychosis. See *ibid.*

33 Bourke, 1999, p. 67, see *supra* note 31.

34 *Ibid.*, p. 58. A new recruit writes: "The first two weeks here you are torn down to nothing; they make you feel lower than a snake in a pit, and then the following 8-10 weeks they proceed to rebuild you, the Marine Corp. way".

35 *Ibid.*, pp. 67, 58.

36 O'Sullivan, 2016, p. 6, see *supra* note 20.

37 Wilson, 2008, p. 19, see *supra* note 8.

38 *Ibid.*

personal appearance and behaviour.[39] Soldiers work and live together. Common social activities such as recreations, mental testing, medical measurement and examinations reinforce bonds within the military.[40] The uniform makes soldiers virtually indistinguishable. Soon new members "look, smell, speak, respond and act the same".[41] Historian Joanna Bourke observes that "uniformity of environment creates uniformity of character and of spirit".[42] In sum, elements characteristic of military life – depersonalization, assimilated appearance, lack of privacy, institutionalized social relations, precise schedules, sleep deprivation – all contribute to the breaking down of the individual.[43]

The repression of individuality is coupled with the cultivation of collective solidarity. The disoriented, confused new recruits are re-built with "military codes, arbitrary rules, and strict punishment".[44] Institutional values promptly fill the void of individual consciousness. As individual souls are assimilated into a collective spirit, the crowd turns into "a psychological one".[45] Through "words, actions, commands, organized behaviour",[46] the military creates a new category of human being – soldiers. They comply with, identify with and may even internalize military rules and standards. The sense of self is eroded. The military becomes the primary source of social reference. The recruit turns to his superior and immediate group for validation and recognition. Being a soldier becomes more important than being any other kind of human being. Obedience and conformity replace autonomy and individuality. They are prepared to do what may go against their personal beliefs, such as killing another human being.

6.2.2. Obedience to Authority

Human beings have a natural tendency to obey authority. Sheer existence of authority suppresses individual agency, especially when the authority is trusted, legitimate, stable and nearby.[47] Social psychologist Stanley Milgram's experiments show that ordinary people are willing to administer electric shocks to a

---

39 O'Sullivan, 2016, p. 82, see *supra* note 20.

40 Mark Osiel, "Obeying Orders: Atrocity, Military Discipline, and the Law of War", in *California Law Review*, 1998, vol. 86, no. 5, p. 1052.

41 O'Sullivan, 2016, p. 83, see *supra* note 20.

42 Bourke, 1999, p. 74, see *supra* note 31.

43 *Ibid.*, p. 67.

44 *Ibid.*, p. 67.

45 *Ibid.*, p. 74.

46 Berreby, 2018, p. 269, see *supra* note 21.

47 Robert Sapolsky, *Behave: The Biology of Humans at Our Best and Worst*, Penguin Press, New York, 2017, p. 470.

screaming victim at the polite, non-coercive request of an experimenter.[48] Milgram discerns "an internalized basis" for obedience. That is, the principle reason for obedience comes from the actor's sense of obligation, not coercion or potential sanctions.[49] Authority is different from naked power because it invokes the right to command and expect obedience.[50] Kelman suggests three levels of legitimacy: legitimacy of the system, legitimacy of specific authorities within the system, and legitimacy of their specific demands.[51] Presumption of legitimacy enjoyed by authorities carries over to the demands they issue.[52] The apparent legitimacy of the military institution contributes significantly to the legitimacy of specific orders and instructions. The sense of institutional legitimacy is transmitted through buildings, military symbols, official documents, procedures, legal and administrative rules, appearance, rituals, *et cetera*. These cues and expectations create a typical authority situation which psychologically binds those involved: both the superior and subordinate are supposed to play their prescribed parts.[53] Once people are in an "action sequence", they tend to react "mindlessly" and to enact routine scripts.[54] They often do not consciously choose to enact a script, they simply do what is expected of them in such a situation.[55] The authority situation channels the individual into automatic, unquestioning obedience.[56]

Legitimate authority therefore creates a perception of a "nonchoice situation" where people suspend their right to make choices.[57] The superior does not need to convince subordinates that carrying out an order is a preferred alternative among others. What happens is an activation of commitments or a sense of obligation which are built into the definition of the soldier's role.[58] Faced with what they deem as legitimate authority, the subordinate focuses on what is required of him, not his own preference, interests or moral judgment.[59] Milgram argues that the "typical soldier" kills out of a sense of duty to obey orders.[60]

---

48 See Stanley Milgram, *Obedience to Authority: An Experimental View*, Harper & Row, New York, 1974.

49 *Ibid.*, pp. 140–141.

50 Kelman and Hamilton, 1989, p. 55, see *supra* note 2.

51 *Ibid.*, p. 102.

52 *Ibid.*, p. 92.

53 *Ibid.*, p. 90.

54 *Ibid.*, p. 90.

55 *Ibid.*, p. 90.

56 *Ibid.*, p. 138.

57 *Ibid.*, p. 91.

58 *Ibid.*, p. 89.

59 *Ibid.*, p. 89.

60 Milgram, 1974, p. 166, see *supra* note 48.

Kelman explains that official authorization carries "automatic justification" for actors. He observes that, behaviourally, authorization makes it no longer necessary for people to make judgment or choices themselves.[61] The actor is not an independent moral agent but "an extension of the authority".[62] Personal attitudes and preferences are not important to a person's entry into a script.[63] In fact, people are willing to go very far to please the power. Kelman argues that situations of legitimate authority can make individuals focus on their role obligations "at the expense" of their personal interests and preferences.[64] He explains that authority can induce actions that call for considerable personal sacrifices or even go against the actor's own moral judgment.[65] This is possible because the actors have relinquished control and responsibility to the authority.[66] For example, someone who personally disapproves stealing, assault and killing may easily perform these acts when commanded by authority. Suppression of individual agency can indeed reduce a soldier's guilt for performing harmful tasks.[67] When a soldier does not want to carry out an order, he may choose to evade or reinterpret the order rather than directly contradict authority.[68]

Furthermore, even when people can state clearly the right moral requirement at the cognitive level, they do not necessarily translate it into actual behaviour in an authority situation. Milgram describes this gap between thought and behaviour in his lab experiments. He observes that many people were simply "unable to realize their values in action and found themselves continuing in the experiment even though they disagreed with what they were doing".[69] This is not necessarily because people profess ungenuine, self-glorifying moral opinions. Rather, it shows that people are not aware of the power of authority situations. That is, although these people were convinced of the wrongness of their acts, they simply "could not bring themselves to make an open break with authority".[70] This is because relatively few people have the necessary mental resources to confront authority, or the authority's definition of the situation.[71]

61 Herbert C. Kelman, "Violence without Moral Restraint: Reflections on the Dehumanization of Victims and Victimizers", in *Journal of Social Issues*, 1973, vol. 29, no. 4, p. 39.

62 *Ibid.*, 39.

63 Kelman and Hamilton, 1989, p. 90, see *supra* note 2.

64 *Ibid.*, p. 97.

65 *Ibid.*, p. 96.

66 *Ibid.*, p. 96.

67 Kelman, 1973, p. 39, see *supra* note 61.

68 Kelman and Hamilton, 1989, p. 97, see *supra* note 2.

69 Milgram, 1974, p. 6, see *supra* note 48.

70 *Ibid.*, p. 10.

71 *Ibid.*, p. 6.

Unless the individual steps outside the definition of situation, he or she is not able to redefine the situation and challenge the legitimacy of the command.[72] In most cases, the thought of disobedience does not even arise. Soldiers have become so integrated into the military structure that they are unable to mentally detach from it, at least not without significant "psychic cost".[73] Joanna Bourke observes that where there is a "permissive attitude" towards harming non-combatants, it takes "enormous courage" for a soldier who thinks it is unlawful to refuse to participate.[74] Milgram reminds us that values or moral convictions are not the only reasons for performing an act. Rather, values are merely "one narrow band of causes in the total spectrum of forces" influencing behaviour.[75]

Needless to say, obedience is crucial to the military organization and mission. One of the key aspects of the military "total institution" is strict hierarchy. An armed force without obedience cannot succeed or survive, it cannot even be called an armed force. Due to the complexity of overall operations and division of tasks, decision-making can be highly centralized. Implementation of top-down decisions may require predictable and co-ordinated acts among large numbers of troops. Consequently, it is often very difficult, if not impossible, for the individual soldier to make informed decision on his own. Disobedience of orders can put oneself and fellow soldiers in danger and seriously undermine the mission. It is warned that displays of "individual valor and initiative might have positively catastrophic consequences".[76] Most of the time, the best course of action is to follow the order. Moreover, dangerous orders are common in war: soldiers are ordered to kill others while facing probable or almost certain death.[77] This means past instances of successful disobedience may be seized upon as precedent to disobey "unpalatable orders that are an innate and necessary aspect of war".[78] It is thus imperative to have consistent obedience throughout the hierarchy at all times in all contexts.

Given the fundamental importance of hierarchy and obedience, the military goes through great lengths to condition automatic obedience in its training. Orders, small or big, serious or ridiculous, easy or difficult, have to be followed strictly without any hesitation.[79] Failure to show absolute obedience is met with

---

72 Kelman and Hamilton, 1989, p. 139, see *supra* note 2.

73 Milgram, 1974, pp. 163, 166, see *supra* note 48.

74 Bourke, 1999, p. 189, see *supra* note 31.

75 Milgram, 1974, p. 6, see *supra* note 48.

76 Cited in Osiel, 1998, p. 1032, see *supra* note 40.

77 O'Sullivan, 2016, p. 85, see *supra* note 20.

78 *Ibid.*

79 The new recruits can receive abnormal orders, such as to march in trunks and boots into the shower and to pour ice-cold water on themselves. See *ibid.*, p. 84.

certainty of punishment – even a minor infraction can receive serious punishment.[80] As is shown in the next section, military training ensures that formality and rigidity of implementing orders are learned by heart. Following orders becomes an instinct. When recruits adopt institutional standards and seek institutional affirmation, it reinforces their submission to superiors' authority.[81]

Compared to citizens in a civilian context, soldiers are under extreme control and influence. The military authority presents greater "urgency" to obey orders than an experimental environment.[82] The propensity to obey orders is strengthened and reinforced regularly in soldiers. The military creates powerful authority situations which impair critical judgment, deny personal agency and induce unquestioning obedience.

6.2.3. Influence of the Group

An individual behaves differently when he is subject to group dynamics. Psychoanalyst Wilfred Bion observes that "the individual is, and has always been, a member of a group", and "no individual, however isolated in time and space, should be regarded as outside a group or lacking in active manifestations of group psychology".[83] Vetlesen comments that when an individual feels, experiences and acts emphatically as a group member, he may show hidden or dormant features which are not seen when acting alone.[84] The group imparts a feeling of power with sheer quantity of members, reduces the sense of individual distinctiveness hence responsibility, and spreads sentiments like a contagion.[85] Group attitudes tend to be absolute rather than ambivalent: suspicions become certainties; antipathy becomes hatred.[86] Intensified emotions in a group can radically compromise one's rational thinking.[87] It is not unusual to see that with heightened negative feelings such as anger or aggression, the group enables violent acts which the individual alone would not think of committing.

Military life cultivates group solidarity. Within the highly ordered and monotonous regime, soldiers live, work and suffer together. Bonds are built in day-to-day routines in peace-time. For the individual soldier, the immediate group can be the main source of comfort, meaning and security. Brotherly camaraderie provides emotional comfort in the harsh and impersonal environment.

---

[80] *Ibid.*

[81] *Ibid.*, p. 95.

[82] O'Sullivan, 2016, p. 171, see *supra* note 20.

[83] Cited in Vetlesen, 2009, p. 171, see *supra* note 13.

[84] *Ibid.*

[85] Cited in Frésard, 2004, p. 52, see *supra* note 31.

[86] *Ibid.*

[87] Vetlesen, 2009, p. 171, see *supra* note 13.

Collective training, drills and collective punishment instil group loyalty, a sense of collective honour and instinct of common fate. For example, many tactical drills require tight teamwork – each participant has to perform specific tasks and work closely with others.[88] A participant's performance is evaluated at both the individual and collective level.[89]

Solidarity is enhanced in the danger of combat where soldiers are exposed, vulnerable and interdependent. Soldiers rely on their immediate group to interpret and react to unfamiliar, disorienting and ambiguous situations. The individual is protected and "supported by the formidableness of the group".[90] In the words of an infantry man: "man is a gregarious animal. His greatest steadying force is the touch of his fellows under battle's pressure".[91]

Group solidarity serves important military function. Armed forces tend to promote *esprit de corps* which produces cohesion, high morale and military effectiveness. Identification with the group enhances combat motivation. Group-mindedness helps a soldier cope with psychological stresses of the war and carry out dangerous tasks. When a soldier strongly identifies with his primary group, he tends to displace self-love onto the group, fear less of self-annihilation, and reduce inhibitions of aggression.[92] Focusing on group interests distracts one from self-preservation and motivates him to overcome the innate reluctance to kill.[93] Glenn Gray writes in *The Warriors: Reflections on Men in Battle* that strong loyalty to the group is "the essence of fight morale".[94] War studies report that love for comrades, more than ideology, hatred or pain of punishment, motivates soldiers to fight.[95] A study of combat pilots concludes that "men are

88 For more details, see O'Sullivan, 2016, p. 97, *supra* note 20.

89 *Ibid.*

90 Sara Mackmin, "Why do Professional Soldiers Commit Acts of Personal Violence that Contravene the Law of Armed Conflict?", in *Defence Studies*, 2007, vol. 7, no. 1, p. 82.

91 Bourke, 1999, p. 87, see *supra* note 31.

92 *Ibid.*

93 Mackmin, 2007, p. 82, see *supra* note 90.

94 Cited in Frésard, 2004, p. 51, see *supra* note 31.

95 Bourke, 1999, p. 130, see *supra* note 31. In one of the surveys, 568 American infantrymen who had participated in combat in Sicily and North Africa in 1944 were asked about their primary motivation for fighting. Little mention was made of "leadership and discipline, lack of alternatives, vindictiveness, idealism, and self-preservation ('kill or be killed')". Combatants mentioned "solidarity with the group and thoughts of home and loved ones" as primary enabling factors. Osiel invokes studies of the battlefield persistence of German soldiers during the Second World War which suggest that commitment to Nazi ideology or political goals were not main incentives. See Osiel, 1998, p. 1054, *supra* note 40. See also, O'Sullivan, 2016, p. 176, *supra* note 20.

fighting for each other" as group interests take over their self-interest.[96] This explains high morale under soaring casualty rates.[97] The extreme feeling of camaraderie creates motivation to fight "even in the most reluctant warriors and in the most unpopular wars".[98]

The individual soldier thinks and acts under strong influence of the group, especially his primary group. The need to conform is so strong that it can override his personal belief and judgment.[99] The soldier's embeddedness in the primary group undermines his ability for "moral deliberation".[100] He may do anything to win the approval and respect of the group. Disapproval of colleagues can be devastating when the group is the primary source of reference. A soldier who deviates from the group may be excluded, ostracized or ridiculed. This is not just uncomfortable or embarrassing, it can be deadly.[101] A soldier cannot survive on his own in combat. His survival depends on "his ability to make others willing to help him in his own time of need".[102]

6.3. Military Training: Condition to Kill

6.3.1. Function and Techniques of Training

The main goal of military training is to "convert civilians into effective combatants".[103] Military training helps soldiers control their emotions under the stress of war and make reasonable decisions based on an accurate assessment of the circumstances.[104] Soldiers develop "tactical knowledge, situational awareness and resilience" through extremely challenging training regimes.[105] Military effectiveness requires combat skills as well as military ethos such as obedience, loyalty, discipline, vigilance and persistence.[106] Moreover, military training

---

[96] Bourke, 1999, p. 130, see *supra* note 31.

[97] *Ibid.*

[98] Osiel, 1998, p. 1055, see *supra* note 40.

[99] Mackmin, 2007, p. 19, see *supra* note 90.

[100] O'Sullivan, 2016, p. 179, see *supra* note 20.

[101] Bourke, 1999, p. 186, see *supra* note 31.

[102] Cited in Mackmin, 2007, p. 82, see *supra* note 90.

[103] Bourke, 1999, p. 60, see *supra* note 31.

[104] O'Sullivan, 2016, p. 99, see *supra* note 20.

[105] *Ibid.*, p. 80.

[106] For example, values of the Israeli Defence Forces ('IDF') include "Perseverance in the Mission and Pursuit of Victory", "Reliability and Trustworthiness", "Professionalism", "Discipline", "Camaraderie", "A Sense of Mission", *et cetera*. See IDF, "The Spirit of the Israel Defense Forces: What Guides Us" (available on its web site).

must "incite hostility"[107] and promote "offensive spirit"[108] in order to motivate fighting. Studies suggest that military training has become more effective in enabling soldiers to fight. Human beings have a natural aversion to killing, especially at close range.[109] Historically, the lack of "offensive spirit" or "passive combat personnel" was a common concern to armed forces. The percentage of soldiers who were unable to open fire in combat was very high; when they did fire, the accuracy was low.[110] One report during the Second World War noted that the average soldier was "quite amazingly lethargic".[111] Grossman observes that the "average soldier" will not kill unless forced or conditioned to do so.[112] Since reluctance to kill is "an emotional and not an intellectual handicap", objective reasons such as "[k]ill or be killed" does little to persuade men into action.[113] Effective training has to mobilize "free-flow-aggression" and control anxiety and guilt in soldiers.[114] Much moral and psychological preparation is required.

The firing rate has increased significantly in recent wars.[115] Discoveries in behavioural psychology have been used by armed forces to enable killing and enhance aggression. The authoritarian military structure is perfect for behaviourism's top-down conditioning.[116] The military readily becomes the ideal ground for "human engineering".[117] Recruits are trained to carry out combat actions as their "second nature".[118] It is hoped that deeply ingrained battle habits

[107] Cited in Frésard, 2004, p. 51, see *supra* note 31.

[108] Bourke, 1999, p. 59, see *supra* note 31.

[109] Dave Grossman, *On Killing: The Psychological Cost of Learning to Kill in War and Society*, Back Bay, New York, 2009, pp. 18–29. This is exclusively based on the United States' experience in twentieth-century wars.

[110] See Bourke, 1999, pp. 61–63, *supra* note 31.

[111] *Ibid.*, p. 62.

[112] Grossman, 2009, p. 32, see *supra* note 109.

[113] Bourke, 1999, p. 72, see *supra* note 31.

[114] *Ibid.*, p. 88.

[115] In the United States' context, it is estimated that only 15–25 per cent of infantry soldiers fired at an exposed enemy even when their lives and the lives of fellow soldiers were at risk in the Second World War, 50 per cent in Korean War, 90–95 per cent in Vietnam War, and 98 per cent in the First Gulf War, see Grossman, 2009, pp. 16, 253, *supra* note 109; see also, O'Sullivan, 2016, p. 109, *supra* note 20.

[116] Bourke, 1999, p. 97, see *supra* note 31.

[117] In a 1923 address, the President of American Psychological Association suggested that war had transformed the discipline of psychology from a 'science of trivialities' into a 'science of human engineering'. See Bourke, 1999, p. 84, *supra* note 31. Grossman calls techniques to rewire the brains to accept killing in war-time as a natural response the science of "killology", see Grossman, 2009, p. 295, *supra* note 109.

[118] Bourke, 1999, p. 61, see *supra* note 31.

will persist in the most challenging circumstances in war.[119] In the intensity of a fight, the military training "takes over" and enables soldiers to perform the conditioned response "instinctively and automatically".[120] Techniques developed to improve combat performance include "repetitive drills, realistic training, hazing and exceptionally tough standards".[121] Repetitive training in realistic settings can instil in soldiers automatic responses.[122] Conditioning, a classic behavioural tool originated from Pavlov's experiments, is done through a positive response to the subject's desired reaction to a stimulus and negative response to incorrect reactions or failures. The stimulus is usually a threat or an order. After repeating the Pavlovian stimulus–response–reinforcement sequence numerous times and firing numerous shots, the response is "instinctive" and accurate.[123] Successful conditioning makes the recruits shoot at the human target "reflexively" and "without conscious thought".[124] Repetitive training conditions both individual and co-ordinated group responses.[125] It ensures that when soldiers are exhausted and lose "all sharpness of consciousness", they can still do their duties and "function like cells in a military organism".[126]

Other techniques such as harsh treatment and hazing can inoculate soldiers to disorienting combat environments and increase innate aggression.[127] The instructor would shower the troops with "a mixture of enthusiasm, ridicule, threats of sanctions and draconian military law".[128] Exhausting exercises, false accusations, silencing of any explanation from the soldiers, *et cetera*, are familiar recipes.[129] A stream of psychological theory believes frustration encourages aggression.[130] The superior's harsh treatment and arbitrary use of power increase anger and frustration which are subsequently turned into aggression towards the enemy. They are also meant to enhance soldiers' ability to control their emotions and react instantaneously under critical situations.[131] It is believed that these

[119] *Ibid.*, p. 61.

[120] O'Sullivan, 2016, p. 135, see *supra* note 20.

[121] *Ibid.*, p. 107.

[122] *Ibid.*, pp. 80–95.

[123] *Ibid.*, p. 97.

[124] *Ibid.*

[125] *Ibid.*, p. 91.

[126] Cited in Grossman, 2009, p. 19, see *supra* note 109.

[127] There are different theories about whether aggression is innate or learnt through experience. See a summary in O'Sullivan, 2016, p. 89, *supra* note 20.

[128] *Ibid.*

[129] *Ibid.*

[130] Bourke, 1999, p. 71, see *supra* note 31.

[131] O'Sullivan, 2016, p. 89, see *supra* note 20.

training regimes can help soldiers "withstand the rigors of combat".[132] Hazing aims to prepare soldiers for the chaotic and disorienting environment in war, where soldiers face multiple urgent issues and threats at the same time. In military training, several instructors may "yell or issue orders" at the same time and demand immediate reply to each order.[133] A soldier's failure to process and respond to the orders may provoke increased pressure from the instructors.[134] The point is made that any hesitation in taking action can be dangerous either to oneself or one's group.[135]

6.3.2. Mechanisms of Selective Moral Disengagement

In addition to physical and psychological conditioning, moral conditioning is key to such tasks as killing and harming other human beings. Soldiers are required to kill opponents against whom they feel neither personal malice nor moral indignation. Moral disengagement towards the target helps combatants to reconcile their killing experience with their daily life. Moral disengagement means suspension of morality which typically governs "reasoned actions" in inter-human relationship.[136] It is not easy to kill and torture on the job and come home as a loving parent and spouse. When the reality requires drastically different attitudes and actions towards other humans, our ego-defense mechanism compartmentalizes application of moral standards.[137] Conflicting aspects of our experiences are locked into different places and not allowed to mix.[138] Soldiers act "in socially desirable and personally acceptable ways" in their day-to-day life but not when carrying out their military mission.[139] There is a deliberate attempt to block or distort "cognitive controls" towards the target.[140] In addition to traditional cognitive and moral constraints, all the natural human emotions are also suspended. This helps insulate or disassociate the combatants' own daily routine from the "moral ambiguities" of their primary mission.[141]

Moral disengagement is institutionalized by the military. By rationalizing, desensitizing, or even denying killing other human beings in war, the military creates a moral and psychological distance which paves way for moral

[132] Cited in Bourke, 1999, p. 70, see *supra* note 31.

[133] O'Sullivan, 2016, p. 89, see *supra* note 20.

[134] *Ibid.*

[135] *Ibid.*

[136] Zimbardo, 2007, p. 307, see *supra* note 29.

[137] *Ibid.*, p. 214.

[138] *Ibid.*

[139] *Ibid.*, p. 305.

[140] *Ibid.*

[141] Wilson, 2008, p. 35, see *supra* note 8.

disengagement. This does not mean, of course, all soldiers are completely free of moral struggle in carrying out their duties.[142]

6.3.2.1. Cognitive Restructuring

I examine the military's role in three kinds of cognitive restructuring proposed by psychologist Albert Bandura: moral justification, euphemistic labelling and advantageous comparison.[143]

The military typically provides normative justifications for its violent and destructive mission. Such justifications are often stated with strong moral righteousness. The most common justification is self-defence, which in its radical form can be framed as fighting for 'the survival of the nation'. The enemy is simply "too evil to warrant survival".[144] Threat from the enemy justifies, or even glorifies the act of killing. Killing is no longer morally deplorable but can be "a source of self-valuation".[145] Repetitive, continuous and sometimes imperceptible indoctrination enables soldiers to reconstrue harmful conduct as virtuous. Soldiers are able to practice selective moral disengagement towards their target and even "take pride in their destructive accomplishments".[146]

Euphemistic labelling manipulates the language used to describe certain acts. As such, it can disguise harmful activities as neutral or even virtuous. Empirical evidence shows that euphemistic language has a "disinhibitory power".[147] It is also a "language of non-responsibility".[148] The adversaries can be referenced in objectifying terms such as "positions, marks or enemy combatants".[149] This combined with repetitive training allows soldiers to deny, somewhat unconsciously, that they are killing actual human beings. Rather, they are just shooting at a 'target'. The term "surgical strikes" invokes the image of lifesaving medical operation to describe targeted killing.[150] Civilian casualties are "collateral damages", a human-free term that appears morally neutral.[151]

142 O'Sullivan, 2016, p. 106, see *supra* note 20.

143 Albert Bandura, "Selective Activation and Disengagement of Moral Control", in *Journal of Social Issues*, 1990, vol. 46, no. 1, pp. 27 ff. For more on psychological mechanisms of moral disengagement see Zimbardo, 2007, pp. 310–311, *supra* note 29.

144 Bourke, 1999, p. 216, see *supra* note 31.

145 Bandura, 1990, p. 33, see *supra* note 143.

146 *Ibid.*, pp. 29, 33.

147 *Ibid.*, p. 31.

148 *Ibid.*, p. 32.

149 O'Sullivan, 2016, p. 107, see *supra* note 20.

150 Bandura, 1990, p. 32, see *supra* note 143.

151 *Ibid.*

Agentless passive form is another device that creates the illusion that horrible acts are resulted from "nameless forces", not human agents.[152]

Advantageous comparison is often used to convince soldiers that the enemy's atrocities are much worse than one's own conduct. Comparison with worse behaviours helps to rationalize one's own atrocities.[153]

6.3.2.2. Dehumanization of the Enemy

When one sees another as a fellow human being, one tends to react to another's experience empathetically or vicariously through perceived similarity. That is, the joy and suffering of perceived similar persons can arouse emotional reactions. Harming "humanized persons" can cause distress and self-censure.[154] Dehumanization divests persons of human qualities.[155] The "vicarious emotional activation"[156] is manipulated so it is not triggered by certain human beings. The dehumanized are not seen as "persons with feelings, hopes, and concerns", but as "subhuman" or "mindless" objects.[157] The dissociation of the enemy from humanity is a kind of "pseudospeciation".[158] It excludes some human beings from "the moral order" of the human world.[159] Creating "a false species out of the other human" makes it easier to kill.[160]

Hostility fosters dehumanization. It is no accident that dehumanization is a common phenomenon to all wars. Combat would be difficult to maintain if the enemy is not abstract and depersonalized.[161] At the time of killing, a soldier is almost always convinced that the enemy is not human.[162] When the enemy is removed from the normal human category, they no longer engage our moral considerations in the same way. The usual social and moral inhibitions against killing are lifted or at least diminished. Consequently, feelings of guilt and

152 *Ibid.*

153 *Ibid.*

154 *Ibid.*

155 *Ibid.*, p. 38.

156 *Ibid.*

157 *Ibid.*

158 Marlantes, 2012, pp. 43–44, see *supra* note 19.

159 Zimbardo, 2007, p. 307, see *supra* note 29. Marlantes recalls that he killed a teenager in the Vietnam War without feeling empathy. He describes a kind of "psychological mechanism" which allowed him to see the teenager as "the enemy", not a human being. See Marlantes, 2012, p. 32, *supra* note 19.

160 Marlantes, 2012, pp. 43–44, see *supra* note 19.

161 O'Sullivan, 2016, p. 153, see *supra* note 20; see also, Grossman, 2009, pp. 156–160, *supra* note 109.

162 Marlantes, 2012, pp. 232–233, see *supra* note 19.

anxiety about killing are reduced.[163] The military actively promotes a culture of dehumanization and depersonalization. The dehumanization process may start in military training, and is eventually "intensified and cemented in war".[164] One dehumanizing technique is to regard the opponents as an abstract numbers – a 'body count' mentality.[165] The enemy is abstract, hence "insensate".[166] The elimination of human lives becomes "the main index of military prowess".[167] Degrading nicknames are invented to reinforce prejudice and hatred towards the enemy. The more alien the enemy, the easier and more effective the dehumanization. Categorizers such as race and ideology come as convenient in separating 'Us' and 'Them', humanity and inhumanity.[168] Dehumanizing names remind soldiers of the inferior status, barbarous culture or simply utter alienness of their enemy. Past wars supply endless examples of such names: "Japs", "Krauts", "gooks", "slopes", "dinks", "Commies", and "ragheads".[169] A Vietnam veteran says killing a "commie" does not amount to killing a fellow human: "I wasn't shooting at a person. I was shooting a bunch of ideologies".[170] Official racism was practiced by the German military towards Russians during the Second World War. As a result of "a constant diet of racial propaganda", German conscripts were accustomed to seeing Russians as "depraved", "animal-like", and indeed "no longer human beings".[171]

6.4. From Lawful to Unlawful Violence: Institutional Contributions to War Crimes

War crimes is a heterogeneous phenomenon. Genealogically, war crimes law has been designed to deal with past atrocities. As a system of uniform norms, war crimes law applies to a wide range of scenarios with intended formal

---

163 Mackmin, 2007, p. 72, see *supra* note 90.

164 O'Sullivan, 2016, p. 148, see *supra* note 20.

165 Grossman describes the body count mentality in Vietnam in Grossman, 2009, p. 161, see *supra* note 109.

166 Bandura, 1990, p. 39, see *supra* note 143.

167 Bourke, 1999, p. 220, see *supra* note 31.

168 O'Sullivan, 2016, p. 109, see *supra* note 20.

169 Grossman, 2009, p. 254, see *supra* note 109; Mackmin, 2007, pp. 77–78, see *supra* note 90; O'Sullivan explains further in O'Sullivan, 2016, p. 149, see *supra* note 20 (footnotes omitted):

> During the Vietnam War, the American soldiers referred to the Viet Cong as 'gooks'; during World War II, the Nazis called Slavs *untermensch* or inferior men; during the Rwandan genocide of 1994, the Hutus called the Tutsis 'cockroaches' or 'snakes'; and during contemporary conflicts in Afghanistan and Pakistan, targeted children are referred to as 'fun-sized terrorists' or 'tits' (terrorists in training).

170 Bourke, 1999, p. 220, see *supra* note 31.

171 Cited in Doris and Murphy, 2007, p. 39, see *supra* note 28.

consistency. Not all war crimes are the same, despite legal efforts to cast them in the same category. Differences come from types of military organization, types of armed conflict, institutional involvement in the commission of the crimes, circumstances at the time of the commission of the crime, *et cetera*. This often gives rise to tension between norm and reality because rules designed to respond to one kind of scenario may not suit others. Instances of war crimes can be caused by very different combinations of reasons.

In this section, I argue that the military, with its authority system, group mentality and training, constitutes a significant and common cause of war crimes. The military may oppose, organize or condone war crimes. Within these three kinds of systemic policies, the military can contribute to war crimes to varying degrees. There is, of course, a difference between training regimes which are rigorous in incorporating laws of war and those deliberately ignoring or violating the law. Yet what I would like to emphasize here is the persistent tension between the way the military operates and the prevention of war crimes, even for military training carried out with the best intentions and most sophisticated techniques. Strict hierarchy and organization, closed environment, the violent nature of training and mission, *et cetera* – how the military typically pursues its mission and priorities – enhance the likelihood of war crimes. Genuine efforts to prevent war crimes require promotion of personal agency and sufficient flexibility in using violence. However, they can risk insubordination, lack of discipline, inaction and, eventually, failure of mission.

6.4.1. Spillover Effects of Violence – Military Training's Indirect Contribution to War Crimes

No doubt, the basic principles of distinction and proportionality dictated by international humanitarian law can be implemented in many situations, with great sophistication and ingenuity. However, it is also important to remember that actions in war are often carried out under time pressure, if not great physical and mental strains. Such war acts tend to follow trained instinct and exaggerate inherent human irrationality. The military's institutional production of violence carries an inherent risk for its excesses. Atrocity is simply a by-product of military operation, regardless of official military policy and rules. Training techniques such as conditioning, brutalization and desensitization facilitate legitimate violence and induce excesses. By elevating aggression and weakening resistance to kill, the military improves combat performance and increases risks of illegitimate violence. Military training often inculcates feelings of aggression towards not just "a potential battlefield adversary", but towards "almost anyone outside the tribe".[172] A soldier conditioned to fire upon stimulus has higher

[172] Cited in Frésard, 2004, p. 52, see *supra* note 31.

tendency to kill than ordinary civilians. Brutalization of soldiers breeds brutalization by soldiers which may spill over to the wrong person under wrong circumstances.

On the normative level, military training instils cognitive changes in the personnel. The military's primary mission dictates that its training must erode inhibitions of interpersonal violence. It creates a sense of exception. The feeling that one's action is not judged by usual social norms may extend to unlawful violence. Cognitive restructuring changes "the soldier's perception of reasonable response and use of force".[173] The training "reconfigures the range of available behavioral options" which may make "reprehensible options" seem legitimate to the individual soldier in the chaos of combat.[174]

To make soldiers only kill lawfully, the military must balance between combat effectiveness and restraint. These two goals are not quite compatible. Many war crimes are committed as a result of spill-over aggression and desensitization towards killing. A Vietnam veteran observed that soldiers who had been trained to act in a 'blood thirsty' manner simply could not be expected to protect Vietnamese civilians.[175] No matter how refined the training, facilitating and legitimizing killing do have an indiscriminate impact.

Military training can facilitate both individual war crimes and collective war crimes by reducing the physical and moral restraints towards killing. Especially in cases of individual war crimes, where the perpetrator uses violence in breach of rules and policy of the army, the spill-over effect of military training should not be neglected.

6.4.2. Influence of Authority System

Violence can also be facilitated by authorization and routinization. As Kelman explains, processes of authorization define the situation in a way that "standard moral principles do not apply and the individual is absolved of responsibility to make personal moral choices".[176] Moreover, processes of routinization organize actions in a way that minimize "opportunity for raising moral questions and making moral decisions".[177] As elaborated in previous sections of this chapter, these processes are normally applied to legitimate military performance. They

173 O'Sullivan, 2016, p. 110, see *supra* note 20.

174 Emphasis omitted. Doris and Murphy, 2007, p. 39, see *supra* note 28.

175 Bourke, 1999, p. 58, see *supra* note 31.

176 Kelman, 1973, p. 38, see *supra* note 61.

177 *Ibid.*

can be easily extended to excessive violence when the military hierarchy decides violence against civilians is "rational and instrumental".[178]

6.4.2.1. Direct Order to Commit War Crimes

Unlike individual war crimes which are committed against the military's wishes, organized war crimes are committed pursuant to rules and policy. While in a law-abiding institution, the individual breaches his duty by committing atrocity; in an armed force with a criminal policy, the individual performs his duty by committing atrocity. Systemic factors override individual agency in the perpetration of crimes. The organization and practice of military institution, which are normally used for lawful violence, also provides ideal infrastructure for unlawful violence. Nazi war criminals, for example, committed atrocities in "an all-encompassing institutional context", supported by their peers and superiors.[179] Mark Osiel highlights the acutely social nature of this type of war crimes: "Atrocity derives precisely from the nature of social organization, especially military organization, not from its collapse. It reflects the workings of such organization in strength, rather than in dissolution".[180]

The military creates its own norms according to which atrocities are approved or even required. Soldiers need to fulfil their social role as defined by the system, regardless of what that role entails. One Vietnam veteran who had followed orders to kill a civilian expressed the psychological effect of activating role commitment in authority situations: "I didn't feel right about it, but I thought I was doing my job when I did it".[181] Misinterpretation of the law also gives unlawful violence the appearance of legality. Doris and Murphy give the example that the United States' ('US') military instructed its personnel to fire white phosphorous at the enemy's equipment, not the enemy soldier, in an effort to circumvent moral and legal prohibitions. Such distortion of abstract rules distracts one from the fact that the enemy are nevertheless burnt to death as a result of the phosphorous attack. It creates sufficient ambiguity to allow an ordinary soldier to follow the order.[182]

---

[178] David Mendeloff, "The Coercive Effects of International Justice: How Perpetrators Respond to Threats of Prosecution", in Susanne C. Knittel and Zachary J. Goldberg (eds.), *The Routledge International Handbook of Perpetrator Studies*, Routledge, Abingdon, 2020, p. 145. For more on violence against civilians, see Hugo Slim, *Killing Civilians: Method, Madness and Morality in War*, Oxford University Press, 2010.

[179] John M. Doris, *Lack of Character: Personality and Moral Behavior*, Cambridge University Press, 2005, p. 56.

[180] Osiel, 1998, p. 1032, see *supra* note 40.

[181] Doris and Murphy, 2007, p. 44, see *supra* note 28.

[182] *Ibid.*, p. 42.

The authority system alienates the actor from his own act, hence from the responsibility of the act. People tend to see their actions as coming from the command of authorities, not their personal agency.[183] Social psychologists find that people can act in ways they normally disapprove if a perceived legitimate authority takes responsibility for their act.[184] Vetlesen claims that evil is often an unintended "by-product of obedience to authority".[185] When individuals feel they are not "the actual agent" of their actions, they feel less moral restraints.[186] People concern themselves only with how to implement the order, not what the order is about.[187] The military deliberately encourages their personnel to displace responsibility of their act onto their superior.[188] The subordinate acts behind his superior. Consequently, subordinates only feel responsible to their superior but not for their own actions. It is reported that many soldiers readily deny responsibility for their own acts, saying: "When I raised my right hand and took that oath, I freed myself of the consequences for what I do. I'll do what they tell me and nobody can blame me".[189] Under orders of the military authority, soldiers can carry out legitimate killing *and* mass atrocities such as the My Lai massacre, where a group of US soldiers killed several hundred unarmed Vietnamese civilians, including women and children.[190] Renouncing personal agency to superiors also minimizes emotional and moral conflicts caused by interpersonal violence, in particular unlawful violence against defenceless civilians. Some military instructors claim that instantaneous obedience to orders enables men to "sleep like a child and awaken refreshed – to kill and fear not".[191]

The sophisticated organizational network can further distance soldiers from consequences of their own act. The individual acts among his fellows: anonymity and division of labour within the group diffuse responsibility in the mind of the individual.[192] Milgram argues that "it is psychologically easier to ignore responsibility when one is only an intermediate link in a chain of evil action but is far from the final consequences of the action".[193] Specialization of

[183] Bandura, 1990, p. 34, see *supra* note 143.

[184] *Ibid.*

[185] Vetlesen, 2009, p. 5, see *supra* note 13.

[186] Bandura, 1990, p. 34, see *supra* note 143.

[187] Milgram, 1974, p. 8, see *supra* note 48.

[188] Talbert and Wolfendale, 2018, pp. 40–41, see *supra* note 23.

[189] Cited in Frésard, 2004, p. 52, see *supra* note 31.

[190] For more on obedience to authority and the My Lai massacre, see Kelman and Hamilton, 1989, *supra* note 2.

[191] Bourke, 1999, p. 214, see *supra* note 31.

[192] Bandura, 1990, p. 39, see *supra* note 143.

[193] Milgram, 1974, p. 11, see *supra* note 48.

tasks fragments the moral burden of killing. Complex operations require multiple people to perform tasks, some of which are seemingly harmless. In drone operations or missile strikes, for example, tasks of target selection, decision to fire and the release of the bomb are performed by different persons who are physically removed from the operational scene and from each other.[194]

The different steps and tasks need to come together with great precision and efficiency. They are part of the "routine, mechanical, highly programmed" operation.[195] Routinization reduces "the necessity of making decisions", thus minimizing opportunities for moral deliberation.[196] It further distracts the actor from the ultimate consequences of the overall operation by focusing him on "the details of his job rather than on its meaning".[197] The participants contribute their part in an "automatic, regularized fashion".[198] Through compartmentalization of work and routinization, technical aspects of the task are separated from their ultimate consequences.

6.4.2.2. Through Covert Policy, Tacit Approval and Condonement

The social influence of the military authority is not limited to instances of direct orders. The authority system may also facilitate war crimes through tacit approval and condonement. Some kind of authorization from legitimate authorities greatly enhances people's "readiness" to commit or condone certain acts, including acts of violence.[199] Even mere inaction towards certain behaviours sends the message that such behaviours are permitted. A permissive environment is gradually created. Through the authority's acquiescence, unlawful behaviours can be legitimized in the eyes of the subordinates. The line between explicit order and implicit approval may not be clearly drawn in many cases. They fall into a wide spectrum of institutional support. Together, they may have a concerted effect of legitimizing and normalizing unlawful violence. As will be discussed below, the case of the My Lai massacre shows that general condonement of atrocities can lead military personnel to interpret an ambiguous order into requiring atrocity.

Excesses of violence is sometimes allowed implicitly to channel emotional stress, incentivize combatants, achieve certain military goal, or simply maintain

---

[194] O'Sullivan, 2016, p. 152, see *supra* note 20.

[195] Kelman, 1973, p. 46, see *supra* note 61.

[196] *Ibid.*

[197] *Ibid.* Milgram also emphasizes "the tendency of the individual to become so absorbed in the narrow technical aspects of the task that he loses sight of its broader consequences", Milgram, 1974, p. 7, see *supra* note 48.

[198] Kelman, 1973, p. 47, see *supra* note 61.

[199] *Ibid.*, p. 39.

the level of aggression. For example, throughout history, wanton killing, brutality, rape, looting, *et cetera*, have been passively allowed as a kind of reward for the soldier's war efforts.[200] Troops understand from their superiors that their spontaneous atrocities towards enemy soldiers and civilians will be tolerated and not punished. Mark Osiel characterizes these instances as crimes of "connivance".[201] There is a certain meeting of mind between the military hierarchy and its members in carrying out atrocities.

Armed forces may permit aggressive operational practices which go beyond the law because of perceived military advantage. For example, certain counterinsurgency tactics induce, secretly encourage or condone war crimes in order to stop co-operation between the insurgents and a "sufficiently sympathetic public".[202] Insurgents, although fighting the guerrilla war out of despair and with scarce resources, still have certain tactical advantages such as familiarity with the local environment and population. Such tactical advantages can be crucial and persistent. In a counterinsurgency war, especially one that is failing, the military high command tends to adopt policies which "necessarily target the civilian population who hide and support the insurgents".[203] The military leadership may conclude that the only way to improve their own chances of survival is to terrorize the civilian population.[204] In order to show the civilian population that it is not "cost-free" to support the insurgency,[205] punitive measures and excessive violence are used: "accidental" bombings from the air, excessive "collateral damages" from drone strikes, house destruction programmes, "zero tolerance" force-protection measures which permit the use of deadly violence against those who come too close, *et cetera*.[206] These tactics are institutional reactions to growing frustrations towards the omnipresent enemy. They confirm that local civilian lives are not as important as one's own soldiers' lives, and that civilian deaths are inevitable and necessary. At the end of the day, local civilians are seen as part of the enemy even if they are not insurgent fighters.[207] Self-restraint against cruelty is suspended, not only towards insurgent fighters, but also towards civilians.

---

200 Osiel, 1998, p. 1038, see *supra* note 40.

201 *Ibid.*

202 Daniel Ellsberg, "Counterinsurgency Tactics Led to Haditha, My Lai", in *New Perspectives Quarterly*, 2006, vol. 23, no. 3, p. 49.

203 *Ibid.*

204 *Ibid.*

205 *Ibid.*

206 *Ibid.*

207 "'Simple Failures' and 'Disastrous Results'", in *The Washington Post*, 21 April 2007, Excerpts from Major General Eldon A. Bargewell's report.

An example is the practice of "night raids" or "kill or capture missions" in Afghanistan, where US forces raid homes of suspect insurgent fighters in the middle of the night. This is an important tactic of the US military in the counterinsurgency operations in Afghanistan. Due to over-broad criteria to determine targets, faulty intelligence and contingencies in carrying out the missions, night raids often result in significant civilian casualties, and many among the victims are women and children.[208] The US forces tend to interpret 'hostile acts' or 'hostile intent' out of benign acts of those who are in the house. This allows use of lethal force according to the rules of engagement.[209] For example, US forces interpret "hostile acts" out of actions of protecting one's homes, and "hostile intent" out of mere possession of a weapon, or the fact that one steps out of the house during the raid, or the fact that people try to escape from the attacking forces.[210] Not surprisingly, such practices lead to unnecessary and tragic civilian deaths.[211] There exists an institutional culture which is conducive to war crimes.

Similarly, in the Vietnam War, the very rules of engagement of the US military made atrocities "overwhelmingly probable".[212] Michael Walzer argues, in *Just and Unjust Wars*, that, in Vietnam, the US military abandoned the distinction between combatants and non-combatants; instead, they invented a new distinction "between loyal and disloyal, or friendly and hostile noncombatants".[213] The rules essentially allow soldiers to err on the side of killing suspected enemies even if they are most likely civilians. One of the most striking tactics is the designation of so-called "free-fire zones" where soldiers are ordered to "shoot first and ask questions later".[214] In addition, the practice of "body count" makes the number of total enemy fighters killed a key criterion for combat

[208] Badalič lists three criteria in target selection:

> The first criterion introduced by the U.S. military was that individuals were legitimate targets if they frequently communicated through mobile phones with combatants, the second criterion was based on the idea that individuals were legitimate targets if they provided food and shelter to combatants, while the third criterion presupposed that individuals were legitimate targets if they were suspected of possessing incidental information on the insurgency.

See Vasja Badalič, *The War Against Civilians: Victims of the "War on Terror" in Afghanistan and Pakistan*, Palgrave Macmillan, Cham, 2019, pp. 47–55.

[209] See *ibid.*, p. 57.

[210] *Ibid.*, pp. 57–62.

[211] *Ibid.*

[212] Christopher Hitchens, "The Hell of War: Why Haditha isn't My Lai", in *Slate*, 5 June 2006.

[213] Cited Frésard, 2004, p. 36, see *supra* note 31.

[214] Ellsberg, 2006, p. 49, see *supra* note 202; See Hitchens, 2006, *supra* note 212.

effectiveness.[215] It provides incentives to include innocent civilians killed in combat and to even deliberately kill civilians to increase the count. Throughout the chain of command, the pre-occupation is the number of bodies, not "which bodies to count".[216] The overall policy has certainly contributed to the perpetrators' interpretation of superior orders in the My Lai massacre. As Kelman explains: "It was not entirely bizarre for Calley to believe that what he was doing at My Lai was to increase his body count, as any good officer was expected to do".[217] According to an officer interviewed not long after the incident, My Lai embodies "a very good tactic": "if you scare people enough they will keep away from you".[218] My Lai is "neither a unique nor an isolated incident".[219] 'Tiger Force', an elite platoon operating more or less alone in Vietnam for a certain period, deliberately murdered scores of civilians. One former member invokes the enabling effect of the permissive social environment: "I knew it was wrong, but it was an acceptable practice". According to another member: "There was a period when just about everyone had a necklace of ears". No charges were filed against members of Tiger Force.[220] In fact, the record of court martials attests to the permissive attitude of the institution: between January 1965 and August 1973, excluding My Lai trials, only 36 court martials took place for war crimes committed by American troops.[221] It was the view of many military commanders that laws of war impose "unnecessary" and "unrealistic" restraints and undermine the success of military mission.[222] Senior military officers were reluctant to enforce regulations.[223] There was extensive "military complicity" in atrocities.[224]

In detention facilities, the military may allow their personnel to torture and abuse prisoners to obtain information. In Abu Ghraib, prison guards are encouraged by intelligence personnel to "facilitate interrogations". According to an investigative report, interrogators "actively" request the guards to "set physical and mental conditions for favorable interrogation of witnesses". For example,

[215] More details on the policy and practice of body count as a "corrupted measurement system", see Marlantes, 2012, pp. 115–129, *supra* note 19.

[216] Doris and Murphy, 2007, p. 44, see *supra* note 28.

[217] Kelman, 1973, p. 40, see *supra* note 61.

[218] Bourke, 1999, p. 176, see *supra* note 31.

[219] *Ibid.*, p. 166. See also, Doris and Murphy, 2007, *supra* note 28.

[220] Doris and Murphy, 2007, p. 44, see *supra* note 28. See also, M.D. Sallah and M. Weiss, "Buried Secrets, Brutal Truths", in *Toledo Blade*, 23 October 2003.

[221] Bourke, 1999, p. 196, see *supra* note 31.

[222] *Ibid.*, p. 175.

[223] *Ibid.*, p. 168.

[224] *Ibid.*

one guard receives the following instructions: "Loosen this guy up for us", "Make sure he has a bad night", and "Make sure he gets the treatment".[225] The military's failure to establish basic discipline among its soldiers and unambiguously oppose prisoner abuse provides social approval to atrocities.[226]

In other occasions, excessive violence and prisoner abuse are tolerated to cultivate aggression in the troops. It is believed that prisoner abuse is an "effective tactic" to improve subsequent combat performance. Military commanders recognize that aggression towards prisoners behind the lines encourage the "offensive spirit" and punishing offenders undermines subsequent use of violence in the battlefield. It is important not to jeopardize the emerging spirit of aggression.[227] A senior military lawyer says that "in practice no commander in his right mind is going to impair the efficiency of his combat unit by trying people who think they're doing the right thing. [...] It's a little like the Ten Commandments – they're there, but no one pays attention to them".[228] Excessively aggressive behaviour is often praised rather than condemned to achieve combat effectiveness.[229] In particular, atrocities tend to be tolerated in "heat of combat" situations: soldiers are in an aroused state, full of anger, fear or desire for revenge. Civilian casualties are usually rationalized as incidental to military self-defence or an "unfortunate tragedy inherent to war".[230] In 2005, in what is subsequently known as the 'Haditha Massacre', US forces methodically killed 24 Iraqi civilians after having been attacked by a roadside bomb in Haditha, Iraq. The squad leader told his men to "shoot first and ask questions later" after suffering the bombing attack. In 2008, the US forces fired indiscriminately at cars and bystanders in a road in Afghanistan, killing 19 people and injuring 50 others.[231] The shootings came after a suicide bomber attacked the unit. Self-defense was claimed in both cases. Those participating in the shootings were either not charged or punished leniently.[232] These are by no means isolated incidents committed by derailed individuals.[233] They are results of top-down condonement

225 Cited in Talbert and Wolfendale, 2018, pp. 10–11, see *supra* note 23.

226 Zimbardo, 2007, p. 386, see *supra* note 29; see also, Doris and Murphy, 2007, p. 48, *supra* note 28.

227 Bourke, 1999, p. 176, see *supra* note 31.

228 *Ibid.*, p. 195.

229 *Ibid.*, p. 195.

230 Office of the Inspector General, Department of the Army, *No Gun Ri Review*, Washington, D.C., January 2001, p. 10.

231 Charlie Savage and Elisabeth Bumiller, "An Iraqi Massacre, a Light Sentence and a Question of Military Justice", in *The New York Times*, 28 January 2012.

232 Hitchens, 2006, see *supra* note 212.

233 *Ibid.*

and bottom-up frustration and revenge-seeking. In these cases, the military hierarchy permits its soldiers to use maximum force where there is the slightest doubt, even when such suspicion of threat is created out of a need for revenge.

6.4.3. Impact of Group Solidarity

There is no doubt that group solidarity is a double-edged sword. The force that produces heroic acts and incredible self-sacrifice can also facilitate collective evil. Internal cohesion can strengthen inside-outside distinction and dehumanization of the enemy. Atrocities may follow. The soldier may participate in war crimes which he would never commit alone, simply to not disappoint his group. The individual is often under "very considerable pressure to conform" to the subculture of his immediate group.[234] When smaller military units such as that of special forces operate alone, they have relative independence from the main command structures.[235] Moral isolation and intense interdependency make conformity imperative in these sub-structures. It is observed that reluctant members of the group typically resolve emotional and moral conflicts in favour of group norms – they end up participating in atrocities.[236] The group may also develop narratives and story-telling which transform horrible atrocities into amusing campfire entertainment.[237] Group dynamics certainly influence its members' perception of atrocity. It takes "great strength of character" to stand up to group norms.[238] Moral and behavioural autonomy in face of enormous group pressure is exceptional.[239]

A Vietnam veteran painfully recalled his "uncontrollable, numbed" conformity to group norms.[240] Another veteran described gross practices, "ridiculous and senseless killing" by his group: the grotesque pranks played upon corpses, the rapes and wanton killings to achieve a higher "kill record". "And no conscience whatsoever", he said. Worse still, he found himself acting like his group.[241] Loyalty to the group also prevents individuals from denouncing atrocities of fellow soldiers. One can be fairly confident in the complicity of fellow servicemen. Love for comrades can condone any kind and number of

[234] Doris and Murphy, 2007, p. 43, see *supra* note 28.

[235] Bourke, 1999, p. 176, see *supra* note 31.

[236] Doris and Murphy, 2007, p. 32, see *supra* note 28.

[237] *Ibid.*

[238] Mackmin, 2007, p. 82, see *supra* note 90.

[239] See argument along this line in, for example, Zygmunt Bauman, *Modernity and the Holocaust*, Polity Press, Oxford, 2007.

[240] Bourke, 1999, p. 197, see *supra* note 31.

[241] *Ibid.*, p. 205.

atrocities.[242] Similarly, in the Abu Ghraib prison, anonymity within the group, pressure to conform and desire to please colleagues all contribute to participation in the abuse of Iraqi prisoners by a small group of American soldiers.[243]

6.4.4. Impact of Moral Disengagement

Selective moral disengagement promoted by the military is a kind of "social production of moral indifference".[244] While dehumanization of the enemy serves important military purposes, it may also spill over to civilians. Bandura argues that the process of dehumanization is essential to the perpetration of inhumanities.[245] To convince soldiers that the enemy has committed atrocities or injustice creates the feeling that the enemy do not deserve fair and humane treatment.[246] Senses of self-righteousness and moral superiority may also legitimate unnecessary violence against civilians. This is illustrated by the words of a US senator regarding the 'War on Terror': "Extremism in the defense of liberty is no vice […] moderation in the pursuit of justice is no virtue".[247]

Dehumanization enables killing of not only enemy combatants, but also enemy civilians. Racial and ideological propaganda cannot distinguish between combatants and civilians. It is as if the compassionate responses are "short-circuited".[248] It facilitates both individual and organized atrocities. The objectifying effect of such racial propaganda is illustrated by the practice of taking human body parts as "trophies or souvenirs" in the Second World War, the Vietnam War and Iraq war.[249] Dehumanization is practiced by the Japanese military in their massacre of Chinese civilians during Japan's invasion of China right before the Second World War. A Japanese general said, "we thought of them as things, not people like us".[250] The Japanese themselves were subject to race-based dehumanization in the Pacific War. During the Second World War, drill instructors reportedly told recruits: "You're not going to Europe, you're going to the Pacific. Don't hesitate to fight the Japs dirty".[251] Richard Holmes argues that in Vietnam,

---

[242] *Ibid.*, p. 131.

[243] Zimbardo, 2007, p. 402, see *supra* note 29.

[244] Cited in Frésard, 2004, p. 65, see *supra* note 31.

[245] Bandura, 1990, p. 38, see *supra* note 143.

[246] For example, the threat of weapons of mass destruction was used as the reason for initiating war against Iraq. The Iraqi regime was also said to have perpetrated injustices against its own population. See Mackmin, 2007, pp. 77–78, *supra* note 90.

[247] Quote of late United States Senator Barry Goldwater, cited in Zimbardo, 2007, p. 437, see *supra* note 29.

[248] Marlantes, 2012, p. 74, see *supra* note 19.

[249] O'Sullivan, 2016, p. 153, see *supra* note 20. Doris and Murphy, 2007, p. 40, see *supra* note 28.

[250] Zimbardo, 2007, p. 307, see *supra* note 29.

[251] Bourke, 1999, p. 193, see *supra* note 31.

"the road to My Lai was paved, first and foremost, by the dehumanization of the Vietnamese and the 'mere gook rule' which declared that killing a Vietnamese civilian did not really count".[252] In other words, the Vietnamese population becomes "totally expendable".[253] After the My Lai massacre, Calley is initially charged with the murder of "[o]riental human beings" rather than 'human beings'.[254] After another "horrific recital of rape and murder" in Vietnam, a solider said: "it wasn't like they were humans. We were conditioned to believe that this was for the good of the nation, the good of our country, and anything we did was okay".[255] A veteran explained the prevalence of the 'gook syndrome' in Vietnam: "I've seen men bat around people, hit them on the head with rifles, act like gods, do anything they want with human beings".[256] When the Chinese, Japanese and Vietnamese are classified as less than human, they become "fair game".[257] Kelman explains how "the process of dehumanization feeds on itself": "Those who participate in the massacre directly are reinforced in their perception of the victims as less than human by observing their very victimization".[258] Race-based dehumanization is still present in more recent conflicts.[259]

Dehumanization of the other, self-righteousness, combined with diminished moral restraints towards killing and hatred towards the enemy, can be a recipe for disaster. To balance between "depersonalisation and humanity"[260] is a virtually impossible task, not to mention that oftentimes depersonalization is actively promoted at the expense of humanity.

6.5. A Cosmopolitan War Crimes Law Mediated and Undermined by the Military Institution

This chapter focuses on the relationship between the military institution and ordinary soldiers as potential perpetrators of war crimes. The military structure is both enabling and constraining for its members: it unleashes the destructive force and suppresses the "creative or transformative power"[261] of the individual. The constraints can be ideological and relational.[262] This chapter explains social

[252] Cited in Grossman, 2009, p. 190, see *supra* note 109.

[253] Kelman, 1973, p. 50, see *supra* note 61.

[254] Bourke, 1999, p. 193, see *supra* note 31.

[255] *Ibid.*

[256] *Ibid.*, p. 220.

[257] *Ibid.*, p. 193.

[258] Kelman, 1973, p. 50, see *supra* note 61.

[259] O'Sullivan, 2016, p. 109, see *supra* note 20.

[260] *Ibid.*, p. 153.

[261] Hays, 1994, p. 65, see *supra* note 28.

[262] *Ibid.*, p. 66.

psychological mechanisms behind the strong influence and control imposed by the military over its members. Through authority and group dynamics, obedience and conformity, the individual is assimilated into the military structure. The immediate community is of enormous normative and practical importance to the ordinary soldier. It is the exclusive source of identity, meaning, values, standards of behaviour, security and comfort in a deliberately closed social environment.

The 'total institution' can support, oppose or ignore a cosmopolitan war crimes law through its rules, policy and practices. For the perpetrator, the cosmopolitan normative framework must be mediated and may be challenged by the immediate normative framework present at the time of the commission of war crimes. This complicates the relationship between the imagined cosmopolitan community and the individual perpetrator. The application of a cosmopolitan war crimes law is not linear and uniform, but mediated and varied. Although the law is guided by "normative individualism", its success depends on the structural efforts of the military institution. Military life diminishes individual capacity and will to think and act as an independent moral agent. This is in direct opposition to human agency, personal judgment and responsibility advocated by the cosmopolitan normative framework. There is permanent tension between the military's organizational practice and the individual-centred narrative of criminal law. A cosmopolitan approach to war crimes law exacerbates such tension. Such is the embodiment of the clashes of values of cosmopolitanism and war within the structure of war crimes law, as described in Chapter 4. A "moral distance"[263] to a cosmopolitan war crimes law is deliberately created and forcefully maintained by the military structure.

[263] Roger Cotterrell, *Law's Community: Legal Theory in Sociological Perspective*, Clarendon Press, Oxford, 1995, pp. 304–305.

7

Influence of Combat Environment on the Perpetrator

A cosmopolitan war crimes law has to be implemented in social structures and concrete social situations. The military structure is intimately linked to the environment of war. The "moral distance"[1] between cosmopolitanism and war has its concrete manifestation in both the organization of the military operation and in the environment of war. This chapter situates the impact of military training and indoctrination in conditions of war. I examine factors which are temporally more "proximate"[2] to war crimes. All wars are different. Conditions of combat described below may correspond to some wars more than others. While both structural influence of the military institution and immediate circumstances induce war crimes, the former contribute more to organized war crimes, and the latter typically feature in individual war crimes.

7.1. The Combat Environment

"War teaches violence."[3] In military training, aggression-inducing techniques such as desensitization and brutalization, as effective as they are, do not entail actual killing or threat to be killed. Military training is consummated in combat, where life and death are real. The smallest mistake can have serious consequences: "Combat magnifies small acts terribly".[4] Combat violence is inherently "irrational".[5] Mechanical killing and often accidental death make war "unsportsmanlike".[6] There is hardly any logic, meaning or sense in most war casualties. Perpetual exhaustion, intense emotions, cognitive impairment and moral disorientation are common symptoms of war. Statistics show that a significant

1 Roger Cotterrell, *Law's Community: Legal Theory in Sociological Perspective*, Clarendon Press, Oxford, 1995, pp. 304–305.

2 John M. Doris and Dominic Murphy, "From My Lai to Abu Ghraib: The Moral Psychology of Atrocity", in *Midwest Studies in Philosophy*, 2007, vol. 31, no. 1, p. 39.

3 Carmel O'Sullivan, *Killing on Command: The Defence of Superior Orders in Modern Combat*, Palgrave Macmillan, London, 2016, p. 146.

4 Karl Marlantes, *What It Is Like to Go to War*, Corvus, London, 2012, p. 157.

5 Joanna Bourke, *An Intimate History of Killing: Face-to-Face Killing in Twentieth-Century Warfare*, Basic Books, 1999, p. 228. Gerry Simpson also points out that death in war is often experienced as "arbitrary" and "without purpose", see Gerry Simpson, *Law, War and Crime*, Polity Press, Cambridge, 2007, p. 179.

6 *Ibid.*, p. 223.

number of soldiers suffered from mental breakdown in the twentieth century battlefield – they became "psychiatric casualties".[7] In many conflicts, the number of soldiers discharged for mental collapse is much higher than the number of those killed in combat.[8]

This section examines a number of situational factors affecting the cognitive and behavioural capacities of soldiers in war.

7.1.1. Overload of Senses, Fear and Stress

Combatants' cognitive competence is corrupted by radical conditions in the battlefield. The combat experience is visceral. With loud noise in live battle – aircraft, armoured vehicles, weapons, *et cetera* – soldiers can literally not "hear themselves think".[9] Grossman describes "a sea of horrors" that "assails" a soldier's senses. The soldier can:

> *Hear* the pitiful screams of the wounded and dying. *Smell* the butcherhouse smells of feces, blood, burned flesh, and rotting decay, which combine into the awful stench of death. *Feel* the shudder of the ground as the very earth groans at the abuse of artillery and explosives, and *feel* the last shiver of life and the flow of warm blood as friends die in your arms. *Taste* the salt of blood and tears as you hold a dear friend in mutual grieving, [...].[10]

When senses are overloaded, rational thinking atrophies. One experiences "furious thinking", with "blood in the throat" and chaos in the background.[11] In this world of "uncertainty and agony",[12] it is usually impossible for an ordinary soldier to know fully about what is happening. Threats can come from anywhere.

The duty to kill and fear of being killed have profound psychological repercussions.[13] The terror of war evokes a primitive fear, deep-wired concern for

---

[7] *Ibid.*, p. 234.

[8] *Ibid.* According to Bourke:

> Levels of collapse varied dramatically by conflict, theatre of war, and unit. […] 25 per cent of all discharges during the 1914-18 war and between 20 and 50 per cent during the 1939-45 war were labelled 'psychiatric casualties'. Men fighting in Korea were twice as likely to become psychiatric casualties as to be killed by enemy fire, since over 25 per cent of combatants were diagnosed as being 'severe' psychiatric casualties while only 12 per cent of combatants were killed.

[9] Doris and Murphy, 2007, p. 36, see *supra* note 2.

[10] Dave Grossman and Loren W. Christensen, *On Combat: The Psychology and Physiology of Deadly Conflict in War and in Peace*, Human Factor Research Group, 2004, p. 73.

[11] Marlantes, 2012, p. 160, see *supra* note 4.

[12] Jean-Jacques Frésard, *The Roots of Behaviour in War: A Survey of the Literature*, International Committee of the Red Cross, Geneva, 2004, p. 23.

[13] O'Sullivan, 2016, p. 41, see *supra* note 3.

one's own life, and more often than not, helplessness. Overwhelming fear can cause combatants to "lose control of their bladder and bowels, shake, freeze, cry, or curl into a fetal position".[14] A terrified solider may not be able to act upon his judgment, if there is any judgment left at all.[15] The highly stimulative environment causes intense and continuous stress in those participating in the firefight. A reasonable amount of stress can facilitate mental and physical performance. However, too much stress for too long can be mentally and physically detrimental. Laboratory experiments show that the relationship between performance and stress follows an inverted U-shaped curve.[16] Excessive stress can impair a person's "cognition, impulse control, emotional regulation, decision making, empathy, and prosociality".[17] Acute stress activates the sympathetic nervous system, which affects the soldier's heart rate, motor performance, "sensory and perceptual awareness", and "attention, memory and cognitive function".[18] This can result in "changes in mental processes, moods, attitudes and motivation" and "a loss of working efficiently".[19]

Overload of senses, fear and stress typical of combat experience can significantly undermine a person's abilities to think, to act and to feel. Military training, as illustrated in Chapter 6, can help soldiers cope with radical conditions of live combat, but only to a certain extent.[20] After all, no training can transform humans into superhumans who are invulnerable to extreme environments.

7.1.2. Extreme Physical Discomfort

Non-violent elements in the operational environment also affect a participant's physical and mental functions. Lack of sleep is often reported. Combatants sometimes have to sleep in open fields, lie on cold and wet ground and wake up whenever needed.[21] Deleterious effects of sleep deprivation include "irritability, inattention, inability to concentrate, and excessive physiological responses to

14 Doris and Murphy, 2007, p. 35, see *supra* note 2.

15 Bourke, 1999, p. 229, see *supra* note 5.

16 Ole R. Holsti, "Crisis Decision Making", in Philip E. Tetlock, *et al.* (eds.), *Behavior, Society, and Nuclear War*, Volume 1, Oxford University Press, 1989, pp. 8–84.

17 Robert Sapolsky, *Behave: The Biology of Humans at Our Best and Worst*, Penguin Press, New York, 2017, p. 134.

18 O'Sullivan, 2016, p. 203, see *supra* note 3.

19 Cited in *ibid.*, p. 130.

20 O'Sullivan, 2016, p. 194, see *supra* note 3.

21 Doris and Murphy, 2007, p. 37, see *supra* note 2.

stress".[22] A defendant on trial for his unit's killing of prisoners of war claimed to have not slept for nine days in a row during the fight.[23]

Extreme weather and unhygienic environment evoke strong emotional reactions. A soldier wrote in his family letter that rain, mud, insects, rats and "very tedious work" frustrate him – life at the front is "a proper hell".[24] Another soldier reported that with rotting human flesh, human excrement, and discarded army rations in the immediate environment, everyone kept inhaling "hot, humid air heavy with countless repulsive odors" at every breath.[25] A veteran recalled that "we cried all the time, not from fear but because we were so dirty".[26] Harsh conditions are present not only next to the battlefield, but also in behind-the-line facilities. In the Abu Ghraib torture scandal, the prison had no adequate infrastructure to sustain proper hygiene. Lack of a sewage system produces a persistent and horrible stench in a closed and crowded environment. Extremely high temperature in Iraq during summer time makes everything worse. A former staff there described the detention environment as "hell on earth".[27] Such prolonged harsh conditions can cause obnoxious emotions which in turn contribute to antisocial behaviour.[28]

7.1.3. Omnipresent Threat

Omnipresent threat, which is typical in counterinsurgency missions, challenges combatants' normative competence. In asymmetrical conflicts, there are "no clear demarcations of war zones, enemies or ground gained".[29] It is "a people's war".[30] The insurgent fighters are mobile and flexible in their manoeuvre. They simply disappear into the environment and blend with the civilian population. This gives them operational advantages such as surprise attack and civilian shelter. The invisibility of the enemy and unpredictability of attacks make every location a potential battlefield. A participant in the Iraq war said that "everybody that's out there at the moment who […] steps foot on that dusty country is fair

[22] *Ibid.*, cited in American Psychiatric Association, *Diagnostic and Statistical Manual of Mental Disorders*, 4th ed., 2000, pp. 599–602.

[23] *Ibid.*

[24] Bourke, 1999, p. 231, see *supra* note 5.

[25] Cited in Doris and Murphy, 2007, p. 36, see *supra* note 2.

[26] *Ibid.*

[27] Philip Zimbardo, *The Lucifer Effect: Understanding How Good People Turn Evil*, Random House Trade Paperbacks, London, 2007, pp. 334–335.

[28] Doris and Murphy, 2007, p. 36, see *supra* note 2.

[29] O'Sullivan, 2016, p. 145, see *supra* note 3.

[30] Bourke, 1999, p. 192, see *supra* note 5.

target [...] there is nowhere safe".[31] Perpetual threat requires perpetual vigilance and preparedness, which is unsustainable for mere mortals. The impossible task of watching out for constant danger can in itself create high levels of fear, stress and anxiety.[32] The psychological burden is exacerbated by the foreign environment and lack of resources and personnel.[33] Military experts and historians had rightly warned in the context of the Iraq war, for example, that it would become increasingly difficult for the American troops to maintain military discipline when they were fighting against an elusive enemy under the intense pressures of war.[34]

Blending of insurgent fighters and civilians also prompts perceptions which justify killing civilians. Overreaction is expected. When a soldier knows through personal and collective experiences that apparent civilians can suddenly open fire or use daily devices such as mobile phones to detonate bombs, he may think shooting at civilians is reasonable and necessary even when it is not.[35] With distorted normative judgment and anger from losses suffered, a soldier may retaliate indiscriminately when he is unable to retaliate against the lawful target.[36] These are "atrocity-producing" situations, said one commentator.[37]

In what is known as the Kandahar massacre, US soldier Robert Bales killed 16 civilians and wounded six others in their homes in the early morning of 11 March 2012, in the Panjwai District of Kandahar Province, Afghanistan.[38] The operational environment played an important role in this seemingly senseless killing. The Panjwai District of Kandahar, the birthplace of the Taliban, was, at the time, "one of the most hostile places on the planet".[39] It was the scene of heavy fighting.[40] Taliban fighters were omnipresent, blended perfectly with the local population. Shortly before the massacre, Bales had personally experienced ambushes and had been pre-occupied with his own failure to protect a fellow

[31] Ross McGarry and Sandra Walklate, "The Soldier as Victim: Peering Through the Looking Glass", in *British Journal of Criminology*, 2011, vol. 51, no. 6, p. 905.

[32] O'Sullivan, 2016, p. 127, see *supra* note 3.

[33] *Ibid.*, p. 130.

[34] Anna Badkhen, "Atrocities are a Fact of All Wars, Even Ours", *SFGATE*, 13 August 2006.

[35] O'Sullivan, 2016, p. 128, see *supra* note 3.

[36] *Ibid.*, p. 145.

[37] Daniel Ellsberg, "Counterinsurgency Tactics Led to Haditha, My Lai", in *New Perspectives Quarterly*, 2006, vol. 23, no. 3, p. 49.

[38] Jack Healy, "Soldier Gets Life Without Parole in Deaths of Afghan Civilians", *The New York Times*, 23 August 2013.

[39] Brendan Vaughan, "Robert Bales Speaks: Confessions of America's Most Notorious War Criminal", *GQ*, 21 October 2015.

[40] Taimoor Shah and Graham Bowley, "G.I. Kills Afghan Villagers; Children Among 16 Dead", *The New York Times*, 12 March 2012.

solider in an incident involving an improvised explosive device (IED).[41] Bales attacked innocent civilians in two villages thinking there were insurgent activities.[42] Anger, frustration and hypervigilance in fighting an invisible enemy may have well facilitated the eventual atrocity.

7.1.4. Prolonged Deployment and Exhaustion

Another factor is prolonged deployment. Continuous combat deployment can create severe exhaustion which can cause mental disorders.[43] Combatants may experience "extreme fear, insecurity, and vulnerability" not only during the combat but throughout the entire deployment period.[44] A "[m]alevolent environment" undermines combatants' ability to see meaning in what they are doing and to feel that they have control over their experiences in war. Senses of meaninglessness and lack of control in turn become stressors in themselves.[45] Human capacities are simply unsustainable in the ecology of the battlefield. It is easy to maintain discipline for a short time, the challenge comes with protracted and repeated missions.[46] It is observed that the process of moral atrophy starts the moment the combatant is deployed.[47] Studies show that long-term deployment has adverse effects on physical and psychological well-being. With increased length of deployment, military personnel are more likely to take part in harmful, indulgent behaviours such as excessive alcohol consumption.[48] Longer deployment also increases stress from the "home front", such as concern for close ones and difficulty in maintaining family relationships.[49] The risk of depression increases with the length of deployment.[50] People who are deployed repeatedly over many years tend to see their time in combat as "endless and repetitive".[51]

---

41 Vaughan, 2015, see *supra* note 39.

42 *Ibid.*

43 Dave Grossman, *On Killing: The Psychological Cost of Learning to Kill in War and Society*, Back Bay, New York, 2009, p. 68.

44 Matthew Talbert and Jessica Wolfendale, *War Crimes, Causes, Excuses, and Blame*, Oxford University Press, 2018, pp. 34–35.

45 *Ibid.*

46 Badkhen, 2006, see *supra* note 34.

47 Robert H. Scales, "Consumed by Wars Without End", *The Salt Lake Tribune*, 14 March 2012.

48 Joshua E.J. Buckman *et al.*, "The Impact of Deployment Length on the Health and Well-Being of Military Personnel: A Systematic Review of the Literature", in *Occupational and Environmental Medicine*, 2011, vol. 68, no. 1, p. 73.

49 *Ibid.*

50 One study finds that "for mid-ranked, married, male soldiers, at 4 months into deployment there would be a 14.8% risk of their developing depression, at 6.5 months this risk would increase to 17.9%, and at 9 months this risk would be 21.6%". Cited in *ibid.*, p. 74.

51 *Ibid.*

They are emotionally drained. This is illustrated by atrocities committed by US soldiers in the continued occupation of Iraq, which sociologist Raymond Scurfield says are entirely predictable – the longer the military force stays in the country, the higher the risk of new crimes against civilians.[52] A participant in Iraq war reported that he is constantly tired because of the continuous pressure from the operation. "You can't maintain that level of intensity for that long", he says.[53] Individuals and units become "battle fatigued, stressed or numbed", and act "abnormally".[54] The mind and body of soldiers keep score of the hardship. The barometer is bound to reach the explosive point when it stays long enough in the pressure cooker.

The perpetrator of the Kandahar massacre, Robert Bales, had done four combat tours in nine years. Five years before the killing of civilians, in a post-combat media interview in Iraq, Bales was the military's exemplary figure. He professed moral and professional values which sounded quite honourable: "I've never been more proud to be a part of this unit than that day, for the simple fact that we discriminated between the bad guys and the non-combatants, and then afterward we ended up helping the people that three or four hours before were trying to kill us".[55] A proud soldier projecting moral superiority is only a few deployments away from a desperate killer shooting innocent civilians. Bales did not recover from his psychological trauma before the next deployment – if he should be re-deployed at all.[56] A military commentator argued that "overuse of infantry personnel […] for close combat" was the main cause of the Kandahar massacre.[57]

Military psychiatrists confirm that battle fatigue is not caused by individual weakness, but is a "normal and natural consequence of extended combat".[58] In other words, it can happen to anyone who has been in a hostile environment for long enough. Unsustainable deployment of personnel simply exacerbates already severe battlefield hardship.

---

[52] Badkhen, 2006, see *supra* note 34.

[53] McGarry and Walklate, 2011, p. 907, see *supra* note 31.

[54] Sara Mackmin, "Why do Professional Soldiers Commit Acts of Personal Violence that Contravene the Law of Armed Conflict?", in *Defence Studies*, 2007, vol. 7, no. 1, p. 74.

[55] Vaughan, 2015, see *supra* note 39.

[56] Craig Whitlock and Carol D. Leonnig, "Seeking Clues in Afghan Killings", *The Washington Post*, 13 March 2012; Peter Finn and Carol D. Leonnig, "Afghan Shootings Refocus Attention at Fort Lewis-McChord Base", *The Washington Post*, 14 March 2012; William Yardley *et al.*, "Home Base of Accused Soldier Has Faced Scrutiny", *The New York Times*, 14 March 2012.

[57] Scales, 2012, see *supra* note 47.

[58] Mackmin, 2007, p. 74, see *supra* note 54.

7.1.5. Emotional Arousal and Pleasure-Seeking in the Use of Violence

The use of violence also has inherent risks. In peace-time situations, an ordinary person rarely has difficulty in controlling his or her aggressive impulse. To be an effective soldier, one has to "break free of the normal civilised constraints".[59] Military training enables soldiers to overcome their reluctance to use violence and to kill. Combat environment may further enhance aggression in trained soldiers. Emotional and physical arousal caused by using violence impairs one's rational cognitive abilities.[60] Numerous first-hand accounts attest to this uncontrollable aggression: one "lost his head completely", his "blood was up", or "all primitive instincts were on top".[61] A soldier recalled that, in the midst of combat, he:

> '[saw] red'. The primitive 'bloody-lust', kept under all his life by the laws and principles of peaceful society, surged through his being, transforming him, maddening him with the desire to kill, kill, kill![62]

The soldier is said to have been "taken over" during intense violence and has to return to his normal self afterwards.[63] A First World War colonel even said that atrocities are to be expected: "you can't stimulate and let loose the animal in man and then expect to be able to cage it up again at a moment's notice".[64] Taking no quarter in the middle or at the end of an intense fight is often recorded. Grossman explains the psychological vulnerability of the no-quarter prohibition as follows:

> In order to fight at close range one must deny the humanity of one's enemy. Surrender requires the opposite – that one recognize and take pity on the humanity of the enemy. A surrender in the heat of battle requires a complete, and very difficult, emotional turnaround by both parties.[65]

For example, soldiers who participated in the Second World War and the Falklands recount many incidents where enemy combatants are killed as they try to surrender during the fight.[66] A Second World War infantry officer recalled that a soldier shot a surrendering German combatant after fighting had ceased

---

59 Quote of David Cooper, a padre in the Falklands war, cited in *ibid.*, p. 75.

60 *Ibid.*

61 Bourke, 1999, p. 219, see *supra* note 5.

62 *Ibid.*

63 *Ibid.*

64 *Ibid.*, p. 175.

65 Grossman, 2009, p. 199, see *supra* note 43.

66 Mackmin, 2007, p. 76, see *supra* note 54.

because the soldier was probably "half off his head" and thus could only continue the killing.[67] Another soldier acknowledged that he could not "change his feelings again during the last rush with a veil of blood before his eyes". This former participant in war said that he did "not want to take prisoners but to kill".[68] Yet another soldier, who bayonetted a prisoner, confessed that he could not help it and was overcome by feelings.[69] The list goes on. Mackmin concludes that the period immediately after the fight carries great risk for war crimes because the combatants' emotional arousal has not rescinded, but lawful targets are no longer there.[70] Aggression cannot be turned on and off instantaneously like an engine.[71]

Combat may even become a "strong motivation and source of pleasure" in its own right.[72] This is another paradox created by war: killing in battle can "invoke a wave of nauseous distress", it can also "incite intense feelings of pleasure".[73] Despite the initial reluctance, many soldiers confess that they have come to enjoy killing.[74] One soldier admitted that "the thrill of destruction was irresistible" and that "war was a turn on".[75] Another wrote that during the war, he sometimes "swelled with pride at the immense destruction" he was capable of and felt "a deep savage joy" which was more than simple "ego enhancement".[76] One may be experiencing some sort of "transcendence through violence".[77] Inflicting death and destruction can somehow create a feeling that one is transformed into something larger than oneself.[78] The thrill and exhilaration generated by violence can become addictive and motivate excessive violence.[79] War crimes may become an enthusiastic group activity. A veteran recalled that his unit slaughtered a group of surrendering enemy combatants with much

[67] *Ibid.*

[68] *Ibid.*, p. 75.

[69] Bourke, 1999, p. 219, see *supra* note 5.

[70] Mackmin, 2007, p. 76, see *supra* note 54.

[71] A Second World War infantry officer said that "if you start a man killing, you can't turn him off again like an engine", cited in *ibid.*

[72] *Ibid.*, p. 79.

[73] Bourke, 1999, p. 1, see *supra* note 5.

[74] Mackmin, 2007, p. 79, see *supra* note 54.

[75] *Ibid.*

[76] Marlantes, 2012, pp. 63–64, see *supra* note 4.

[77] *Ibid.*

[78] *Ibid.*, p. 233.

[79] Mackmin, 2007, p. 79, see *supra* note 54.

"[l]aughing and howling, hoo-ha-ing and cowboy and good-old-boy yelling".[80] Participants in war can find themselves seeking pleasure in the utmost human tragedy.

7.1.6. Revenge and Hatred for the Enemy

Hatred for the enemy and desire for revenge are powerful motivations for killing and excessive violence. Hatred is "an enduring organization of aggressive impulses toward a person or class of persons […] composed of habitual bitter feeling and accusatory thought".[81] Doris argues that repeatedly seeing death and injury of fellow soldiers "adversely affects the moral functioning" of combatants.[82] Hatred for the enemy can even suppress the instinctive fear of death – it is like "a steel helmet for the mind".[83] Many people only become motivated to kill after seeing their comrades killed by the enemy. Losing a comrade and close friend can create "overwhelming emotions such as hostility and rage".[84] It gives soldiers a "big score to settle" and makes them "snap into action".[85] Author and journalist Philip Caputo said that he was "burnt with hatred" for the enemy and that he did not resent the enemy for their politics, but for killing his comrades. This caused him to seek "a chance to kill somebody".[86] A commentator claimed that the burst of rage and desire for revenge can have the same effect as intoxication with alcohol or drugs.[87]

The "justice of vengeance" was frequently invoked in the Vietnam War to rationalize both lawful and unlawful killing. A sniper said:

> It's not too pleasant to have a fellow human in one's sights, with such clarity as to be almost able to see the colour of his eyes, and to have the knowledge that in a matter of seconds, another life has met an untimely end. However, one had to be callous, after all it was, an eye for an eye, a tooth for a tooth.[88]

Hatred and revenge are ways to seek meaning in deaths and sufferings in war. They render the seemingly "senseless and wholesale slaughter" of

[80] Cited in Doris and Murphy, 2007, p. 32, see *supra* note 2.

[81] Bourke, 1999, p. 140, see *supra* note 5.

[82] Doris and Murphy, 2007, p. 38, see *supra* note 2.

[83] Bourke, 1999, p. 139, see *supra* note 5.

[84] Talbert and Wolfendale, 2018, pp. 34–35, see *supra* note 44.

[85] Bourke, 1999, p. 215, see *supra* note 5.

[86] *Ibid.*, p. 144.

[87] Peter Rowe, "Military Misconduct during International Armed Operations: Bad Apples or Systemic Failure", in *Journal of Conflict & Security Law*, 2008, vol. 13, no. 2, p. 181.

[88] Bourke, 1999, p. 216, see *supra* note 5.

comrades significant or heroic.[89] Grief is converted into rage. Revenge easily spills over to unlawful targets – surrendering enemy combatants, civilians, prisoners of war, *et cetera*. If one is not able to engage legitimate targets in the desired manner, one seeks "to create an enemy out of defenceless peasants".[90] The "justice of revenge" can rationalize any atrocity. In the three months prior to the My Lai massacre, the perpetrator unit had lost one quarter of their personnel to enemy attacks – sniper fire, mines and booby traps.[91] The high death toll incited a vengeful attitude which eventually contributed to the atrocity. A former platoon leader during the Vietnam War acknowledged that he planned and participated in "a no-quarter fight", fuelled with desire for revenge for a lost comrade.[92] Similar motivations were present at the Haditha massacre where a group of US soldiers killed 24 Iraqi civilians nearby after having been attacked by a roadside bomb in Haditha, Iraq in 2005.[93] Other than civilians, prisoners tend to serve as "a captive audience" on whom soldiers can take out their negative and intense emotions.[94] A priest recalled that their soldiers, out of frustration and anger, routinely killed prisoners after suffering booby trap casualties: "It seemed like there was nobody else to take it out on, so they just killed people". The priest himself was tempted to lash out at prisoners after seeing the senseless death and suffering caused by booby traps.[95]

7.2. Combat Environment Conducive to Antisocial Behaviour

Elements of combat environment introduced above have a significant impact on a person's inclinations and behaviours. Alone or accumulatively, these factors can prompt antisocial behaviours, in particular, aggression. This section explains in greater detail the connection between negative external environments and emotional and behavioural changes.

7.2.1. Insubstantial Situational Elements and Serious Moral Failures

The environment shapes our behaviour in a short time without us knowing it.[96] Immediately before our decision to act, our brain registers a lot of information from the environment which affects the probability of pro- or antisocial

[89] *Ibid.*, p. 215.

[90] *Ibid.*

[91] *Ibid.*, p. 192.

[92] Marlantes, 2012, pp. 99–106, see *supra* note 4.

[93] Charlie Savage and Elisabeth Bumiller, "An Iraqi Massacre, a Light Sentence and a Question of Military Justice", *The New York Times*, 28 January 2012.

[94] Mackmin, 2007, p. 80, see *supra* note 54.

[95] Bourke, 1999, p. 192, see *supra* note 5.

[96] Sapolsky, 2017, p. 98, see *supra* note 17.

behaviour.[97] When we make decisions, even those of great consequences, we tend to be "less rational and autonomous" than we think.[98] Indeed, psychological research consistently shows that normative cognition and behaviour are "extremely sensitive" to situational changes.[99] For example, the environment affects one's mood, often in an imperceptible way, and the mood change in turn affects behaviour. Emotion is proven to have a powerful impact on a wide range of human functioning, including risk-taking, memory, co-operative behaviour and problem-solving.[100] Research on helping behaviour shows that a favourable environment enhances the likelihood of helping while an unfavourable environment inhibits helping behaviour. For example, antecedent good fortune, as small as finding a dime, and pleasant smells have been found to facilitate helping behaviour and co-operation.[101] On the contrary, time pressure (caused by being in a hurry) and loud noises prevent a lot of people from helping a stranger in distress.[102] Importantly, very modest environmental variation can lead to significant moral failures. The situational input is alarmingly disproportionate to the behavioural output.[103] As Doris explains, many dangerous features of the situation are so subtle that they are very difficult, if not impossible, to discern. Our normative competence, that is, our cognitive and motivational structures, are much more "subversive" than we know.[104] Many mental activities occur within

---

97 *Ibid.*

98 *Ibid.*

99 For reviews of this experimental tradition, see Doris and Murphy, 2007, p. 33, *supra* note 2. See also, John M. Doris, *Lack of Character: Personality and Moral Behavior*, Cambridge University Press, 2005; Lee Ross and Richard E. Nisbett, *The Person and the Situation: Perspectives of Social Psychology*, Temple University Press, London, 1991.

100 Doris, 2005, p. 30, see *supra* note 99.

101 See Alice M. Isen and Paula F. Levin, "Effect of Feeling Good on Helping: Cookies and Kindness", in *Journal of Personality and Social Psychology*, 1972, vol. 21, no. 3, pp. 384 ff.; Robert A. Baron, "The Sweet Smell of… Helping: Effects of Pleasant Ambient Fragrance on Prosocial Behavior in Shopping Malls", in *Personality and Social Psychology Bulletin*, 1997, vol. 23, no. 5, pp. 498 ff.; Robert. A. Baron and Marna. I. Bronfen, "A Whiff of Reality: Empirical Evidence Concerning the Effects of Pleasant Fragrances on Work-Related Behavior", in *Journal of Applied Social Psychology*, 1994, vol. 24, no. 13, pp. 1179 ff., cited in Doris and Murphy, 2007, pp. 34, 37, see *supra* note 2.

102 See John M. Darley and Daniel C. Batson, "'From Jerusalem to Jericho': A Study of Situational and Dispositional Variables In Helping Behavior", in *Journal of Personality and Social Psychology*, 1973, vol. 27, no. 1, pp. 100 ff.; and Kenneth E. Mathews and Lance K. Cannon, "Environmental Noise Level as a Determinant of Helping Behavior", in *Journal of Personality and Social Psychology*, 1975, vol. 32, no. 4, pp. 571 ff., cited in Doris and Murphy, 2007, p. 34, see *supra* note 2.

103 Doris and Murphy, 2007, p. 34, see *supra* note 2.

104 Doris, 2005, pp. 148, 153, see *supra* note 99.

us without our will or even awareness. The environment may simply make some people fail to perceive the situation as requiring normative judgment.[105]

Compared with the insubstantial situational factors in psychological experiments, the adversity in war is extreme and lasting. We can reasonably expect that conditions of war are conducive to impaired normative competence and moral failures.[106] In combat, soldiers are exposed to persisting loud noises, disturbing sights and smells, frequent death and sufferings, and experience acute stress, anxiety, aggressive urges, and perhaps pleasure in killing. They can endure "extreme fatigue" caused by combat missions and exacerbated by prolonged deployment.[107] These factors can significantly affect soldiers' perception of and propensity towards appropriate use of force. They can cause combatants to lose their "moral compass" and commit crimes.[108] "War rage", a "battlefield frenzy" and determined revenge-seeking reflect the human experience of war: "anger and fury towards being attacked by the enemy", "bitterness over their own casualties and their frustration at the tenacity of the enemy".[109] War creates not just physical and emotional hot zones, but also "ethical hot zones".[110] Despite their training, soldiers are more likely to behave irrationally or unethically than an ordinary civilian in peace-time.[111]

7.2.2. Aggression as a Coping Mechanism

Human beings automatically seek to restore the inner equilibrium of emotions when their natural balance is disrupted by radical changes. To cope with external changes, one can "act on, abstain from or withdraw" from the environment.[112] Aggression is a common coping mechanism to restore certain inner equilibrium of emotions.[113] The so-called "stress-induced displacement aggression" is familiar to us in daily life. It is illustrated by the correlation between domestic violence and stressful occasions such as economic downturns or watching a football game.[114] According to military psychologist Ben Shalit, in combat, stressful emotions such as anger and frustration, or harsh environments such as threat and

---

105 Doris and Murphy, 2007, p. 36, see *supra* note 2.

106 *Ibid.*, p. 34.

107 O'Sullivan, 2016, p. 130, see *supra* note 3.

108 Zimbardo, 2007, p. 417, see *supra* note 27.

109 O'Sullivan, 2016, p. 130, see *supra* note 3.

110 Doris, 2005, p. 149, see *supra* note 99.

111 O'Sullivan, 2016, p. 130, see *supra* note 3.

112 Mackmin, 2007, p. 71, see *supra* note 54.

113 *Ibid.*

114 Sapolsky, 2017, pp. 131–132, see *supra* note 17.

danger, can heighten the propensity for aggression.[115] When intense emotions and harsh external environments induce powerful displacement aggression, it can be directed towards both lawful and unlawful targets. Crimes against civilians is, according to one military expert, "a classic combat stress symptom".[116] In some cases, the aggressive reaction is delayed until conditions are more favourable, as this was not possible when the stress occurred.[117] Such delayed coping behaviour separates the reaction and the source of reaction, which can make violence seem unprovoked or senseless.[118]

Certainly, obnoxious emotions do not always cause aggression in all people. Usually, a person with a normal predisposition to violence can control aggressive instincts using normal coping and inhibiting mechanisms. But when the person's emotional excitement reaches a certain threshold (the level varies individually), he becomes pre-occupied with doing something to alleviate the intense feeling of annoyance.[119] The person simply has no mental flexibility to seek an alternative, less harmful outlet when obnoxious emotions are overwhelming.

7.3. Distortion of Norms: Intrinsic Criminality and Pathology of War

> In all wars, at all times, in every country, wars transform ordinary, even good men into killers.[120]

7.3.1. Inversion of Civilian Norms

As we have seen, combat environment undermines normative competence through extreme physical and psychological strains. This section shows that war-time norms can in themselves cause moral disorientation in soldiers. On the normative level, the intrinsic link between war and crimes lies in the reversal of the peace-time prohibition against killing and destruction. War is essentially consisted of large-scale and organized crimes – if judged by peace-time norms. Some authors consider whether war channels aggression and violence within the population to a legitimate external target.[121] The right to kill is, according to an instructor of the International Committee of the Red Cross, "the first principle

---

[115] Ben Shalit, *The Psychology of Conflict and Combat*, Praeger, New York, 1988, p. 43, cited in Mackmin, 2007, p. 71, see *supra* note 54.

[116] Quote of John Pike, Director of GlobalSecurity.org, a Washington-based military think tank, cited in Badkhen, 2006, see *supra* note 34.

[117] Mackmin, 2007, p. 72, see *supra* note 54.

[118] *Ibid.*

[119] *Ibid.*

[120] Zimbardo, 2007, p. 417, see *supra* note 27.

[121] See O'Sullivan, 2016, p. 4, *supra* note 3.

of the law of war".[122] Participating in and witnessing lawful killings in war force soldiers to break from the prohibitions of civilian norms. As such, war creates freedom from conventional social and moral constraints on violence and killing. This is one of the biggest leaps of faith in the moral realm. Such a dramatic change of the moral landscape, which is required by law and duty, can result in moral disorientation. War is conducive to social disorder and normlessness.[123] It operates as a "school of crime" imparting violence and aggression.[124]

Harming human life often causes a lot of distress even when it is clearly lawful. A veteran said what scared him more than being shot at was his callous attitude towards human life.[125] A Second World War infantryman went into hysteria after killing an enemy soldier: "that bothered me", he stammered, "my father taught me never to kill".[126] The cognitive shock is profound. Boundaries between right and wrong are blurred:

> There is no clarity. Everything swirls. The old rules are no longer binding, the old truths no longer true. Right spills over into wrong. Order blends into chaos, love into hate, ugliness into beauty, law into anarchy, civility into savagery.[127]

In addition to lawful killing, witnessing unlawful violence further uproots the fundamental moral structure. One soldier wrote after seeing atrocities:

> There was no honor here, no virtue. The standards of behaviour taught in the homes, churches, and schools of America had no place in battle. They were mythical concepts good only for the raising of children, to be cast aside forever from this moment on.[128]

As Joanna Bourke observes, atrocities can be "difficult to define" and are often ignored because violence is "ubiquitous" in combat situations.[129] The level of violence, lawful or unlawful, greatly challenges soldiers' moral sense and rational thinking. Battlefield norms tend to "propel even the most civilized of individuals into a more primitive mindset".[130] The "bewilderment", "stupefaction", and "sense of growing strangeness"[131] which the ordinary soldier

[122] Frésard, 2004, p. 22, see *supra* note 12.

[123] O'Sullivan, 2016, p. 4, see *supra* note 3.

[124] McGarry and Walklate, 2011, p. 901, see *supra* note 31.

[125] Bourke, 1999, p. 58, see *supra* note 5.

[126] *Ibid.*, p. 235.

[127] Cited in Mark Osiel, "Obeying Orders: Atrocity, Military Discipline, and the Law of War", in *California Law Review*, 1998, vol. 86, no. 5, p. 965.

[128] Cited in O'Sullivan, 2016, p. 142, see *supra* note 3.

[129] Bourke, 1999, p. 225, see *supra* note 5.

[130] Osiel, 1998, p. 965, see *supra* note 127.

[131] *Ibid.*, p. 966.

experiences stand in stark contrast with the common sense, normality and moral certainty in an ordinary citizen in peace-time. The ordinary soldier struggles to find "some logic and meaning" in the normative chaos.[132] Civilian values cannot save them from the verge of psychological collapse, only military ethos which eradicates human sensibilities can restore a sense of order, albeit an inverted one.[133]

7.3.2. Desensitization towards Killing

Frequent exposure to death and suffering creates numbness. The ordinary soldier lives the "atrocity triangle"[134] of being the perpetrator, victim and witness: the soldier is obliged to attack, liable to being attacked, and bears witness to violent attacks carried out by others. The average infantryman's daily routine is replete with killing, death and brutal incidents. Routinized or habitual killing desensitizes the soldier to the nature of the act.[135] Seeing dead and mutilated bodies often enough tends to immunize the soldier to the sight of human suffering.[136] Eventually, desensitization reaches the point where killing another human being is a "routine act that requires little to no moral reflection".[137] When killing is accepted as business as usual, there is little empathy or fellow feeling towards other human beings. The most fundamental moral injunction against killing is broken; nothing is sacred anymore. One does not feel sad or is in any other way affected when killing other human beings or witnessing death. There is a sense of "transcendence" beyond good and evil.[138] Many servicemen kill the enemy with a sense that they are performing "a slightly distasteful but necessary" task. The act of killing becomes "a programmed response", according to a Vietnam veteran, "no emotion attached".[139] Respect for human life is lost. A "human being becomes so unimportant", said a veteran, who was happiest when counting "kills" – the number of people he killed.[140] A 21-year-old American soldier who killed an Iraqi civilian said afterwards: "It was like nothing. Over here, killing people is like squashing an ant".[141]

---

132 Bourke, 1999, p. 232, see *supra* note 5.

133 *Ibid.*

134 McGarry and Walklate, 2011, p. 906, see *supra* note 31.

135 O'Sullivan, 2016, p. 146, see *supra* note 3.

136 *Ibid.*

137 *Ibid.*

138 Marlantes, 2012, p. 174, see *supra* note 4.

139 Bourke, 1999, p. 154, see *supra* note 5. See first person account in Marlantes, 2012, pp. 61 ff., *supra* note 4.

140 Bourke, 1999, p. 58, see *supra* note 5.

141 Cited in Zimbardo, 2007, p. 417, see *supra* note 27.

Indifference towards the lives of others is mirrored by helplessness towards one's own fate. The conditions of war remind soldiers of their own mortality. The reality of war constrains the soldier's options – including his freedom to act humanely.[142] Psychiatrist Jonathan Shay observes that in war, all sides are trying to break the will of the opponent through "competing attempts to enslave" the soldier's mind, heart and soul.[143] Soldiers do not have the freedom to quit. They are "captives" of war.[144] A soldier who runs away from the enemy faces the same fate as one who runs toward them: capture, confinement or possible death.[145] Shay accurately summarizes the soldier's dilemma: "The front line is thus a narrow zone of fear and death lying between two prisons".[146] An "unfocussed, and uncontrolled, fear of death" is often behind group actions and atrocities committed by soldiers.[147] The brutality of war induces "even in the fit and willing soldier a sense of his own unimportance", which in turn prompts the soldier to treat the lives of others, especially those in vulnerable positions, such as surrendering enemies or innocent civilians, as equally unimportant.[148] In sum, war alienates the soldier from his own humanity. Moral drift results in loss of humanity in both the soldier's self-perception and his attitude towards others. It is the embodiment of Arendtian "double-dehumanization" in the battlefield. It is matched by the philosophy of war as described in Chapter 4 above.

Where fighting is not carried out face to face, physical distance also contributes to desensitization and depersonalization towards killing. Albert Bandura explains that it is easier for an actor to inflict harm when the victims' suffering is not seen and when actions are "physically and temporally" separated from their consequences.[149] Distance between the soldier and target can be created through technological superiority. In the twentieth century, weapons which can kill remotely were already appreciated by their users for reducing the psychological burden of killing. A Vietnam veteran said that the grenade launcher is a good thing because it does not kill directly – in the sense that you do not have to "put your eye on a particular person and shoot him and kill him".[150]

[142] Osiel, 1998, p. 1041, see *supra* note 127.

[143] David Berreby, *Us and Them: The Science of Identity*, University of Chicago Press, 2018, p. 269.

[144] *Ibid.*

[145] *Ibid.*

[146] *Ibid.*

[147] O'Sullivan, 2016, p. 145, see *supra* note 3.

[148] Osiel, 1998, p. 1041, see *supra* note 127.

[149] Albert Bandura, "Selective Activation and Disengagement of Moral Control", in *Journal of Social Issues*, 1990, vol. 46, no. 1, p. 37.

[150] Bourke, 1999, p. 205, see *supra* note 5.

Contemporary weapon systems are becoming more and more depersonalized. The act of killing becomes abstract. According to one commentator, the soldier has become "the servant of a weapons system", whose role "is reduced to triggering a series of complex material mechanisms".[151] Certain weapon operators such as pilots, drone operators, artillery or missile crews launch attacks against remote targets.[152] Weapon systems make killing "more clinical", "clean" and "less personal".[153] There is much less visual and sound exposure to death and suffering. Shooting through a night vision camera makes the soldier feel that he is not killing real human beings but just moving images.[154] Hence, a commentator's conclusion about the striking effects of modern weapons on their operators: "The perpetrator can now kill his victims without touching them, without hearing them, without seeing them. He may feel sure of his success and safe from its repercussions".[155] Killing is mentally and physically depersonalized. There is a "psychic split" between killing on the job and one's daily routines.[156] Distance makes the killer feel less intentionality and responsibility towards the death of other human beings.

7.3.3. From Sanctioned Criminality to Pathology

When war encourages its participants to treat questions of "utmost moral importance" – killing, violence and aggression – as "morally uninteresting", it is not surprising that people simply lose interest in any moral requirements.[157] Violence tends to escalate and feed upon itself.[158] As Richard Wasserstrom writes in 1974: "war has, in some important ways, made psychopaths of them all". Soldiers can become accustomed to violence which does not discriminate. Once morally repellent behaviours are accepted as morally appropriate. This kind of moral drift, Doris and Murphy contend, is "a persistent feature of atrocity". It is illustrated by the statement of an Auschwitz doctor who participated in

151 Frésard, 2004, p. 64, see *supra* note 12.

152 O'Sullivan, 2016, p. 151, see *supra* note 3. See also, Marlantes, 2012, p. 18, *supra* note 4. Marlantes describes in detail the physical and psychological distance created by targeted killing from the air.

153 O'Sullivan, 2016, p. 151, see *supra* note 3.

154 Grossman, 2009, p. xx, see *supra* note 43.

155 Cited in Arne Johan Vetlesen, *Perception, Empathy, and Judgment: An Inquiry into the Preconditions of Moral Performance*, Penn State University Press, Pennsylvania, 1994, p. 90.

156 Marlantes, 2012, p. 18, see *supra* note 4.

157 Richard Wasserstrom, "War and its Crimes", in Virginia Held *et al.* (eds.), *Philosophy, Morality, and International Affairs*, Oxford University Press, 1974, p. 61.

158 Zimbardo, 2007, p. 422, see *supra* note 27.

"medicalized killing": "In the beginning it was almost impossible. Afterward it became almost routine".[159]

War itself constitutes an "intrinsically pathological"[160] environment which can "distort and rechannel"[161] behaviours in destructive ways. Conditions of war and dynamics of detention facilities carry "inherent risks" for abuses.[162] The feelings of acting outside the normal society – free from usual social and moral constraints and of almost absolute power towards the potential victims – contribute to arbitrary and pathological behaviours. In the Stanford prison experiment, ordinary college students serving as guards in a prison simulation rapidly came "to derive pleasure from insulting, threatening, humiliating and dehumanizing their peers".[163] Those normal, healthy college students entered the prison experiment thinking they are going to play their role in a calm, controlled manner; ordinary people go to war to conduct lawful fighting. Both can end up doing strange things and indulging in "entrepreneurial cruelty"[164] – cruelty improvised by individual initiative and creativity. The pathological and dehumanizing environment creates a "morally dangerous situation"[165] where the probability of moral failure is increased.

7.4. War Crime as a Corollary to War

Gwynne Dyer describes the moral cost of war for "ordinary", "decent" soldiers:

> You put those same kids in the jungle for a while, get them real scared, deprive them of sleep, and let a few incidents change some of their fear to hate. Give them a sergeant who has seen too many of his men killed by booby traps and by lack of distrust, and who feels that Vietnamese are dumb, dirty, and weak, because they are not like him. Add a little mob pressure, and those nice kids who accompany us today would rape like champions. Kill, rape and steal is the name of the game.[166]

This chapter highlights the inevitability and predictability of war crimes in war.[167] One military expert puts it plainly: "If you get enough soldiers into

[159] Doris and Murphy, 2007, p. 47, see *supra* note 2.

[160] Craig Haney, Curtis Banks and Philip Zimbardo, "Interpersonal Dynamics of a Simulated Prison", in *International Journal of Criminology and Penology*, 1973, vol. 1, no. 1, p. 90.

[161] *Ibid.*

[162] Zimbardo, 2007, p. 353, see *supra* note 27.

[163] Haney, Banks and Zimbardo, 1973, p. 89, see *supra* note 160.

[164] Doris, 2005, p. 53, see *supra* note 99.

[165] *Ibid.*, p. 147.

[166] Gwynne Dyer, *War*, Guild Publishing, Reading, 1985, cited in Grossman, 2009, p. 191, see *supra* note 43.

[167] See some examples in wars waged by Western States in Badkhen, 2006, *supra* note 34.

enough combat, some of them are going to murder civilians".[168] Atrocities "aren't surprising at all", says a military historian in relation to several war crimes against Iraqi civilians and prisoners; the "fact that we maybe weren't expecting them is surprising".[169] War crimes have been a persistent feature of war.

This chapter explains how the extreme environment and subversive normative framework of war influence its participants. The objective environment of war creates and sustains an ecology of irrationality. Extreme physical and mental hardships wear down the finite human will power and rational agency. War propagates its own normative framework. The violent nature of war creates moral ambiguities and legal uncertainties in the most fundamental questions. War reduces moral restraints towards violence and provides opportunity for excesses. It is no mystery that identity-based war crimes are committed in the context of identity-based war. There is a conceptual and ideological continuity between lawful and unlawful violence, war and war crimes. This chapter demonstrates practical implications of such conceptual indivisibility. Categorizing the continuum of violence in war poses psychological difficulty in its implementation. The rational distinction between law and unlawful violence is designed with the rational agent alone in mind, not the irrational environment.

A cosmopolitan war crimes law has to be applied in the normative and physical environment of war. War is all-encompassing and all-consuming for those participating in it. For those who are fatefully immersed in the combat situation, cosmopolitan norms can be either alien or simply inaccessible. They cannot detach themselves from their immediate environment and conduct impartial reasoning like in peace-time or in the courtroom. The war has significant normative and practical impact on the individual.

The system of criminal law focuses on the direct, tangible perpetrator, not the pervasive, often unmeasurable environment. It perceives conscious intentionality instead of unconscious mental activities, active choices instead of passive reactions to environment. It coerces rational human agency in an environment where agency is extremely vulnerable. The gap between the legal fiction of agency and the reality can undermine the normative claim of criminal law. The perpetrator may simply not have the normative competence to consider criminal law's reason. Just as war crimes are corollary to war, the rational agent is a corollary to cosmopolitanism. War and cosmopolitanism may not speak together but talk past each other.

[168] Quote of John Pike, Director of GlobalSecurity.org, cited in *ibid.*

[169] Quote of Andrew Wiest, Professor of Military History at the University of Southern Mississippi, cited in *ibid.*

8

A Cosmopolitan Criminal Law's Response to Human Vulnerabilities in War

This chapter turns to normative implications of war-time moral psychology for cosmopolitan criminal law. What are the consequences of the gap between criminal law's fiction of agency and ordinary soldiers' experience of war? How can criminal law respond to the characteristic social environment of war? Is the cosmopolitan meaning of war crimes law still meaningful in the anti-cosmopolitan social reality of war? I suggest some changes of perspective in the application of criminal law in light of empirical findings. The final section considers the role of the crime of aggression in justifying the conception and practice of a cosmopolitan war crimes law.

8.1. Consequences of the Gap Between Norm and Reality

Chapters 6 and 7 above show that coercing individual agency in agency-suppressing institutions and demanding consistent rational thinking in an ecology of irrationality create a gap between cosmopolitan law and social reality. True, there is always a gap between norms and facts. Cosmopolitanism has been a living ideal, not reality, since ancient times. Criminal law seeks to guide, not reflect, behaviour. Indeed, it is the very nature of norms to be different from facts. The schism shows the power and ambition of the law. Some constructivist spirit is needed to build a better world. It cannot be ruled out that a cosmopolitan law in itself can help to create a more cosmopolitan world and transform individual perceptions. A cosmopolitan criminal law asserts the authority of a cosmopolitan community over other, parallel communities. It tends to operate on the assumptions that the cosmopolitan community provides the dominant normative and cultural framework for individuals around the world, and that a cosmopolitan war crimes law gives "a determinate answer"[1] to complex and controversial issues.

Nevertheless, mere postulation of authority is not enough. Norms need a material basis. Too big a gap between norm and reality, or between realities projected by norms and realities observed and experienced by concrete people, undermines the legitimacy and efficacy of the norms. The gap between norm and

[1] Nicolas Lamp, "The 'Practice Turn' in International Law: Insights from the Theory of Structuration", in Moshe Hirsch and Andrew Lang (eds.), *Research Handbook on the Sociology of International Law*, Edward Elgar Publishing, Cheltenham, 2018, p. 289.

fact should be reasonable, not abyssal. The discrepancy between a cosmopolitan criminal law's conception of human agency and social psychology's measurement is acute and consequential. It shows the contrast between a courtroom-style, calm, back-and-forth reasoning and snap judgment in an ethical hot zone, under time pressure and immersed in an obnoxious environment. A cosmopolitan war crimes law risks prioritizing a kind of "superficial reckoning"[2] with atrocities. The individual is singled out to take responsibility for the institution. Moreover, a decontextualized conception of individual agency ultimately distracts us from the moral cost of war. I now elaborate three consequences for the ordinary soldier: 'disabling effect on the law', risks of scapegoating, and distraction from the moral cost of war.

8.1.1. 'Disabling' Effect on the Law

The threat of criminal law is not the same for an ordinary citizen in peace-time and for an ordinary soldier who is integrated into the military institution and experiencing radical emotions and physical exhaustion in the battlefield. Cognitive controls are required for persons to behave in socially acceptable ways. Suspension of cognitive control means suspension of key functions which are required for criminal law to have an impact: sense of personal responsibility, obligation, guilt, and analysis of one's conduct in cost-benefit calculations. It is as if there is a "short circuit" in the brain – action replaces thought.[3] If people are not aware of their determinative motives induced by situational stimuli, they cannot scrutinize or endorse such motives. They are therefore not in a position to evaluate behaviour informed or moved by such motives and desires.[4] Or in cases where persons lose control over their behaviour due to intense fear or disorientation, they are not able to act in accordance with their judgment. The environment of war may elicit behaviour independently of an agent's judgment.[5] In light of what is already discussed in Chapters 6 and 7, I illustrate the following five scenarios where, to different degrees, institutional and situational forces in war can have "disabling"[6] effects on criminal law.

---

2 Mark Goodale, "After International Law: Anthropology Beyond the 'Age of Human Rights'", in *AJIL Unbound*, 2021, vol. 115, p. 291.

3 Philip Zimbardo, *The Lucifer Effect: Understanding How Good People Turn Evil*, Random House Trade Paperbacks, London, 2007, pp. 305–306.

4 Matthew Talbert and Jessica Wolfendale, *War Crimes, Causes, Excuses, and Blame*, Oxford University Press, 2018, p. 76.

5 *Ibid.*, p. 101.

6 Roger Cotterrell, *Law's Community: Legal Theory in Sociological Perspective*, Clarendon Press, Oxford, 1995, pp. 304–305.

8.1.1.1. Erosion of Morals

First, erosion of moral perception and judgment of soldiers. Military life and combat conditions constitute "cognitive environment" which are often "inimical" to one's cognitive feats.[7] Such a cognitive environment can cause "moral drift" – "a slide into evil" as people are "gradually acclimated to destructive norms".[8] When the institution devises a normative framework which allows or requires war crimes, it can transform its members' moral judgment. Participants in organized war crimes often do not lose all senses of morality, rather they act according to inverted virtues, duty and practical wisdom.[9] Here, 'the wisdom of repugnance' in moral judgment, a kind of moral intuition widely affirmed in atrocity trials, cannot function as expected. Moral intuition may be an unreliable guide when it is shaped by a highly manipulative normative regime.

A person's mental life is fundamentally re-organized when immersed in an authority system.[10] Military life reduces the kind of critical capacity needed for a person's "ethical sensitivity".[11] When soldiers are instrumentalized as "thinking bayonet",[12] "men-the-weapon"[13] or "walking weapon guidance system",[14] their capacity and opportunity for moral deliberation are reduced. Long-term exposure to dehumanizing ideologies in a closed environment can impair ordinary soldiers' normative competence.[15] According to Bandura, dehumanization fosters self-exonerative thinking towards victims. People rationalize, rather than condemn, harmful conduct towards dehumanized persons.[16] What used to be unthinkable becomes normal. The "supportive organizational context" may well induce a "shared illusion" that members "are engaged in a legitimate

7 John M. Doris and Dominic Murphy, "From My Lai to Abu Ghraib: The Moral Psychology of Atrocity", in *Midwest Studies in Philosophy*, 2007, vol. 31, no. 1, p. 41.

8 John M. Doris, *Lack of Character: Personality and Moral Behavior*, Cambridge University Press, 2005, p. 57.

9 Talbert and Wolfendale, 2018, pp. 151–152, see *supra* note 4. Talbert and Wolfendale give the example of how the US military quickly accepted and implemented so-called "enhanced interrogation techniques" which amount to torture in the aftermath of 9/11 terrorist attacks.

10 Stanley Milgram, *Obedience to Authority: An Experimental View*, Harper & Row, New York, 1974, pp. 209–210.

11 Doris and Murphy, 2007, p. 15, see *supra* note 7.

12 Joanna Bourke, *An Intimate History of Killing: Face-to-Face Killing in Twentieth-Century Warfare*, Basic Books, 1999, p. 59.

13 *Ibid.*, p. 60.

14 Karl Marlantes, *What It Is Like To Go To War*, Corvus, London, 2012, p. 3.

15 Doris and Murphy, 2007, p. 39, see *supra* note 7.

16 Albert Bandura, "Selective Activation and Disengagement of Moral Control", in *Journal of Social Issues*, 1990, vol. 46, no. 1, p. 39.

enterprise".[17] That is, the soldier internalizes norms and values of the military. For him, war crimes, just like regular war fighting, can be moral and legal.

Similarly, moral drift can be induced by war itself. War-fighting can change standards of appropriate behaviour for a reasonable soldier.[18] Normative competence is also affected by battlefield norms and experiences, as is shown in Chapter 7. Moreover, the "radical confusion of the battlefield" makes it difficult to make normatively appropriate decisions.[19] Doris argues that "difficult-to-interpret situations that prevent acquisitions of morally significant information" amount to "local impairments of normative competence".[20]

8.1.1.2. Immoral but Legal

Even if the soldier maintains the right moral values, his understanding of what is legal is greatly constrained by the institution's authority and combat realities. Authorization creates the *perception* of legality. It can make one think that certain behaviour is immoral but legal. After all, this can be said about most lawful killings in war. In addition to explicit orders, Doris and Murphy argue that policies and sub-structures can degrade soldiers' ability to determine the illegality of unnecessary killing and other atrocities.[21] For example, the "war-fighting culture" in Vietnam can make orders to kill civilians and prisoners not "manifestly illegal" in the eyes of the ordinary soldier.[22] Certain behaviour can be perceived as legal through a continuum of violence, that is, legality of lawful violence can have *persuasive effect* on the legality of unlawful violence. Unlawful violence may simply be regarded as "an additional, unavoidable, though abominable, act of war".[23] Intense pressures and confusion from the combat can also impair the legality judgment.

In sum, the social environment of war can make atrocities appear *morally unfortunate* but legal. This also raises the question of effectiveness of criminal law: if it is nearly impossible for the reasonable soldier to identify the illegality of the orders he receives under certain circumstances, the punishment for

[17] Herbert C. Kelman, "Violence without Moral Restraint: Reflections on the Dehumanization of Victims and Victimizers", in *Journal of Social Issues*, 1973, vol. 29, no. 4, p. 47.

[18] Doris and Murphy, 2007, p. 38, see *supra* note 7.

[19] *Ibid.*, p. 35.

[20] Doris, 2005, p. 138, see *supra* note 8.

[21] Doris and Murphy, 2007, p. 48, see *supra* note 7.

[22] *Ibid.*, p. 45.

[23] Bourke, 1999, p. 175, see *supra* note 12.

obeying an unlawful order cannot enter his calculation or reasoning.[24] This may account for situational difficulties to live up to the requirement not to follow *manifestly unlawful* orders of the commander, as prescribed, for example, in Article 33 of the Rome Statute of the ICC. Acts which appear manifestly unlawful for a remote bystander may not appear the same way for the perpetrator there and then. Legal rules, like moral standards, can be relative in particular social contexts.

8.1.1.3. Illegal but not Responsible

Even if the soldier knows the act is both immoral and illegal, he may still follow it through because he feels not responsible for his own action. As is shown in Chapter 6, the military system alienates the individual from his act and its consequences. Responsibility can be displaced to the superior or diffused among the group. Bandura explains the relationship between restraints against violence and perception of agency: "Self-sanctions are activated most strongly when personal agency for detrimental effects is unambiguous".[25] Military training and combat environment can reduce self-sanctions through "obscuring causal agency",[26] reconstruing prohibited conduct, distancing harmful consequences, and blaming and dehumanizing the enemy.

8.1.1.4. Gap Between Thinking and Acting

One legal adviser says that "[i]mmediate and certain approval from comrades overrides any reason for complying with legal standards or any fear of the consequences of engaging in criminal behavior".[27] Even when one knows what is unlawful and wishes not to carry out the act at the cognitive level, one may not be able to act accordingly. This is because reason, or normative conclusion, is but one source of action. There is not necessarily a connection between the normative reasoning and motivation.[28] Recall Milgram's observation that in an actual situation, multiple forces other than one's values are impinging on a person.[29] Although a certain behavioural option is theoretically available, it is often

---

[24] See Mark Osiel, "Obeying Orders: Atrocity, Military Discipline, and the Law of War", in *California Law Review*, 1998, vol. 86, no. 5, p. 1007; Talbert and Wolfendale, 2018, p. 80, see *supra* note 4.

[25] Bandura, 1990, p. 34, see *supra* note 16.

[26] *Ibid.*, p. 28.

[27] Cited in Osiel, 1998, p. 1062, see *supra* note 24.

[28] R. Jay Wallace, "Moral Psychology", in Frank Jackson and Michael Smith (eds.), *The Oxford Handbook of Contemporary Philosophy*, Oxford University Press, 2007, p. 89.

[29] Milgram, 1974, p. 6, see *supra* note 10.

not "psychologically available"[30] to the ordinary soldier. It takes mental strength to act in line with one's reasoned judgment under countervailing circumstances. A soldier who is conditioned to kill, placed in the authority situation and embedded in his group is less autonomous in his behaviour than an ordinary person in peace-time.

8.1.1.5. Physical Control over Behaviour

A more straightforward case is loss of control over one's behaviour. The relationship between the act and the actor should be one of possession: it is the perpetrator's purposive act rather than something that happened to him.[31] This is especially true in some combat situations. The extreme battlefield environment may simply cause a person to lose "reflective self-control" over his behaviour.[32] The impairment of certain physical capacities is typically temporary or transient, yet still real and consequential.

In sum, when criminal law cannot engage the agent in reasoned deliberation, it has no effect in its persuasion of compliance and threat of punishment. Situational forces help soldiers ignore, minimize, distort or disbelieve the harmful consequences of their own acts.[33] Their senses of personal agency, personal responsibility, and ability to make rational and independent decisions often do not support presuppositions of criminal law. When the agent's ability of reasoned deliberation is seriously compromised, the law is deprived of the "deliberative impact".[34]

8.1.2. Risks of Scapegoating

Crimes are physically committed by individual persons. But the solution does not necessarily lie solely with the individual. The Chinese proverb 'treat the head when there is headache; treat the foot when the foot hurts' reminds us of limitations of a reactive and fragmented approach. The most obvious place may not be the only place to look at. Problems in the head or foot may be caused by systemic illness. War crimes may not entirely result from isolated individuals, but also from the system and the environment. In behavioural and responsibility assessment, artificial separation of the individual soldier from the social group and war crimes from conditions of war obscure rather than clarify the problem.

---

30 Herbert Kelman and V. Lee Hamilton, *Crimes of Obedience: Toward a Social Psychology of Authority and Responsibility*, Yale University Press, New Haven, 1989, p. 76.

31 Doris, 2005, p. 140, see *supra* note 8.

32 Talbert and Wolfendale, 2018, p. 101, see *supra* note 4.

33 See Bandura, 1990, pp. 27–46, *supra* note 16.

34 Doris and Murphy, 2007, pp. 51–52, see *supra* note 7.

As Chapters 6 and 7 show, operational tactics and other institutional policies have significant impact on individual perception and behaviour. The length and frequency of deployment, for example, is a policy issue. The decision can be seen as a trade-off between the benefits of experienced personnel, group cohesion, and costs of mental and physical health of the military personnel. There is tension between the needs of the military and those of the individual.[35] Armed forces of different States have different deployment policies and practices.[36] There seems to exist a certain threshold of deployment length beyond which psychological problems of military personnel increase significantly.[37] Overuse of combat personnel exhausts the finite human resource. The exploitation of combat soldiers over a long time is certainly a problem at the institutional level. Those who are in charge of making such policy should be proportionately responsible for consequent crimes in war.

Shifting responsibility down the hierarchy effectively exonerates institutional policy, practice and culture. Criminal law may be instrumentalized to scapegoat individuals at the bottom of the hierarchical structure. Common communicative tactics of political and military leaders include minimization and disassociation. Through minimization, authorities downplay the seriousness and scope of the crime, and limit blame to "misguided or overzealous" individual soldiers.[38] Through disassociation, authorities preserve their legitimacy by distancing themselves from deviant soldiers. The deviant is characterized as the "black sheep" who is unworthy of group membership.[39] Minimization and disassociation are characteristic of political statements post war crimes. Political and military leaders assure the public that atrocities are committed by a few 'bad apples' and are completely "foreign to the normal character and actions"[40] of the armed force. Former US President Barack Obama says that the Kandahar massacre does not represent the "exceptional character" of the American military

[35] Joshua E.J. Buckman *et al.*, "The Impact of Deployment Length on the Health and Well-Being of Military Personnel: A Systematic Review of the Literature", in *Occupational and Environmental Medicine*, 2011, vol. 68, no. 1, pp. 69–70.

[36] *Ibid.*, pp. 70, 74. The United Kingdom's army, for example, sets a six-month limit for a single deployment and a 12-month limit for every 36-month period. The US army typically deploys personnel for 12 months at a time, every two years. Some studies propose the threshold to be approximately 6 months per deployment or 12 months within 3 years.

[37] *Ibid.*, p. 74.

[38] Bandura, 1990, p. 35, see *supra* note 16. See also, Charles M. Rowling, Penelope Sheets and Timothy M. Jones, "American Atrocity Revisited: National Identity, Cascading Frames, and the My Lai Massacre", in *Political Communication*, 2015, vol. 32, no. 2, p. 314.

[39] *Ibid.*, p. 315.

[40] Cited in Doris and Murphy, 2007, p. 31, see *supra* note 7.

and the perpetrator, Robert Bales, is "a lone gunman who acted on his own".[41] Similarly, in the aftermath of prisoner abuses at Abu Ghraib, then President George W. Bush was quick to distance his country from the bad apples: "They don't represent America. They represent the actions of a few people".[42] Perpetrators are said to have been punished through criminal justice – black sheep purged and institutional moral sanctity reaffirmed by the 'rule of law'.

Perhaps, it is not so much what criminal law emphasizes, but what it distracts from, that deserves our attention. If a cosmopolitan war crimes law's reaction to State-sponsored or -facilitated atrocity is to empower the individual and relativize the power of the State, an unexpected side-effect of disempowering the State and its institutions is minimization of their responsibility. Power corresponds to responsibility. Our belief in the myth of human invulnerability to situational forces directs our attention to perfecting our imperfectible humanity, rather than maintaining sufficient vigilance towards negative situational forces. In this sense, we almost 'set ourselves up for a fall'. As Zimbardo points out, we must recognize the power of "negative situational forces" to "infect us" before we can "avoid, prevent, challenge and change" them.[43] We simply cannot ignore the situational power out of existence. By isolating and localizing responsibility, the narrative of criminal law overshadows alternative narratives which seek out responsibility of the military and political establishments.

8.1.3. Distraction from the Moral Cost of War

The normative individualism practiced by a cosmopolitan war crimes law distances war crimes from not only the military institution, but also conditions of war. Excessive spotlight on individual failures distracts us from the intrinsic moral cost of war. As I mention in Chapters 6 and 7, the description of the military institution and war here is largely based on the experiences of Western States, in particular the experience of the US and its allies in past wars. This is because the US stands out for the sheer number of wars she has fought since the twentieth century. Secondly, when it comes to compliance with laws of war, Western democracies tend to believe that their armies have the best chance to succeed. A book on the My Lai massacre questions such self-perceptions:

> Until My Lai, it had been possible (although perhaps not quite accurate) to believe that the authors of the twentieth century's greatest atrocities were to be found in distant, primitive, or at least

---

[41] Taimoor Shah and Graham Bowley, "U.S. Sergeant Is Said to Kill 16 Civilians in Afghanistan", *The New York Times*, 11 March 2012; "Obama: Afghan Shooting Rampage was Work of Lone Gunman", *Reuters*, 13 March 2012.

[42] Cited in Doris and Murphy, 2007, p. 31, see *supra* note 7.

[43] Zimbardo, 2007, p. 211, see *supra* note 3.

deluded peoples. With My Lai the heart of darkness came home to America.[44]

In other words, if all the resources and training cannot avoid frequent war crimes under difficult conditions of war, can we hope that much less privileged others successfully abide by the law?

The reality is that there is an unavoidable and often invisible moral cost of war. A cosmopolitan criminal law's egocentric logic seems to suggest that if participants have stronger self-discipline, deeper philosophical insight, and more practical wisdom, the war can be fought with moral perfection. It is simply wishful thinking. Military training that is most sensitive to ethical imperatives pales in the face of the intense pressure of war.[45] No amount of individual or institutional effort can offset the moral cost of war. Many training programmes include mandatory courses on ethics and law.[46] Case studies are employed to immerse soldiers in realistic scenarios and cultivate ethical judgment in difficult situations.[47] However, efforts to sensitize moral judgment should be viewed in light of other countervailing institutional policies and realities of war. Desperate tactics are intrinsic to certain types of war and have ideological roots way beyond the war itself; prolonged and frequent deployment are driven by the need to fight too many wars in a short period. Oftentimes, it is not entirely failures of individuals or even institutions; rather, it is war itself that makes individuals and institutions fail. Carmel O'Sullivan makes the sharp observation that war crimes are not just the result of human failures but "symptomatic" of war.[48] Doris and Murphy reveal what is precisely at stake when governments send their citizens to fight war: "they endanger not only their lives, but also their souls".[49] In the fateful tragedy of war, normal people become criminals, and crimes become normal.

By creating a narrative of what is wrong, criminal law distracts us from what it rights. It is what war crimes law legitimizes, not what it criminalizes, that is the crux of the problem. Overemphasis of the solution of criminal law in the aftermath of war-time atrocity prevents critical thinking about the war itself

44 Michael Bilton and Kevin Sim, *Four Hours in My Lai*, Penguin Press, London, 1993, cited in Rowling, Sheets and Jones, 2015, p. 323, see *supra* note 38.

45 Doris and Murphy, 2007, pp. 40–41, see *supra* note 7.

46 Anna Badkhen, "Atrocities are a Fact of All Wars, Even Ours", *SFGATE*, 13 August 2006.

47 See Osiel, 1998, p. 1077, *supra* note 24.

48 Carmel O'Sullivan, *Killing on Command: The Defence of Superior Orders in Modern Combat*, Palgrave Macmillan, London, 2016, p. 157.

49 Doris and Murphy, 2007, p. 54, see *supra* note 7.

at the collective level.[50] It represents a missed opportunity to ask bigger questions about justifications for the initiation and continuation of war. Military and political leaders should not be allowed to put soldiers in extreme environments and to offload the burden of war entirely on them.[51]

8.2. Remedies Within Criminal Law and Beyond

8.2.1. Incorporating Empirical Insights into a Cosmopolitan War Crimes Law

Criminal law's attribution of responsibility distinguishes it from other descriptive and prescriptive frames in a significant way. A complete change of structure, such as deviating from its focus on individuals, would make criminal law unrecognizable – we do not know if it could be called criminal law anymore. The discipline's self-image is illustrated by the judges of the Eichmann trial:[52]

> It is the purpose of every criminal trial to clarify whether the charges in the prosecution's indictment against the accused who is on trial are true, and if the accused is convicted, to mete out due punishment to him. Everything which requires clarification in order that these purposes may be achieved, must be determined at the trial, and everything which is foreign to these purposes must be entirely eliminated from the court procedure.

Faced with numerous important questions raised by the Holocaust, the Court cautions against entering into "provinces which are outside its sphere".[53] The Court concedes that it has neither the mandate nor the necessary tools to investigate general questions outside criminal law. To do so would derail the trial off its own track.[54] Law's "deliberate blindness towards certain empirical causes" is not considered a defect but a "functional necessity".[55] The profession is very conscious of its goals and paths, which in turn constitute its own limitations. "Reductionism" may well be necessary for legal reasoning.[56]

---

50 Denying collective responsibility for war, according to Marlantes, is like "scurrying around the house of an alcoholic hiding empty bottles and never mentioning drinking". See Marlantes, 2012, p. 216, *supra* note 14.

51 O'Sullivan, 2016, p. 156, see *supra* note 48.

52 Israel, District Court of Jerusalem, *Attorney General v. Adolf Eichmann*, Judgment, 11 December 1961, Criminal Case No. 40/61, p. 2 (https://www.legal-tools.org/doc/aceae7/).

53 *Ibid.*

54 *Ibid.*

55 Ino Augsberg, "Some Realism About New Legal Realism: What's New, What's Legal, What's Real?", in *Leiden Journal of International Law*, 2015, vol. 28, no. 3, p. 462.

56 Fuad Zabiyev, "On the Judge Centredness of the International Legal Self", in *The European Journal of International Law*, 2021, vol. 32, no. 4, p. 1162.

Nevertheless, the discrepancies between legal norms and reality invite us to reconsider law's closure to insights from other disciplines. As Mark Drumbl points out:

> The reductive parsimony of criminal trials may also distort the historical record and neglect the reality that many individuals who harm others in times of atrocity may themselves be compromised, victims, or individuals who exercised their agency in contradictory ways.[57]

As the field of international criminal law becomes more and more established, it is justified to ask whether war crimes law should integrate insights from sociology and moral psychology and how it can do so within its own "controlling framework".[58] These questions are in fact inseparable or even derived from law's search for moral meaning, which is a central concern in this book. My answer is that war crimes law should import social psychological insights and can do so within its own "logic and boundaries".[59] This is by no means to say that insights from these other knowledge fields are superior to law. Rather, my claim is that law can better accommodate empirical findings by adjusting its own standards of what is relevant and meaningful. Criminal law can take up empirical challenges by augmenting its cognitive openness without sacrificing its normative closure. It can incorporate new knowledge and insights and, at the same time, maintain its self-referentiality.

In particular, criminal law's attributional biases, as they are guided by the cosmopolitan ethos and applied in war, can be partly mitigated within its own frame. Criminal law can be practiced in a way that is more sensitive to the unique situational elements surrounding war crimes. Throughout history, criminal law has evolved through various determinist accounts. Self-reform based on new scientific discoveries is never alien to the discipline. I argue that in the case of war crimes, the frame of attribution should depart from the predominantly rationalist fiction of human agency and reflect situational influences on the individual. The application of war crimes law should take core insights of social psychology seriously and strive for a better balance between person and environment in attribution. The critical features of war crimes are the institutional and combat elements. The application of law should, to the extent possible,

---

57 Mark A. Drumbl, "When Perpetrators Become Defendants and then Convicts", in Susanne C. Knittel and Zachary J. Goldberg (eds.), *The Routledge International Handbook of Perpetrator Studies*, Routledge, Abingdon, 2020, p. 122.

58 Andrew Lang, "New Legal Realism, Empiricism, and Scientism: The Relative Objectivity of Law and Social Science", in *Leiden Journal of International Law*, 2015, vol. 28, no. 2, p. 248.

59 Uğur Ümit Üngör and Kjell Anderson, "From Perpetrators to Perpetration Definitions, Typologies, and Processes", in Knittel and Goldberg (eds.), 2020, p. 8, see *supra* note 57.

take these two features into account. After all, a criminal law that exhibits greater understanding of the social realities and causes of war crimes has a better chance to influence attitude and behaviour.

Among all the scenarios listed in the previous section where criminal law's intervention is disabled, only lack of physical control is readily recognized as a condition to exclude responsibility. When a person is physically not able to act in accordance with his character and judgment, he should be excused from criminal responsibility. All the other scenarios – failure to recognize immorality or unlawfulness of the conduct, feeling no personal responsibility, not able to resist situational forces – are not readily recognized for exclusion or mitigation of responsibility. Failure to recognize illegality of a conduct or mistake of law, for example, was discussed in the *Al Hassan* trial before the ICC. In 2012, Al Hassan joined an Islámic extremist group which occupied the city of Timbuktu in Mali. He became a leader of the Islámic Police created by the occupying force. The Islámic Police, together with other institutions of the group, enforced certain rules derived from *Sharí'ah* such as flogging. These punishments were subsequently characterized by the Trial Chamber as torture. Al Hassan was convicted of various war crimes and crimes against humanity in virtue of his role in the Islámic Police. Al Hassan is a Muslim. The rules enforced can be regarded as reasonable interpretations of *Sharí'ah* and have been practiced in a number of Muslim countries. The majority of the Trial Chamber refused to grant mistake of law as an excusing condition. Judge Antoine Kesia-Mbe Mindua, however, held that there is a valid case for mistake of law in relation to flogging, given Al Hassan's religious background and the general social environment he was in.[60] Judge Mindua's dissent deserves attention.

Faced with "complexity, fluidity, and contingency of perpetration",[61] it is of course by no means an easy task for criminal law to provide normative guidance that is uniform and effective. Based on tentative conclusions from psychology literature, my suggestions in this section are similarly tentative. They can be debunked and replaced by further empirical findings.

8.2.2. Responsibility of the Ordinary Soldier

Doris and Murphy argue that cognitive and motivational capacities are prerequisites for individual responsibility. Cognitive capacities, including "perceptual,

[60] See ICC, *Prosecutor v. Al Hassan Ag Abdoul Aziz Ag Mohamed Ag Mahmoud*, Trial Chamber X, Trial Judgment, 26 June 2024, ICC-01/12-01/18, paras. 1763–1774 (https://www.legal-tools.org/doc/o613gxre/); and *id.*, Opinion individuelle et partiellement dissidente du Juge Antoine Mindua, 28 June 2024, ICC-01/12-01/18-2594-OPI3, paras. 91–101 (https://www.legal-tools.org/doc/zlv5eyl2/).

[61] Üngör and Anderson, 2020, p. 7, see *supra* note 59.

interpretive, and deliberative" capacities, are required to evaluate and select appropriate actions.[62] It is a kind of "normative competence" which is necessary for an individual to "appreciate ethical considerations, ascertain information relevant to particular ethical judgments, and identify behavior implementing their ethical judgments".[63] Motivational capacities motivate and regulate behaviour in light of the identified action. These two types of capacities can also be understood as "powers of reflection" and "powers of self-control".[64] External environment can cause degradation of these factors to varying degrees. Military life and combat environment combined can significantly diminish individual capacity and will to think and act as an independent moral agent. Military life reduces moral and social restraints against violence through deliberate training and indoctrination, its authority, structure, and group cohesion; while war itself imparts ethical standards which are radical and subversive. Compared to the insubstantial situational factors present in experiments, factors present in military life and in combat are dramatic and radical. In fact, they are typically extreme and prolonged compared to peace-time situations.

The scenarios of war-induced mental impairment are borderline cases where criminal law can seek evolution and adaptation in the context of war. The ultimate question is: should the law or the judiciary abandon legal intervention when the law clearly has no effect on the perpetrator's behaviour? It is certainly not necessary or desirable to renounce criminal law's intervention altogether. How, then, should criminal law address significant impairment of normative competence in the perpetrator of war crimes? The court may consider it an excusing condition for lack of the requisite mental element, a mitigating circumstance because of significant moral and behavioural challenges, or proceed with full responsibility because there is requisite intentionality. There is no uniform answer to this question. In sentencing, for example, there is also statutory support for considerations of "the individual circumstances of the convicted person".[65] Judges should simply be more open-minded towards excusing or mitigating conditions that are seemingly unobtrusive or not conventionally considered in criminal trials.

In fact, war crimes trials cannot import the mode of thinking from peacetime criminal cases without any adaptation to the social realities of war. The difference between social contexts of war crimes and ordinary domestic crimes is consequential. True, war is war – the cruelty, the hardship, the death and the

[62] Doris and Murphy, 2007, p. 26, see *supra* note 7.

[63] *Ibid.*, p. 30.

[64] *Ibid.*, p. 29.

[65] Rome Statute of the International Criminal Court, 17 July 1998, Article 78(1) ('Rome Statute') (https://www.legal-tools.org/doc/7b9af9/).

destruction are taken for granted. But a criminal trial cannot take *human performance* in war for granted. Some suggest that responsibility should be assessed against difficulties of compliance: the harder the obstacles to acting legally, the less responsibility should the agent take.[66] O'Sullivan argues that judges should consider "the soldier's environment and the factors that shape their perceptions, standards and behaviour", in particular "the social, behavioural, psychological, biological and cultural" factors specific to war crimes.[67] Interdisciplinary research, not just legal research, according to O'Sullivan, is required for the court to fully understand the behavioural environment of the soldier.[68] The court, in other words, should be conscious that the soldier in action typically makes judgment in "ethical hot zones", not normal deliberative contexts in peace-time.[69] In assessing a "manifestly unlawful"[70] order, for example, the court should take into account the 'cognitive environment' of the individual in question. If the court finds the perpetrator in his cognitive environment could have reasonably believed that his conduct pursuant to a superior order is lawful, the court should recognize an excuse for responsibility.[71] In such cases the cognitive environment may have made it unreasonable to expect an ordinary soldier to detect the unlawfulness of superior orders.

The court has to consider the cumulative effects of all the normatively degrading factors, from military structure to combat experience. Collectively, they may have a serious impact on the mental competence of the perpetrator in question. Different situations can cause impairments of normative capacities to different degrees. The same situational factors may have different impact on different individuals in a given situation. The assessment of contextual influence therefore has to be done on a case-by-case basis to see if normative capacities have been substantially degraded to warrant potential exclusion or mitigation of responsibility.[72]

---

66 Paul Formosa, "Moral Responsibility and Evil", in Knittel and Goldberg (eds.), 2020, p. 248, see *supra* note 57.

67 O'Sullivan, 2016, pp. 75, 113, see *supra* note 48.

68 *Ibid.*, p. 155.

69 Doris, 2005, p. 149, see *supra* note 8.

70 Rome Statute, 1998, Article 33, see *supra* note 65.

71 Doris and Murphy, 2007, p. 41, see *supra* note 7. Saira Mohamed suggests that judges should take into account the complexity of choice and situation, and that atrocity trials should be "sites of storytelling, providing an opportunity for understanding how individuals choose to perpetrate unspeakable crimes" and serve an aspirational function for future behaviours. See Saira Mohamed, "Deviance, Aspiration, and the Stories We Tell: Reconciling Mass Atrocity and the Criminal Law", in *The Yale Law Journal*, 2015, vol. 124, no. 5, p. 1628.

72 *Ibid.*, p. 33.

The criminal court's role is to assign individual responsibility, so it should not attribute to the individual what is due to the institution or the war for the sake of moral expediency. Otherwise, the court becomes, perhaps unconsciously, part of the effort to apologize for the institution and the war. These borderline cases present an opportunity for the discipline to reinvent itself facing new challenges in a new context.

Moreover, the acute but temporary nature of many defects of normative competence suggests that *ex post facto* assertion of legal and moral authority of a cosmopolitan war crimes law can be necessary and effective. The corruption of mental capacity is often situation-specific. Through the criminal trial, the cosmopolitan community communicates the wrongfulness of the conduct to the perpetrator and condemns such conduct. Although the perpetrator's responsibility may be excused or mitigated for his mental state at the time of the crime, the harm to fundamental values can still be examined and deliberated, with a view to restoring the integrity of such values both in the eyes of the general public *and* the perpetrator. The perpetrator is not treated as an instrument to norm pronouncement or expression, but is given an opportunity to distance him- or herself from moral wrongs and restore the sense of moral self.

8.2.3. Responsibility of Leaders and Institutions

Seeking leadership responsibility can be part of the effort to improve the behavioural environment of ordinary soldiers. Military leaders and ultimately the State should bear responsibility for running the military organization and going into war. Larry May, for example, suggests that when interpreting principles of attribution, one should bear in mind that it is leaders who are "most deserving of being prosecuted for war crimes".[73] Leaders create rules and expectations of "approved behaviours" within their sphere of influence.[74] They play key roles in determining the direction that the institution is taking, more so than the participants therein. The often 'systemic' ethical failure in military institutions is the result of "regulation, policy, culture and ideology".[75] Military leaders may bear different degrees of responsibility. The responsibility of an individual soldier and that of the commander should be seen in proportion. Their power and agency should correspond to their responsibility. The greater control and influence exercised by the commander, the more responsibility should be assigned to him or her, and less to the individual soldier.

[73] Larry May, *War Crimes and Just War*, Cambridge University Press, 2007, p. 18. See also, *id.*, pp. 256–278.

[74] Zimbardo, 2007, p. 438, see *supra* note 3.

[75] Doris and Murphy, 2007, p. 52, see *supra* note 7.

When it comes to isolated war crimes committed by deviating individuals, often perceived as 'bad apples' cases, the institution should not be pronounced innocent so quickly. The military is responsible for providing the opportunity to commit atrocity and encouraging aggression and violence in its training. Training techniques and operating tactics which facilitate lawful killing can also facilitate war crimes. Operational guidelines which are overly suspicious of and aggressive towards civilians can easily lead to excessive violence. Organizational practices and policies which have more implicit links to seemingly isolated atrocities, such as deployment lengths and frequency, monitoring and treatment of acute mental distress, management of premises, disciplinary oversight of individual behaviour (such as consumption of alcohol), *et cetera*, should be considered. Leaders should share responsibility for deviations and excesses to the degree that these violations are caused by what they actively encourage and what they omit to do. The responsibility may go beyond individual leaders. State responsibility can also be invoked in these cases.[76] Blame should be justly allocated, says a Vietnam veteran regarding the My Lai massacre.[77] War correspondent Louis Heren further argues that "the major guilt surely rests with the then Secretary of Defence who decided that the war would be fought with indiscriminate firepower of megaton proportions and inhuman practices such as free fire zones and body counts".[78] Heren is right. The more 'top-down' war crimes are, the more responsibility should be attributed to the leadership rather than lower-level participants.

The idea that responsibility may lie higher up is not entirely alien to policy and practice, at least at the international level. The strategy of targeting higher-level military and civilian leaders has generally speaking been adopted in international trials. The Chief Prosecutor of the Nuremberg Tribunal, Robert H. Jackson, pointed out that all of the Nuremberg defendants had "broad discretion" and "great power" in their participation in the mass crimes, and that their responsibility should be correspondingly great.[79] Various *ad hoc* tribunals and the ICC also seek, in their policy and practice, to pursue higher-level leaders who are most responsible for atrocity crimes. The Prosecutor of the ICC, for example, prioritizes mid- and high-level perpetrators in case-selection, assuming leaders

[76] See O'Sullivan, 2016, p. 3, *supra* note 48.

[77] Bourke, 1999, p. 180, see *supra* note 12.

[78] *Ibid.*, p. 224.

[79] Robert H. Jackson, "Opening Statement Before the International Military Criminal Tribunal", in *Trial of Major War Criminals Before the International Military Tribunal, Nuremberg, 14 November – 1 October 1946*, Volume 2: Proceedings, IMT, Nuremberg, 1947, pp. 98–102 (https://www.legal-tools.org/doc/3c08b1/).

typically bear greater responsibility.[80] This may be driven by practical and principled reasons which are not examined in this book. The insight of social psychology provides an additional principled reason for pursuing leadership responsibility.

There exist sophisticated attribution rules in international criminal law for the role of the leadership: they can be punished as the principal perpetrator, the criminal mastermind, for ordering or soliciting crimes, or through command responsibility for failure to prevent or punish war crimes. These rules are clear-cut. They reflect the powerful influence of inter-personal relationships in commission of war crimes.[81] That being said, even applied with skilfulness, creativity and the best intentions, these attribution rules cannot fully capture the influence of the leadership and the atrocity-inducing environment they create. This brings us back to the inherent limitations of criminal law and its fictions. Criminal law's internal remedies cannot eradicate but only mitigate the fundamental biases of its attribution frame.

8.3. Residual Responsibility in the Crime of Aggression

The previous section calls for a better balance between person and environment in the attribution of responsibility. The attribution of crimes to military organization and battlefield environment leads us to think about the responsibility of war itself. The core insight is that war not only causes death and destruction which are deemed 'normal', but also induces excesses of violence which are 'pathological'. Together, the 'normal' and 'pathological' violence of war constitute the "specific evil"[82] of the crime of aggression. The criminalization of aggression therefore plays a crucial role in the cosmopolitan justification of punishing war crimes in two ways. First, it mitigates the compromises made of cosmopolitan values in war. The incomplete protection of human life and dignity in war, as specified in Chapter 4 above, can be seen as a "transitional stage"[83] to a full cosmopolitan condition of peace. The ambivalence, the selectivity of war crimes law when it comes to the protection of cosmopolitan values can only be

[80] Office of the Prosecutor of the ICC, "Policy Paper on Case Selection and Prioritisation", 15 September 2016 (https://www.legal-tools.org/doc/182205/).

[81] To mitigate the inadequacies of the current rules, Neha Jain proposes doctrinal reforms of individual responsibility to reflect the role and function of high-level participants in mass atrocity. See Neha Jain, *Perpetrators and Accessories in International Criminal Law: Individual Modes of Responsibility for Collective Crimes*, Hart Publishing, London, 2016.

[82] Frédéric Mégret, "What is the Specific Evil of Aggression?", in Claus Kreß and Stefan Barriga (eds.), *The Crime of Aggression: A Commentary*, Cambridge University Press, 2017, p. 1443.

[83] *Ibid.*, p. 1446.

justified if the reason for such conditionality and compromise is addressed by a parallel regime of criminal law.[84]

Second, where appropriate, the responsibility of war crimes not accounted for due to insufficient normative competence caused by war can be attributed to the crime of aggression. It is not exactly in the simple logical sense that war is a precondition to war crimes – if there were no war, war crimes would never have been committed. It is rather a psychologically-informed understanding that corruption of soldiers' mental competence in war partly causes excessive violence. War produces anti-cosmopolitan conditions – suppression of human agency and individuality, promotion of hatred, dehumanization, desensitization of violence. The propensity and intentionality to commit war crimes should be seen as preceding from both the human agent and the war. The root cause of war crimes is war. If war crimes law addresses the symptom, then prohibition of war addresses the real disease of excesses in war. While war crimes are condemned for their immediacy to 'unnecessary' sufferings, the crime of aggression has an indirect yet indispensable role to play in accounting for human tragedies in war.

A cosmopolitan criminal law may excuse or mitigate responsibility of war crimes for the soldier's diminished normative competence; it may also resort to moral expediency in punishing individuals for their typical reactions to conditions of war. Any residual responsibility from excusal or mitigation of responsibility and the burden of moral expediency can be seen as displaced to the aggressor. From a cosmopolitan perspective, war must be criminalized for making law and cosmopolitan ethos unavailable to its participants. This is prior and indispensable to promoting cosmopolitan values in war. In other words, responsibility for war crimes should be seen as captured by both war crimes and the crime of aggression. This provides a better understanding of the gravity of aggression as not just creating 'necessary' sufferings in war but also making 'unnecessary' sufferings inevitable.

For war crimes prosecution not to distract the public from the true moral cost of war, it is crucial to prosecute the crime of aggression, where applicable. The structural arbitrariness in the criminalization of excesses in war, as laid out in Chapter 4, and its psychological consequences for war participants, as described in Chapters 6 and 7, can be mitigated by the prosecution of the crime of aggression. A cosmopolitan war crimes law is not self-justifying, but can only be justified by simultaneous criminalization of war. Cosmopolitan morality requires fighting against the crime of war before war crimes.

[84] See, for a critical analysis of an isolated approach to war crimes, Samuel Moyn, *Humane: How the United States Abandoned Peace and Reinvented War*, Farrar, Straus and Giroux, New York, 2021.

Where the war is fought not because there is an aggressor, such as the case of 'humanitarian intervention', or most non-international armed conflicts, it is more complicated to attribute responsibility of the war. More value trade-offs should be recognized. Cosmopolitan values are more ambiguous and unsustainable in these situations.

9

Conclusion: Unique Paradoxes of a Cosmopolitan War Crimes Law

This book is a quest for the moral meaning of war crimes law. It starts with an attempt to build cosmopolitan morality into war crimes law. Universalist, individualist and rationalist cosmopolitan principles can provide moral meaning to the law. A cosmopolitan war crimes law embodies a cohesive and concerted cosmopolitan community. Individuals can be bound by universal moral links or certain models of political organization such as cosmopolitan constitutionalism or cosmopolitan democracy. Community values underlying such a law are universal and homocentric. The social foundation of the cosmopolitan law is linked to certain assumptions of the moral nature of human beings. The cosmopolitan community relies on its rational and autonomous members to achieve consensus on fundamental values and account for war crimes.

On the ideational level, the eminent legitimacy conferred by cosmopolitan morality is compromised by the need to accommodate war-time norms. Cosmopolitan values are inevitably curtailed in the criminalization process for the law to have any relevance in war. A cosmopolitan war crimes law's ambivalent, partial and relative moral message is matched by its uncertain effect in practice. On the experiential level, cosmopolitan legal legitimacy is diluted by the bond among remote strangers, and diminished by countervailing social environments. Sociological and psychological findings challenge the constancy and impartiality of the moral nature of human beings as presupposed in cosmopolitan moral and legal thinking. Hence, the *moral distance* between the embedded person and a cosmopolitan community. The moral distance is further expanded by cosmopolitanism's ideological opposite – war. In particular, war affects the law's target of regulation in an empirically and normatively significant way. Neglect of the social and psychological impact of war can undermine cosmopolitan law's effectiveness and relevancy. It may be legitimate to promote personal choice and responsibility in peace-time, but under conditions of war, it is often not fair to require the ordinary soldier to behave consistently as rational and autonomous agents. It is equally unfair to let the individual take the blame for the system and be burdened with the inevitable consequences of the decision to go to war.

This book does not claim exclusivity on the cosmopolitan vision which can guide war crimes law. The cosmopolitan blueprint painted here is only one possible version, one that is informed by, and independent from, the substance and practice of war crimes law. Nevertheless, the challenges of war described in this book may remain relevant for any other cosmopolitan approaches to war crimes law or international criminal law in general.

9.1. Composition and Conditions of a Cosmopolitan War Crimes Law

This book conceives a possible cosmopolitan war crimes law with its social foundations, underlying values, and conception of human agency and responsibility. The social foundations of war crimes law can be a cosmopolitan community. The cosmopolitan community should be a more or less coherent entity capable of articulating common values and producing concerted reactions. It can be a kind of minimalist cosmopolitan morality which is concerned with human vulnerabilities in reaction to the worst sufferings in war. Such a moral community can be "slender but robust".[1] Alternatively, possible models of cosmopolitan political organization include cosmopolitan constitutionalism and cosmopolitan democracy. A cosmopolitan war crimes law identifies values which are important to the cosmopolitan community. These values are human-centred and universal. That is, the law seeks to protect individual interests and worth which are primary and absolute compared to material objects or collective rights. Meanwhile, the cosmopolitan criminal law, as it applies in the context of war, has to acknowledge that certain violations of the most fundamental values such as human life and freedom in war are necessary, as established in Chapter 4.

Within a relational conception of criminal law, the individual is linked to the community in both the creation and application of the law. Criminal law connects the community to the individual through shared interests and values, selective criminalization of certain conducts, and normative demands on each member. For the general public, criminal law serves as a vehicle to express common values, denounce serious wrongs, and communicate with the perpetrator. The relationship between the individual and the community as required by and embodied in criminal law may not fully reflect the reality. But some degree of fiction is necessary for the justification and legitimation of criminal law.

The cosmopolitan community relies on its rational and autonomous members to achieve consensus on fundamental common values and account for war crimes. In an ideal world, a cosmopolitan war crimes law is supported by a cosmopolitan solidarity for maximum protection of human values in war, and is applied to the individual agent who can appreciate the cogency of the law and act rationally. The argument comes down to rational human agency. A rational human being, as the subject of cosmopolitan solidarity, would support the

[1] Jürgen Habermas, *The Postnational Constellation: Political Essays*, ed. and trans. by Max Pensky, MIT Press, Cambridge, Massachusetts, 2001, pp. 107–112.

creation of a cosmopolitan war crimes law in order to alleviate the worst human suffering. Anyone who disagrees with such fundamental preoccupation with human vulnerability is considered partial and irrational. A rational human being as the object of the regulation of criminal law would, after reviewing all behavioural options, conclude that the best course of action is to refrain from committing war crimes. Anyone who is not able to adopt this conclusion and act accordingly is considered irrational. Criminality is associated with intentional irrationality.

A cosmopolitan approach to war crimes law shows how cosmopolitan morality can guide the creation, interpretation and application of criminal law in the context of war. In particular, cosmopolitan principles, as they are applied to war crimes law, require certain assumptions of the moral nature of human beings. By fully appreciating what a cosmopolitan war crimes law entails, this book lays down theoretical building blocks for future development of such a law, if so desired. After all, a cosmopolitan community has to be imagined before it can be realized. Common values must be identified before they can be protected. Human agency must be valued before it can be empowered.

9.2. Cosmopolitan Principles and the Frame of Criminal Law

Cosmopolitanism is a way of imagining criminal law. A war crimes law conceived under the guidance of cosmopolitan morality is universalist in its reach, individualist in its focus, and rationalist in its normative demand. Criminal law originates and is typically applied in the domestic environment and in peacetime. That is, the law traditionally gains meaning and efficacy in a closed community and predictable environment, where bonds among individuals are concrete and assessment of fundamental right and wrong is relatively consistent. The extension of the frame of criminal law to a cosmopolitan community does not mean a simple increase in size, but introduces a whole complexity of parallel relationships between the individual and different communities. Criminal law's authority and efficacy towards potential perpetrators hinge on how individuals perceive their relationship with the collective and with each other. The deeper a collective binds its members, the more power and influence it can assert. The nature and scope of the cosmopolitan community prefigure the nature and extent of its normative authority over its members. The universal reach of a cosmopolitan criminal law dilutes the relationship between the community and its members. The normative influence of a cosmopolitan criminal law suffers consequently.

On the other hand, there is certain affinity between cosmopolitan principles and legal rhetoric. Ideological compatibility can facilitate the cosmopolitanization of law. The "formal equivalence of legal relations" necessarily abstracts and simplifies individual persons by treating them as "formally identical".[2] This correlates with the universal orientation of law which seeks general application through "use of formulas", minimizing individual variation.[3] The universal, egalitarian orientations of law can make its cosmopolitan application seem natural. Criminal law, in particular, also coincides with cosmopolitan morality in its emphasis of individuality and human agency. Criminal law's projection of reality is "egocentric"[4] in that it favours personal features and voluntary action. By isolating the individual mind and behaviour, it deliberately excludes environmental elements such as culture and society. The problem and solution lie solely in the individual person. The individual-centred criminal law receives philosophical approval from cosmopolitan thinking. The individual is both the source of justification behind the law and the target of regulation. The individual provides both meaning and solution for the law. A war crimes law affirmed by cosmopolitan individualism is more confident, righteous and unrelenting in asserting its version of reality and normative dispensation. It describes personal disposition and motivation as the sole causes of war crimes. Consequently, any intervention on human behaviour should be made upon human persons, not their environment.

Similarly, criminal law requires a rational agent who is amenable to its normative demands. Human rationality is deemed consistent and stable. With a few exceptions, the agent should be regarded as rational under all circumstances. After all, if the individual does not have full mental capacity, the intervention of criminal law is neither plausible nor justified. The cosmopolitan ideology lends force to the rationalist assumption of criminal law by highlighting the immanence and impartiality of moral reasoning. In trying circumstances such as war, a cosmopolitan war crimes law demands human beings to be more rational and independent in their thinking. *Human reason*, and reason alone, becomes the hope of reversing atrocities in war. The cosmopolitan advocacy of human value is matched by its high standards for human agency. It justifies the application of criminal law in the context of war without considering any mitigating circumstances not anticipated in peace-time.

If in peace-time, the individualist and rationalist emphases of criminal law may still have a comfortable distance from reality for the law to be reasonable

2 Roger Cotterrell, *Law's Community: Legal Theory in Sociological Perspective*, Clarendon Press, Oxford, 1995, p. 99.

3 Mikael Rask Madsen, "Reflexive Sociology of International Law: Pierre Bourdieu and the Globalization of Law", in Moshe Hirsch and Andrew Lang (eds.), *Research Handbook on the Sociology of International Law*, Edward Elgar Publishing, Cheltenham, 2018, p. 190.

4 See Boaventura de Sousa Santos, "Law: A Map of Misreading. Toward a Postmodern Conception of Law", in *Journal of Law and Society*, 1987, vol. 14, no. 3, p. 292.

and fair, in times of war, these structural emphases may well become structural biases. When the cosmopolitan ideology lends war crimes law its formidable moral authority, it also *exacerbates* these biases.

9.3. Legal and Moral Authorities of a Cosmopolitan War Crimes Law

In legal processes, participants use legal rules "as a means of proof in support of a thesis".[5] A legal argument invites its audience to accept a claim not because of its "intrinsic merits"[6] – such as intellectual or moral merits – but because it is validated by positive law. The legal discourse is believed to be "intellectually and normatively autonomous" and to possess "a self-generated validity through its systematic and logical character".[7] It is "cognitively open" and "normatively closed" to "external knowledge fields" such as morality, politics or sociology.[8] That is, external insights do not gain normative significance automatically, they are only recognized in law's own terms, or reconceived from "law's point of view".[9] The external world needs to be translated into the legal reality through some "consecration mechanisms".[10] Law distributes significance to external information according to "its *own* system imperatives" and transforms exogenous communications into its own terms.[11] For example, war crimes law determines agency based on what part of human nature it considers legally relevant or meaningful. The fact that law's conception of human agency is different from sociological or psychological findings does not undermine the formal validity of the law. Roger Cotterrell points to the capacity of law to "find its own good reasons within its own framework of discourse for ignoring even obvious facts of its environment".[12] Law has a monopoly of meaning in its own "symbolic universe".[13] This "integrated" system devises its own standards for assessing the

5 The cited phrase is originally used to describe personal authority: "an argument from authority 'uses the acts or opinions of a person or group of persons as a means of proof in support of a thesis'", in Fuad Zarbiyev, "Saying Credibly What the Law Is: On Marks of Authority in International Law", in *Journal of International Dispute Settlement*, 2018, vol. 9, no. 2, p. 296.

6 *Ibid.*

7 Cotterrell, 1995, p. 93, see *supra* note 2.

8 See *ibid.*, and p. 52.

9 See Nicole Roughan, "Mind the Gaps: Authority and Legality in International Law", in *European Journal of International Law*, 2015, vol. 27, no. 2, p. 333.

10 Madsen, 2018, p. 196, see supra note 3.

11 Cotterrell, 1995, p. 105, see *supra* note 2.

12 *Ibid.*, p. 52.

13 Sungjoon Cho, "Social Constructivism and the Social Construction of World Economic Reality", in Hirsch and Lang (eds.), 2018, p. 381, see *supra* note 3.

quality of the legal argument.[14] Within the "epistemologies"[15] of law, normative disputes are resolved through the method of logic.[16] There is an internal normative scale according to which some legal reasoning is imaginative rather than unsound, creative rather than idiosyncratic, robust rather than careless.[17]

The "operational code" of law is built upon a "myth system" which ultimately generates law's autonomy and normative force.[18] Law evokes a sense of obligation which is distinctly legal and provides an "exclusionary reason for action".[19] Such reason is "content-independent"[20] because law's authority does not depend on substantive justification from external knowledge fields, but solely on its formal validity according to its own method. It is "pre-emptive" because it precludes "possible countervailing reasons" and overrules "other relevant considerations".[21] Law is thought to have an "independent capacity" to effect compliant behaviour.[22]

Legal authority is therefore neither "coercion" nor "rational persuasion" but a kind of "deference entitlement"[23] which comes from a *belief* in the intrinsic merit of law. Within this belief system, law aspires ideals of justice, emancipation and progress.[24] In particular, law devises a certain form of justification which ensures that regulatory decisions be made on "reasoned not idiosyncratic grounds".[25] Through formalities, procedures and publicity, law makes the exercise of power relatively reasonable and predictable.[26] It creates a sense of security for all subjects of law.[27] This is perhaps a reason why subjects of law believe

---

14 Cotterrell, 1995, p. 109, see *supra* note 2.

15 Gregory Shaffer, "The New Legal Realist Approach to International Law", in *Leiden Journal of International Law*, 2015, vol. 28, no. 2, p. 207.

16 Daniel Bodansky, "Legal Realism and its Discontents", in *Leiden Journal of International Law*, 2015, vol. 28, no. 2, p. 271.

17 Cotterrell, 1995, p. 92, see *supra* note 2.

18 Bodansky, 2015, p. 281, see *supra* note 16.

19 Roughan, 2015, p. 338, see *supra* note 9.

20 Zarbiyev, 2018, p. 294, see *supra* note 5.

21 *Ibid.*

22 Nicolas Lamp, "The 'Practice Turn' in International Law: Insights from the Theory of Structuration", in Hirsch and Lang (eds.), 2018, p. 289, see *supra* note 3.

23 Zarbiyev, 2018, pp. 294–295, see *supra* note 5.

24 Cotterrell, 1995, p. 17, see *supra* note 2.

25 Ian Johnstone, "The Power of Interpretive Communities", in Michael Barnett and Raymond Duvall (eds.), *Power in Global Governance*, Cambridge University Press, 2005, p. 187. See also, Jean D'Aspremont, *International Law as a Belief System*, Cambridge University Press, 2017.

26 Cotterrell, 1995, p. 18, see *supra* note 2.

27 *Ibid.*

they have a stake in the rule of law.[28] Bodansky reminds us that it is the "veneration" for the "majesty" of law that effectuates changes.[29]

Despite the magic a genuine faith in the rule of law can perform, law's inspirational formalities may still be insufficient. The intrinsic morality of law is neutral. Perfect legal arguments can be substantively arbitrary, unjust, or simply cold and boring. As the saying goes: "It is easier to make certain things legal than to make them legitimate".[30] In particular, the nature of issues falling under the realm of criminal law motivates a search for morally meaningful legality. It requires building into criminal law values of a "well-integrated and well-ordered" society.[31] Moral justifications can be deliberately and selectively imported into legal reasoning. Cosmopolitan morality represents a powerful external justification which can reinforce the authority of war crimes law. It provides an additional normative scale which increases the substantive legitimacy of the law. Its universal reach, individualist focus and rationalist beliefs diametrically oppose mentalities associated with war-time atrocity. When a criminal law claims to assert universal values over particular interests, individual agency and responsibility over systemic power and impunity, consistent rationality over situational vulnerability, it appeals to faith in the ultimate triumph of the human person and projects moral strength.

Even where the quality of legal reasoning suffers as a consequence of inadequate positive law, moral authority can make up where legal arguments fall short. In a number of cases of the ICTY discussed in this book, insufficient legal authority is remedied by powerful moral authority. A commentator pointed to the sensitivity behind the relationship between law and morality: "positive law running out, especially in the face of an atrocity, is the worst thing that could happen to the international legal system".[32] Zahar even claims that the lasting impact of the Nuremberg trial and the ICTY comes from the moral authority, not legal quality of their work.[33] There seems to be a smooth transition between law and morality, which is paradoxical from a strict "law's point of view". It is

[28] Lamp, 2018, p. 289, see *supra* note 22.

[29] Bodansky, 2015, p. 281, see *supra* note 16.

[30] Cited in C.A. Thomas, "The Concept of Legitimacy and International Law", LSE Law, Society and Economy Working Papers No. 12, 2013, p. 2.

[31] Cotterrell, 1995, p. 301, see *supra* note 2.

[32] Cited in Payam Akhavan, "The Perils of Progressive Jurisprudence: The *Nullum Crimen Sine Lege* Principle in International Criminal Law", in *Current Legal Problems*, 2022, vol. 74, no. 1, p. 22.

[33] Alexander Zahar, "Civilizing Civil War: Rewriting Morality as Law", in Bert Swart, Alexander Zahar and Göran Sluiter (eds.), *The Legacy of the International Criminal Tribunal for the former Yugoslavia*, Oxford University Press, 2011, p. 493.

paradoxical because acknowledging the independent force of morality in front of law, although done selectively and purposively, inevitably undermines the intrinsic authority of law. Yet, in international criminal law jurisprudence, the combination of legal and moral reasoning often seems to produce a miraculous synergy which increases the overall impact of the law.

The legal-moral authority carried by a cosmopolitan criminal law can be a force for change. It can channel the evolution of law into a more cosmopolitan direction and even bring the reality closer to the cosmopolitan ideals. Indeed, the project of criminal justice can be a forerunner for other cosmopolitan projects in bringing about cosmopolitan conditions. Theory always has practical implications, not to mention long-lasting, deeply inspirational theories such as the cosmopolitan ones. Nevertheless, the discussion of a cosmopolitan war crimes law should not stop at ideational realms. Its claim to legitimacy should be examined not only from a normative perspective, but also from empirical perspectives.

Is the law as morally meaningful to the fictitious cosmopolitan agent as to concrete persons embedded in diverse cultures and societies? This question transitions the discussion from philosophical ideals to empirical observations. War crimes law typically seeks to regulate targets outside its "epistemic community".[34] While within its epistemic community the imperative of the rule of law is more or less respected and recognized as relevant, outside law's epistemologies its authority is relative to other social norms. The same can be said about cosmopolitan morality, whose challenge does not lie in addressing its moral salience to its followers, but in 'converting' bystanders and opponents. Empirical accounts of moral psychology and anti-cosmopolitan conditions of war contextualize and relativize claims of legal authority and cosmopolitan moral authority. They can help detach law from its preoccupation with its own "discipline-effect" which, according to Cotterrell, is not founded in scientific autonomy and certainties, but in "the social-political imperatives of law as an intersection of knowledge and power".[35] Exclusive focus on "postulated" values and moral sentiments of a cosmopolitan community can isolate war crimes law from conditions of war to which it purports to relate.[36]

[34] Mai'a K. Davis Cross, "Rethinking Epistemic Communities Twenty Years Later", in *Review of International Studies*, 2013, vol. 39, no. 1, p. 138.

[35] Cotterrell, 1995, p. 56, see *supra* note 2.

[36] *Ibid.*, p. 301.

9.4. The Relative Authority of a Cosmopolitan War Crimes Law in Multiple Realities and Normative Systems

Normative frameworks project not only norms but also their version of reality. Criminal law is a way of imagining the real.[37] It provides a particular description, evaluation and response to an event. Using its own criteria to determine which details and features of an event to regulate, criminal law creates its own legal reality that fits its application.[38] Within its "edited diagrams of reality",[39] criminal law emphasizes certain facts instead of others. By selectively representing the reality, the frame of criminal law promotes "a particular problem definition, causal interpretation, moral evaluation, and/or treatment recommendation".[40] It is perhaps because of its reductionist approach to reality that criminal law is able to produce "a decontextualized taxonomy of evil"[41] and "solemn and definitive judgments".[42] It can only succeed in describing and regulating acts of war crimes to a certain degree, depending on the relationship between the cosmopolitan community and the individual, between criminal law and other social norms.

A cosmopolitan war crimes law's images of community are "ideological presentations" of social life.[43] They present partial as total.[44] Because of its selective mode of representation, a cosmopolitan war crimes law can be reality-distorting, even when it is applied creatively. Its edited images can be confronted by other versions of norms and realities. As a result, its assumption of supremacy of authority may be diminished by non-legal and anti-cosmopolitan norms in concrete social environments. This may be counter-intuitive to committed legal minds who tend to see other social norms as "derived directly or indirectly from law, as created or maintained by 'delegation' from it, or as sources influencing the content of law".[45]

---

[37] See Santos, 1987, p. 286, *supra* note 4.

[38] See *ibid.*, pp. 287–288.

[39] See *ibid.*, p. 294.

[40] Cited in Charles M. Rowling, Penelope Sheets and Timothy M. Jones, "American Atrocity Revisited: National Identity, Cascading Frames, and the My Lai Massacre", in *Political Communication*, 2015, vol. 32, no. 2, p. 312. Boaventura de Sousa Santos similarly says that "Each legal object favours a specific formulation of interests and a specific concept of disputes and of modes of settling them". See Santos, 1987, p. 291, *supra* note 4.

[41] Akhavan, 2022, p. 25, see *supra* note 32.

[42] Gerry Simpson, "The Conscience of Civilisation, and its Discontents: A Counter History of International Criminal Law", in Philipp Kastner (ed.), *International Criminal Law in Context*, Routledge, Abingdon, 2017, p. 26.

[43] Cotterrell, 1995, p. 325, see *supra* note 2.

[44] *Ibid.*

[45] Cotterrell, 1995, p. 29, see *supra* note 2.

An important sociological insight is that non-legal norms are not necessarily "subordinate"[46] to law. Legal doctrine cannot, just by postulation of normative supremacy, effect "dramatic and meaningful" normative changes in a concrete social environment.[47] Criminal law's reductionist description inevitably produces reductionist solutions. The sometimes "simple-minded and linear"[48] reality projected by criminal justice is constantly destabilized by the complexity of war. The cosmopolitan community and its law co-exist with local communities and their normative frameworks. Meanwhile, legal rules co-exist with formal and informal social norms and customs. These different normative frameworks may coincide, conflict or compete with each other. An individual can find them appealing to different degrees. A cosmopolitan war crimes law's impact on behaviour cannot be seen as automatic and comprehensive, but conditional and relative.[49]

Previous chapters show that a cosmopolitan war crimes law's assertion of normative authority may face competition from normative frameworks of the military institution and war itself. Many of these conflicts are inevitable: the military institution legitimizes killing and dehumanization, promotes group thinking and obedience to authority, opposes values of human life and dignity, and suppresses rational and autonomous agency; the war further desensitizes killing and entrenches a dehumanizing relationship with the enemy. *Those who are subject to law's regulation may not inhabit the same reality or normative climate as projected by the very law*. Furthermore, the ordinary soldier may be caught in incompatible normative demands and interpretations of facts which all seek to influence his mind and behaviour. Law is built upon relationships as "legal capital" is built upon "social capital".[50] The power of legal capital depends not just on its "myth system", but also on its social foundations.[51] While the cosmopolitan community is remote and abstract, the military structure is immediate and concrete. Evidence suggests that effective prevention of crimes depends much less on certainty of criminal prosecution than how soldiers are

[46] *Ibid.*

[47] Moshe Hirsch, "The Sociological Perspective on International Law", in Jeffrey L. Dunoff and Mark A. Pollack (eds.), *International Legal Theory: Foundations and Frontiers*, Cambridge University Press, 2022, p. 283.

[48] Simpson, 2017, p. 26, see *supra* note 42.

[49] See Shaffer, 2015, p. 195, *supra* note 15; and Roughan, 2015, p. 340, see *supra* note 9.

[50] Bryant G. Garth, "Issues of Empire, Contestation, and Hierarchy in the Globalization of Law", in Hirsch and Lang (eds.), 2018, p. 28, see *supra* note 3.

[51] *Ibid.*

organized before and during the combat.[52] Law gives *general* reasons for action which require agents' further practical reasoning in a concrete situation.[53] The "congruence thesis" suggests that "legal norms and authoritative directives can guide self-directed social interaction only if they are broadly congruent with the practices and patterns of interaction extant in the society generally".[54] Ordinary soldiers' experience of law may be "incongruous", "technocratic" or "literal";[55] their failures of recognizing immorality, illegality, personal responsibility, and of realizing personal autonomy show the inefficiency of a cosmopolitan criminal law and the inadequacy of internal remedies alone. These failures are prompted by the immediate normative frameworks and combat environment which may have more power over the individual than the abstract cosmopolitan law.

In light of psychological findings, Ross and Shestowsky already caution in the domestic context that criminal law be modest in its claim of dispensing justice.[56] Criminologists suggest that "informal, extra-legal social sanctions" are often "a much more powerful disincentive" for crimes than formal legal sanctions.[57] In international law practice and literature, confidence in "the transformative potential" of a cosmopolitan legal order has been tempered in the recent decade.[58] Only those who have the most zealous faith in the rule of law would claim that legal doctrine can resolve very difficult moral and political problems.[59] A cosmopolitan legalistic approach to international crimes has been rightly criticized by many for its tendencies to overpromise and underdeliver.[60] Nouwen and Werner, for example, argue that the project of criminal justice

52 See Mark Osiel, "Obeying Orders: Atrocity, Military Discipline, and the Law of War", in *California Law Review*, 1998, vol. 86, no. 5, p. 1028.

53 Jutta Brunnée and Stephen J. Toope, *Legitimacy and Legality in International Law: An Interactional Account*, Cambridge University Press, 2010, p. 23.

54 *Ibid.*

55 Simpson, 2017, p. 26, see *supra* note 42.

56 Lee Ross and Donna Shestowsky, "Contemporary Psychology's Challenges to Legal Theory and Practice", in *Northwestern University Law Review*, 2002, vol. 97, no. 3, p. 1081.

57 David Mendeloff, "The Coercive Effects of International Justice: How Perpetrators Respond to Threats of Prosecution", in Susanne C. Knittel and Zachary J. Goldberg (eds.), *The Routledge International Handbook of Perpetrator Studies*, Routledge, Abingdon, 2020, p. 144.

58 Mark Goodale, "After International Law: Anthropology Beyond the 'Age of Human Rights'", in *AJIL Unbound*, 2021, vol. 115, p. 289.

59 This is paraphrased from Chayes' warning that international lawyers "must avoid the temptation to deal with very difficult political and moral issues as though they could be resolved by rather simple and very general legal imperatives". Cited in Bodansky, 2015, p. 276, see *supra* note 16.

60 See an overview of criticisms and discussion of alternative mechanisms in Darryl Robinson, "A Cosmopolitan Liberal Account of International Criminal Law", in *Leiden Journal of International Law*, 2013, vol. 26, no. 1, p. 140.

marginalizes alternative conceptions of global justice.[61] Criminal law is necessary but certainly not enough in dealing with atrocities. It should not give us the illusion that it can alone align the motivation of actors to refrain from committing war crimes. To be fully informed in finding solutions to war crimes, we need to look beyond the regime of criminal law.

It is therefore important for a cosmopolitan law to not only incorporate sociological and psychological insights as it sees fit, but also to explore its relationship with other social norms which may be not so cosmopolitan or even non-legal. A cosmopolitan war crimes law needs to come to terms with its "relative authority".[62] Co-operation is as important as co-optation. The normativity of law is strengthened by concurrent social norms and undermined by an opposing social environment. No legal solution or cosmopolitan morality is viable in a social or cultural vacuum.[63] Legal discourse cannot replace "imaginative dialogues", "social bonding" or "community building".[64] It is therefore not enough to create more laws and better laws. Additional "ideational routes"[65] should be explored. A favourable social environment can provide a kind of "social grammar"[66] for the abstract law and its cosmopolitan morality. The solution of a cosmopolitan criminal law must be supplemented or seen as supplementary to other social solutions in preventing and denouncing war crimes. Advocates for a cosmopolitan war crimes law should treat "competing versions of rationality" and external "value-spheres"[67] seriously.

9.5. Enchantment and Disenchantment of Norms: Merits and Perils of Empirical Findings

If the construction part of the book portrays an enchanting picture of a cosmopolitan war crimes law, the description of empirical findings may have a somewhat disenchanting effect. The book recognizes that legal discourse, even one that is empowered by a formidable cosmopolitan morality, does not enjoy a privileged vantage point outside its own epistemologies. It tempers "nomological thinking" with contextual thinking.[68] The cosmopolitan law should incorporate

---

61 Sarah M.H. Nouwen and Wouter G. Werner, "Monopolizing Global Justice: International Criminal Law as Challenge to Human Diversity", in *Journal of International Criminal Justice*, 20-15, vol. 13, no. 1, pp. 157 ff.

62 Roughan, 2015, p. 340, see *supra* note 9.

63 Cho, 2018, p. 386, see *supra* note 13. Cho's argument is made in the context of WTO law.

64 *Ibid.*, pp. 385, 387.

65 *Ibid.*, p. 387.

66 *Ibid.*, p. 388.

67 Galit A. Sarfaty, "An Anthropological Approach to International Economic Law", in Hirsch and Lang (eds.), 2018, p. 313, see *supra* note 3.

68 Shaffer, 2015, p. 206, see *supra* note 15.

into its own reference system external rationalities such as those of empirical disciplines. The appliers and advocates of such a law should also seek co-operation with other social norms and mechanisms, to avoid normative imperialism or blindness. This does not mean, of course, that empirically-oriented disciplines, such as sociology and psychology illustrated in this book, are superior to the legal discourse. Just like the legal discourse, empirical disciplines do not enjoy a privileged position in their truth claims. It is readily accepted that "all empirical knowledge is contingent, not absolute".[69] Empirical studies may offer a relatively "reliable access to the objective world", but only in a progressive, provisional or partial manner.[70] They can be considered objective or relevant "in a particular context, for certain purposes, and only for now".[71]

Despite their defects, empirical findings can inform, enrich and disrupt normative discussions in significant and meaningful ways. The description of the effects of war on human institutions and agency turns cosmopolitanism against its own premise – the moral nature of human beings. The confrontation of cosmopolitanism and war is not purely a contestation of wills. The challenges faced by a cosmopolitan war crimes law lie in the subconscious and unconscious mind, not just conscious thinking; in radical emotions, not just rational communications. The cosmopolitan ideal is rivalled not by an alien enemy, but its *alter ego*.

The empirical approach does not seek to prove the irrelevance or irrationality of law or its belief system. Rather, it seeks to improve the legal and moral appeal of a cosmopolitan war crimes law by narrowing the gap between legal norms and "local moral conditions".[72] It seeks to make the law morally meaningful not only to those who support its formation, but also to those subject to its regulation. There is certainly constructive space "between the arrogance of dogmatism, and the despair of skepticism".[73] The question of how the law and its cosmopolitan morality can be "re-enchanted"[74] must be answered with creativity, imagination, understanding and openness. Caveated by war's anti-universalism, anti-agency and irrational nature, this book also suggests incorporation of empirical insights into legal reasoning and creation of conducive social and

---

[69] *Ibid.*, p. 202.

[70] Andrew Lang, "New Legal Realism, Empiricism, and Scientism: The Relative Objectivity of Law and Social Science", in *Leiden Journal of International Law*, 2015, vol. 28, no. 2, p. 232.

[71] *Ibid.*, p. 254.

[72] *Ibid.*

[73] Francis Bacon said this in reference to the mission of political theory. Cited in Albena Azmanova, "The Costs of the Democratic Turn in Political Theory", in Benjamin Martill and Sebastian Schindler (eds.), *Theory as Ideology in International Relations: The Politics of Knowledge*, Routledge, Abingdon, 2020, p. 111.

[74] Bodansky, 2015, p. 279, see *supra* note 16.

normative environments for its compliance. Further empirical studies can be done to shed light on conditions for a cosmopolitan war crimes law to make effective interventions. A cosmopolitan war crimes law can be "rationally planned and purposeful and also deeply rooted in social and cultural life".[75]

9.6. The Unique Paradoxes of a Cosmopolitan War Crimes Law

This book does not claim a perfect moral theory for war crimes law. A cosmopolitan theory, like any theory, has irreplaceable merits and incorrigible defects for the purposes of war crimes law. A cosmopolitan war crimes law is inherently paradoxical. In its unique paradoxes of cosmopolitanism and war lie both its strength and weakness: cosmopolitanism as an ideological counterforce to dehumanization in war; war being subversive of cosmopolitanism through unconscious mental activities, passive reactions and human vulnerabilities.

[75] *Ibid.*

INDEX

D

E

F

G

H

I

J

K

L

V

W

Z

TOAEP TEAM

VOLUMES IN TOAEP'S *PUBLICATION SERIES*

Morten Bergsmo, Mads Harlem and Nobuo Hayashi (editors):
Importing Core International Crimes into National Law
Torkel Opsahl Academic EPublisher
Oslo, 2010
FICHL Publication Series No. 1 (Second Edition, 2010)
ISBN: 978 82 93081-00-5

Nobuo Hayashi (editor):
National Military Manuals on the Law of Armed Conflict
Torkel Opsahl Academic EPublisher
Brussels, 2023
Publication Series No. 2 (Third Edition, 2023)
ISBN print: 978-82-8348-226-3
ISBN e-book: 978-82-8348-225-6

林 伸生 (主编):
国家武装冲突法军事手册研究
Torkel Opsahl Academic EPublisher
Brussels, 2023
Publication Series No. 2 (Chinese Edition, 2023)
ISBN print: 978-82-8348-119-8
ISBN e-book: 978-82-8348-120-4

Morten Bergsmo, Kjetil Helvig, Ilia Utmelidze and Gorana Žagovec:
The Backlog of Core International Crimes Case Files in Bosnia and Herzegovina
Torkel Opsahl Academic EPublisher
Oslo, 2010
FICHL Publication Series No. 3 (Second Edition, 2010)
ISBN: 978-82-93081-04-3

Morten Bergsmo (editor):
Criteria for Prioritizing and Selecting Core International Crimes Cases
Torkel Opsahl Academic EPublisher
Brussels, 2024
Publication Series No. 4 (Third Edition, 2024)
ISBN print: 978-82-8348-238-6
ISBN e-book: 978-82-8348-239-3

Morten Bergsmo and Pablo Kalmanovitz (editors):
Law in Peace Negotiations
Torkel Opsahl Academic EPublisher
Oslo, 2010
FICHL Publication Series No. 5 (Second Edition, 2010)
ISBN: 978-82-93081-08-1

Morten Bergsmo, César Rodríguez Garavito, Pablo Kalmanovitz and María Paula Saffon (editors):
Distributive Justice in Transitions
Torkel Opsahl Academic EPublisher
Oslo, 2010
FICHL Publication Series No. 6 (2010)
ISBN: 978-82-93081-12-8

Morten Bergsmo, César Rodriguez-Garavito, Pablo Kalmanovitz and María Paula Saffon (editors):
Justicia Distributiva en Sociedades en Transición
Torkel Opsahl Academic EPublisher
Oslo, 2012
FICHL Publication Series No. 6 (2012)
ISBN: 978-82-93081-10-4

Morten Bergsmo (editor):
Complementarity and the Exercise of Universal Jurisdiction for Core International Crimes
Torkel Opsahl Academic EPublisher
Oslo, 2010
FICHL Publication Series No. 7 (2010)
ISBN: 978-82-93081-14-2

Morten Bergsmo (editor):
Active Complementarity: Legal Information Transfer
Torkel Opsahl Academic EPublisher
Oslo, 2011
FICHL Publication Series No. 8 (2011)
ISBN print: 978-82-93081-56-2
ISBN e-book: 978-82-93081-55-5

Morten Bergsmo (editor):
Abbreviated Criminal Procedures for Core International Crimes
Torkel Opsahl Academic EPublisher
Brussels, 2017
FICHL Publication Series No. 9 (2017)
ISBN print: 978-82-93081-20-3
ISBN e-book: 978-82-8348-104-4

Sam Muller, Stavros Zouridis, Morly Frishman and Laura Kistemaker (editors):
The Law of the Future and the Future of Law
Torkel Opsahl Academic EPublisher
Oslo, 2010
FICHL Publication Series No. 11 (2011)
ISBN: 978-82-93081-27-2

Morten Bergsmo, Alf Butenschøn Skre and Elisabeth J. Wood (editors):
Understanding and Proving International Sex Crimes
Torkel Opsahl Academic EPublisher
Beijing, 2012
FICHL Publication Series No. 12 (2012)
ISBN: 978-82-93081-29-6

Morten Bergsmo (editor):
Thematic Prosecution of International Sex Crimes
Torkel Opsahl Academic EPublisher
Brussels, 2018
Publication Series No. 13 (Second Edition, 2018)
ISBN print: 978-82-8348-025-2
ISBN e-book: 978-82-8348-024-5

Terje Einarsen:
The Concept of Universal Crimes in International Law
Torkel Opsahl Academic EPublisher
Oslo, 2012
FICHL Publication Series No. 14 (2012)
ISBN: 978-82-93081-33-3

ترجِ آینارسن
مفهوم جرایم جهانی در حقوق بین الملل
ترجمه دکتر فریدون جعفری
Torkel Opsahl Academic EPublisher
Brussels, 2023
Publication Series No. 14 (Persian Edition, 2023)
ISBN print: 978-82-8348-202-7
ISBN e-book: 978-82-8348-203-4

莫滕·伯格斯默 凌岩(主编):
国家主权与国际刑法
Torkel Opsahl Academic EPublisher
Beijing, 2012
FICHL Publication Series No. 15 (2012)
ISBN: 978-82-93081-58-6

Morten Bergsmo and Ling Yan (editors):
State Sovereignty and International Criminal Law
Torkel Opsahl Academic EPublisher
Beijing, 2012
FICHL Publication Series No. 15 (2012)
ISBN: 978-82-93081-35-7

Morten Bergsmo, Cheah Wui Ling and Antonio Angotti (editors):
Old Evidence and Core International Crimes
Torkel Opsahl Academic EPublisher
Brussels, 2024
Publication Series No. 16 (Second Edition, 2024)
ISBN print: 978-82-8348-228-7
ISBN e-book: 978-82-8348-229-4

Yi Ping:
戦争と平和の間——発足期日本国際法学における「正しい戦争」の観念とその帰結
Torkel Opsahl Academic EPublisher
Beijing, 2013
FICHL Publication Series No. 17 (2013)
ISBN: 978-82-93081-66-1

Morten Bergsmo and Song Tianying (editors):
On the Proposed Crimes Against Humanity Convention
Torkel Opsahl Academic EPublisher
Brussels, 2014
FICHL Publication Series No. 18 (2014)
ISBN: 978-82-93081-96-8

Morten Bergsmo and Carsten Stahn (editors):
Quality Control in Fact-Finding
Torkel Opsahl Academic EPublisher
Brussels, 2020
Publication Series No. 19 (Second Edition, 2020)
ISBN print: 978-82-8348-135-8
ISBN e-book: 978-82-8348-136-5

Morten Bergsmo, Cheah Wui Ling and Yi Ping (editors):
Historical Origins of International Criminal Law: Volume 1
Torkel Opsahl Academic EPublisher
Brussels, 2014
FICHL Publication Series No. 20 (2014)
ISBN: 978-82-93081-11-1

Morten Bergsmo, Cheah Wui Ling and Yi Ping (editors):
Historical Origins of International Criminal Law: Volume 2
Torkel Opsahl Academic EPublisher
Brussels, 2014
FICHL Publication Series No. 21 (2014)
ISBN: 978-82-93081-13-5

Morten Bergsmo, Cheah Wui Ling, Song Tianying and Yi Ping (editors):
Historical Origins of International Criminal Law: Volume 3
Torkel Opsahl Academic EPublisher
Brussels, 2015
FICHL Publication Series No. 22 (2015)
ISBN print: 978-82-8348-015-3
ISBN e-book: 978-82-8348-014-6

Morten Bergsmo, Cheah Wui Ling, Song Tianying and Yi Ping (editors):
Historical Origins of International Criminal Law: Volume 4
Torkel Opsahl Academic EPublisher
Brussels, 2015
FICHL Publication Series No. 23 (2015)
ISBN print: 978-82-8348-017-7
ISBN e-book: 978-82-8348-016-0

Morten Bergsmo, Klaus Rackwitz and Song Tianying (editors):
Historical Origins of International Criminal Law: Volume 5
Torkel Opsahl Academic EPublisher
Brussels, 2017
FICHL Publication Series No. 24 (2017)
ISBN print: 978-82-8348-106-8
ISBN e-book: 978-82-8348-107-5

Morten Bergsmo and Song Tianying (editors):
Military Self-Interest in Accountability for Core International Crimes
Torkel Opsahl Academic EPublisher
Brussels, 2015
FICHL Publication Series No. 25 (2015)
ISBN print: 978-82-93081-61-6
ISBN e-book: 978-82-93081-81-4

Wolfgang Kaleck:
Double Standards: International Criminal Law and the West
Torkel Opsahl Academic EPublisher
Brussels, 2015
FICHL Publication Series No. 26 (2015)
ISBN print: 978-82-93081-67-8
ISBN e-book: 978-82-93081-83-8

ولفگانگ کالک
معیارهای دوگانه:
حقوق کیفری بین‌المللی و غرب
Torkel Opsahl Academic EPublisher
Brussels, 2025
Publication Series No. 26 (Persian Edition, 2025)
ISBN print: 978-82-8348-259-1
ISBN e-book: 978-82-8348-260-7

Liu Daqun and Zhang Binxin (editors):
Historical War Crimes Trials in Asia
Torkel Opsahl Academic EPublisher
Brussels, 2016
FICHL Publication Series No. 27 (2015)
ISBN print: 978-82-8348-055-9
ISBN e-book: 978-82-8348-056-6

Morten Bergsmo, Mark Klamberg, Kjersti Lohne and Christopher B. Mahony (editors):
Power in International Criminal Justice
Torkel Opsahl Academic EPublisher
Brussels, 2020
Publication Series No. 28 (2020)
ISBN print: 978-82-8348-113-6
ISBN e-book: 978-82-8348-114-3

Stian Nordengen Christensen:
Counterfactual History and Bosnia-Herzegovina
Torkel Opsahl Academic EPublisher
Brussels, 2018
Publication Series No. 30 (2018)
ISBN print: 978-82-8348-102-0
ISBN e-book: 978-82-8348-103-7

Stian Nordengen Christensen:
Possibilities and Impossibilities in a Contradictory Global Order
Torkel Opsahl Academic EPublisher
Brussels, 2018
Publication Series No. 31 (2018)
ISBN print: 978-82-8348-104-4
ISBN e-book: 978-82-8348-105-1

Morten Bergsmo and Carsten Stahn (editors):
Quality Control in Preliminary Examination: Volume 1
Torkel Opsahl Academic EPublisher
Brussels, 2018
Publication Series No. 32 (2018)
ISBN print: 978-82-8348-123-5
ISBN e-book: 978-82-8348-124-2

Morten Bergsmo and Carsten Stahn (editors):
Quality Control in Preliminary Examination: Volume 2
Torkel Opsahl Academic EPublisher
Brussels, 2018
Publication Series No. 33 (2018)
ISBN print: 978-82-8348-111-2
ISBN e-book: 978-82-8348-112-9

Morten Bergsmo and Emiliano J. Buis (editors):
Philosophical Foundations of International Criminal Law: Correlating Thinkers
Torkel Opsahl Academic EPublisher
Brussels, 2018
Publication Series No. 34 (2018)
ISBN print: 978-82-8348-117-4
ISBN e-book: 978-82-8348-118-1

Morten Bergsmo and Emiliano J. Buis (editors):
Philosophical Foundations of International Criminal Law: Foundational Concepts
Torkel Opsahl Academic EPublisher
Brussels, 2019
Publication Series No. 35 (2019)
ISBN print: 978-82-8348-119-8
ISBN e-book: 978-82-8348-120-4

Morten Bergsmo, Emiliano J. Buis and Song Tianying (editors):
Philosophical Foundations of International Criminal Law: Legally-Protected Interests
Torkel Opsahl Academic EPublisher
Brussels, 2022
Publication Series No. 36 (2022)
ISBN print: 978-82-8348-121-1
ISBN e-book: 978-82-8348-122-8

Terje Einarsen and Joseph Rikhof:
A Theory of Punishable Participation in Universal Crimes
Torkel Opsahl Academic EPublisher
Brussels, 2018
Publication Series No. 37 (2018)
ISBN print: 978-82-8348-127-3
ISBN e-book: 978-82-8348-128-0

Xabier Agirre Aranburu, Morten Bergsmo, Simon De Smet and Carsten Stahn (editors):
Quality Control in Criminal Investigation
Torkel Opsahl Academic EPublisher
Brussels, 2020
Publication Series No. 38 (2020)
ISBN print: 978-82-8348-129-7
ISBN e-book: 978-82-8348-130-3

Morten Bergsmo, Wolfgang Kaleck and Kyaw Yin Hlaing (editors):
Colonial Wrongs and Access to International Law
Torkel Opsahl Academic EPublisher
Brussels, 2020
Publication Series No. 40 (2020)
ISBN print: 978-82-8348-133-4
ISBN e-book: 978-82-8348-134-1

Morten Bergsmo and Kishan Manocha (editors):
Religion, Hateful Expression and Violence
Torkel Opsahl Academic EPublisher
Brussels, 2023
Publication Series No. 41 (2023)
ISBN print: 978-82-8348-141-9
ISBN e-book: 978-82-8348-142-6

Gavin E. Oxburgh, Trond Myklebust, Mark Fallon and Maria Hartwig (editors):
Interviewing and Interrogation: A Review of Research and Practice Since World War II
Torkel Opsahl Academic EPublisher
Brussels, 2023
Publication Series No. 42 (2023)
ISBN print: 978-82-8348-200-3
ISBN e-book: 978-82-8348-201-0

Mark Klamberg, Jonas Nilsson and Antonio Angotti (editors):
Commentary on the Law of the International Criminal Court: The Statute
Volume 1
Torkel Opsahl Academic EPublisher
Brussels, 2023
Publication Series No. 43 (Second Edition, 2023)
ISBN print: 978-82-8348-204-1
ISBN e-book: 978-82-8348-205-8

Mark Klamberg, Jonas Nilsson and Antonio Angotti (editors):
Commentary on the Law of the International Criminal Court: The Statute
Volume 2
Torkel Opsahl Academic EPublisher
Brussels, 2023
Publication Series No. 44 (Second Edition, 2023)
ISBN print: 978-82-8348-206-5
ISBN e-book: 978-82-8348-207-2

Mark Klamberg, Jonas Nilsson and Antonio Angotti (editors):
Commentary on the Law of the International Criminal Court:
The Rules of Procedure and Evidence
Torkel Opsahl Academic EPublisher
Brussels, 2023
Publication Series No. 45 (2023)
ISBN print: 978-82-8348-208-9
ISBN e-book: 978-82-8348-209-6

Song Tianying:
Legal Construction of Common Humanity: Human Agency in a Cosmopolitan War Crimes Law
Torkel Opsahl Academic EPublisher
Brussels, 2025
Publication Series No. 46 (2025)
ISBN print: 978-82-8348-255-3
ISBN e-book: 978-82-8348-275-1

All volumes are freely available online at http://www.toaep.org/ps/. For printed copies, see http://www.toaep.org/about/distribution/. For reviews of earlier books in this Series in academic journals and yearbooks, see http://www.toaep.org/reviews/.

www.ingramcontent.com/pod-product-compliance
Lightning Source LLC
Chambersburg PA
CBHW071337230926
51849CB00006B/506/J
9788283482553

Legal Construction of Common Humanity: Human Agency in a Cosmopolitan War Crimes Law

Song Tianying

2025
Torkel Opsahl Academic EPublisher
Brussels

Dr. **Song Tianying** is a CILRAP Research Fellow and Member of the Steering Group of the Coalition for International Criminal Justice (CICJ). She holds a doctorate from the European University Institute (Florence). Her doctoral thesis was awarded the Antonio Cassese Prize for the Best Doctoral Thesis in International Law. She obtained her master's degree in international law and bachelor's degree in law from China University of Political Science and Law (Beijing). She was formerly a Legal Adviser at the International Committee of the Red Cross East Asia Delegation in Beijing. She has co-edited several books on international criminal law and published articles and book chapters. She was awarded the 2016 M.C. Bassiouni Justice Award for being an outstanding, young East Asian lawyer in the field of international criminal law and justice.

Front cover: *The front cover shows Herod Antipas overwhelmed by regret when presented with the head of St. John the Baptist, counsellors in disbelief – a fresco by Andrea del Sarto (1486–1530) in his Chiostro della Scalzo cycle (1526), across the street from the CILRAP Bottega in Florence. Regret, remorse or contrition speaks to moral agency as much as societal accountability does. Photograph: CILRAP.*

Back cover: *Armed forces and international criminal law both project linearity and clear taxonomies, symbolized here by this newly restored public entrance in the Via dei Canestrari corner of Piazza Navona in Rome. The realities of moral choice and agency in war – the topic of this book – can be much more blurred and interwoven. Photograph: CILRAP.*

ISBNs: 978-82-8348-255-3 (print) and 978-82-8348-275-1 (e-book).

Dedicated to Cosimo Mingyu Bergsmo